Sustainable Dwelling

Caroline Speed

Sustainable Dwelling

A Phenomenography of House, Home and Place

VDM Verlag Dr. Müller

Impressum/Imprint (nur für Deutschland/ only for Germany)
Bibliografische Information der Deutschen Nationalbibliothek: Die Deutsche Nationalbibliothek verzeichnet diese Publikation in der Deutschen Nationalbibliografie; detaillierte bibliografische Daten sind im Internet über http://dnb.d-nb.de abrufbar.

Alle in diesem Buch genannten Marken und Produktnamen unterliegen warenzeichen-, marken- oder patentrechtlichem Schutz bzw. sind Warenzeichen oder eingetragene Warenzeichen der jeweiligen Inhaber. Die Wiedergabe von Marken, Produktnamen, Gebrauchsnamen, Handelsnamen, Warenbezeichnungen u.s.w. in diesem Werk berechtigt auch ohne besondere Kennzeichnung nicht zu der Annahme, dass solche Namen im Sinne der Warenzeichen- und Markenschutzgesetzgebung als frei zu betrachten wären und daher von jedermann benutzt werden dürften.

Coverbild: www.purestockx.com

Verlag: VDM Verlag Dr. Müller Aktiengesellschaft & Co. KG
Dudweiler Landstr. 99, 66123 Saarbrücken, Deutschland
Telefon +49 681 9100-698, Telefax +49 681 9100-988, Email: info@vdm-verlag.de
Zugl.: Melbourne, RMIT University, PhD Diss., 2008

Herstellung in Deutschland:
Schaltungsdienst Lange o.H.G., Berlin
Books on Demand GmbH, Norderstedt
Reha GmbH, Saarbrücken
Amazon Distribution GmbH, Leipzig
ISBN: 978-3-639-22856-4

Imprint (only for USA, GB)
Bibliographic information published by the Deutsche Nationalbibliothek: The Deutsche Nationalbibliothek lists this publication in the Deutsche Nationalbibliografie; detailed bibliographic data are available in the Internet at http://dnb.d-nb.de .
Any brand names and product names mentioned in this book are subject to trademark, brand or patent protection and are trademarks or registered trademarks of their respective holders. The use of brand names, product names, common names, trade names, product descriptions etc. even without a particular marking in this works is in no way to be construed to mean that such names may be regarded as unrestricted in respect of trademark and brand protection legislation and could thus be used by anyone.

Cover image: www.purestockx.com

Publisher:
VDM Verlag Dr. Müller Aktiengesellschaft & Co. KG
Dudweiler Landstr. 99, 66123 Saarbrücken, Germany
Phone +49 681 9100-698, Fax +49 681 9100-988, Email: info@vdm-publishing.com

Copyright © 2010 by the author and VDM Verlag Dr. Müller Aktiengesellschaft & Co. KG and licensors
All rights reserved. Saarbrücken 2010

Printed in the U.S.A.
Printed in the U.K. by (see last page)
ISBN: 978-3-639-22856-4

Contents

1	**Introduction**	**1**
1.1	Introduction	2
1.2	Statement of the Topic	3
1.2.1	Dominant Housing Paradigm in Australia	3
1.2.2	Australian Domestic Architecture	5
1.2.3	Sustainable Domestic Architecture	6
1.2.4	Suburban Development in Australia	7
1.3	Research Aim	9
1.4	Significance of the Study	10
1.5	Thesis Structure	11
2	**House and Home**	**14**
2.1	Introduction	15
2.2	House	16
2.2.1	House as Architecture	16
2.2.2	Architecture and the Human Psyche	19
2.2.3	House and the Human Psyche	21
2.3	Home	24
2.3.1	Home Defined	25
2.3.2	Home as Place	27
2.3.3	House and Home	28
2.4	Conclusion	28
3	**Theories of Place**	**30**
3.1	Introduction	31
3.2	Definition of Place	34
3.2.1	Place and Space	35

		3.2.2 Place and Landscape	37
		3.2.3 Place as a way of Understanding	37
	3.3	**Place as Being-in-the-World**	**38**
	3.4	**Place as Dwelling**	**40**
	3.5	**Place and Placelessness**	**44**
		3.5.1 Rootedness	45
		3.5.2 Insideness	45
		3.5.3 Authenticity	46
	3.6	**Place as *Genius Loci***	**47**
	3.7	**Place as Memory**	**49**
	3.8	**Criticisms of Theories of Place as Experience**	**51**
	3.9	**Conclusion**	**53**
4	**Research Design**		**56**
	4.1	**Introduction**	**57**
	4.2	**Research Questions**	**57**
	4.3	**Research Approach**	**58**
		4.3.1 Phenomenography	58
		4.3.2 Research Paradigm	60
		4.3.3 Ontological Assumptions	60
		4.3.4 Epistemological Assumptions	61
		4.3.5 Methodological Assumptions	61
		4.3.6 Assumptions within Phenomenography	61
	4.4	**Research Techniques**	**64**
		4.4.1 Data Collection	65
	4.5	**Issues of Trustworthiness**	**68**
		4.5.1 Credibility	68
		4.5.2 Transferability	68
		4.5.3 Dependability	69
		4.5.4 Confirmability	70
		4.5.5 Authenticity	70
	4.6	**Issues of Ethics**	**70**

	4.7	Conduct of the Study	71
	4.7.1	Phase 1: Initiating the Study	71
	4.7.2	Phase 2: Data Collection	72
	4.7.3	Phase 3: Data Analysis	78
	4.7.4	Phase 4: Theorising from the Study	79
5	**House**		**80**
	5.1	**Introduction**	**81**
	5.2	**Category of Description 1: House as Self**	**82**
	5.2.1	Theme 1: Holistic Relationship Between House, Home and Place	82
	5.2.2	Theme 2: Profound Connection to House	82
	5.2.3	Theme 3: House is a Place of Peace	85
	5.2.4	Theme 4: House Communicates Themselves	86
	5.2.5	Summary: House as Self	87
	5.3	**Category of Description 2: House as an Agora**	**87**
	5.3.1	Theme 1: Anthropocentric Relationship Between House, Home and Place	88
	5.3.2	Theme 2: Family Connection to House	89
	5.3.3	Theme 3: House Evokes Sentimental Feelings	90
	5.3.4	Theme 4: House Communicates a Simple Lifestyle	92
	5.3.5	Summary: House as an Agora	94
	5.4	**Category of Description 3: House as Refuge**	**94**
	5.4.1	Theme 1: Conflicted Relationship Between House, Home and Place	94
	5.4.2	Theme 2: Intense Connection to House	95
	5.4.3	Theme 3: People Oriented Feelings about House	96
	5.4.4	Theme 4: House Communicates Their Values	97
	5.4.5	Summary: House as Refuge	98
	5.5	**Category of Description 4: House as Shelter**	**98**
	5.5.1	Theme 1: Disjointed Relationship Between House, Home and Place	98
	5.5.2	Theme 2: No Connection to House	99
	5.5.3	Theme 3: House is a Commodity	100

	5.5.4	Theme 4: House Communicates their Commitment to Sustainable Living	100
	5.5.5	Summary: House as Shelter	101
5.6		**Structural Aspect: House**	**101**
6	**Home**		**103**
	6.1	**Introduction**	**104**
	6.2	**Category of Description 1: Home as Symbiosis**	**105**
	6.2.1	Theme 1: Home Means Symbiosis	105
	6.2.2	Theme 2: Memories of Home	110
	6.2.3	Summary: Home as Symbiosis	116
	6.3	**Category of Description 2: Home as People**	**116**
	6.3.1	Theme 1: Home Means Family	116
	6.3.2	Theme 2: Memories of Home	123
	6.3.3	Summary: Home as People	126
	6.4	**Category of Description 3: Homelessness**	**126**
	6.4.1	Theme 1: Home Means Nothing	126
	6.4.2	Theme 2: Memories of Home	131
	6.4.3	Summary: Homelessness	132
	6.5	**Structural Aspect: Home**	**132**
7	**Place**		**133**
	7.1	**Introduction**	**134**
	7.2	**Category of Description 1: Place as Dwelling**	**135**
	7.2.1	Theme: Expansive Place Boundaries and Connections	135
	7.2.2	Summary: Place as Dwelling	141
	7.3	**Category of Description 2: Place as Amenities**	**141**
	7.3.1	Theme: Contained Place Boundaries and Connections	141
	7.3.2	Summary: Place as Amenities	150
	7.4	**Category of Description 3: Alienation from Place**	**150**
	7.4.1	Theme: Fragmented Place Boundaries and Connections	150
	7.4.2	Summary: Alienation from Place	156

7.5		**Category of Description 4: Affinity with Place**	**156**
	7.5.1	Theme: Amorphous Place Boundaries and Connections	156
	7.5.2	Summary: Affinity with Place	161
7.6		**Structural Aspect: Place**	**161**

8 Sustainability   162

8.1		**Introduction**	**163**
8.2		**Category of Description 1: Sustainability as Being**	**164**
	8.2.1	Theme 1: Holistic Definition of Sustainability	164
	8.2.2	Theme 2: House is an Example of Sustainable Living	165
	8.2.3	Theme 3: Sustainability Extends to Place	169
	8.2.4	Summary: Sustainability as Being	171
8.3		**Category of Description 2: Sustainability as Doing**	**171**
	8.3.1	Theme 1: Anthropocentric Definition of Sustainability	172
	8.3.2	Theme 2: Sustainability Contained to the House	180
	8.3.3	Theme 3: No Connection Between Sustainability and Place	182
	8.3.4	Summary: Sustainability as Doing	185
8.4		**Structural Aspect: Sustainability**	**185**

9 Outcome Space: Sustainable Dwelling   187

9.1		**Introduction**	**188**
9.2		**Sustainability as Being**	**189**
	9.2.1	House, Home and Place	189
	9.2.2	House, Home, Place and Sustainability	191
	9.2.3	Childhood Memories and Experience of Home	193
	9.2.4	Summary: Sustainability as Being	193
9.3		**Sustainability as Doing**	**194**
	9.3.1	House, Home and Place	194
	9.3.2	House, Home, Place and Sustainability	196
	9.3.3	Childhood Memories and Experience of Home	198
	9.3.4	Summary: Sustainability as Doing	199
9.4		**Conclusion**	**199**

10 Conclusion		**201**
10.1 Introduction		202
10.2 Research Questions		202
10.2.1 Research Question 1		202
10.2.2 Research Question 2		204
10.2.3 Research Question 3		205
10.3 Implications		**207**
10.3.1 House, Home, Place and the Human Psyche		207
10.3.2 Home and Sustainability		208
10.3.3 Implications for Housing Policy and Trends		209
10.3.4 Development and Application of Methods		210
10.4 Conclusion		**211**
11 References		**213**

Table of Figures

Figure 1	Cultural Probe	74
Figure 2	Cultural probe exercise: What Home Really Means To You . . .	75
Figure 3	Cultural probe exercise: Places of Childhood	75
Figure 4	Cultural probe exercises: For me, 'sustainable' means . . . , notebook, camera and maps	76
Figure 5	Map of House and Garden (Respondent 8)	90
Figure 6	What Home Really Means . . . (Respondent 7)	106
Figure 7	Home (Respondent 1)	107
Figure 8	What Home Really Means . . . (Respondent 2)	109
Figure 9	What Home Really Means . . . (Respondent 2)	110
Figure 10	Childhood Homes (Respondent 1)	112
Figure 11	Childhood Homes (Respondent 2)	115
Figure 12	What Home Really Means . . . (Respondent 8)	117
Figure 13	Home (Respondent 10)	118
Figure 14	What Home Really Means . . . (Respondent 9)	120
Figure 15	What Home Really Means . . . (Respondent 10)	121
Figure 16	What Home Really Means . . . (Respondent 13)	122
Figure 17	Childhood Homes (Respondent 13)	125
Figure 18	What Home Really Means . . . (Respondent 4)	128
Figure 19	What Home Really Means . . . (Respondent 4)	129
Figure 20	What Home Really Means . . . (Respondent 4)	130
Figure 21	Map of Neighbourhood (Respondent 7)	137
Figure 22	Map of Neighbourhood (Respondent 6)	139

Figure 23	Map of Neighbourhood (Respondent 8)	143
Figure 24	Map of Neighbourhood (Respondent 5)	145
Figure 25	Map of Neighbourhood (Respondent 10)	146
Figure 26	Map of Neighbourhood (Respondent 9)	148
Figure 27	Map of Neighbourhood (Respondent 12)	152
Figure 28	Forest with Bridge in Distance (Respondent 11)	157
Figure 29	Map of Neighbourhood (Respondent 11)	158
Figure 30	Map of Neighbourhood (Respondent 4)	160
Figure 31	The Meaning of 'Sustainability' (Respondent 6)	165
Figure 32	Sustainable Home (Respondent 1)	167
Figure 33	The Meaning of 'Sustainability' (Respondent 8)	172
Figure 34	The Meaning of 'Sustainability' (Respondent 9)	173
Figure 35	Footpath (Respondent 8)	176
Figure 36	The Meaning of 'Sustainability' (Respondent 13)	178
Figure 37	The Meaning of 'Sustainability' (Respondent 4)	180
Figure 38	Outcome Space	189

1 Introduction

> *"Existential foothold" and "dwelling" are synonyms, and "dwelling", in an existential sense, is the purpose of architecture. Man dwells when he can orientate himself within and identify himself with an environment, or in short, when he experiences the environment as meaningful. Dwelling therefore implies something more than "shelter". It implies that the spaces where life occurs are* places, *in the true sense of the word (Norberg-Schulz, p. 5).*

1.1 Introduction

The concept and experience of home is central to human history. It is considered such a uniquely human concept that when objects and animals are given anthropomorphic qualities, they are generally also given an environment humans would recognise as a home. The 2008 animated film *WALL-E* is a touching example of this. WALL-E is a Waste Allocation Load Lifter–Earth Class, a solar-powered mustard yellow rubbish compactor. So polluted is the Earth by 2111 that the humans have to flee, with the intention to return to Earth when it is clean enough for humans to live here again, and other life forms have returned. Meanwhile, the WALL–E units are left behind to clean up the rubbish, which is compacted into cubes and neatly stacked into towers that rival skyscrapers in height.

This film deals with many meaningful concepts, the most poignant being the fact that home, and especially the Earth as home, is a universally recognised essential human need. Home for WALL-E is a discarded truck that transported and stored the WALL-E units. He personalised the space with artefacts and objects he collects while sorting through rubbish; he strung up fairy lights, and hooked up a TV. Home for WALL-E is a protected space from which he views the world. It is where he returns to recharge, literally and metaphorically. It is where he finds respite, and the safe space to which he flees when feeling threatened.

WALL-E resonates with us on many levels: his uncertainty about whether a spork should be placed with the forks or the spoons; his frustration and confusion with a Rubik's Cube; and his desire to gather things around him that make his house a home. But our hearts are touched by his loneliness, and the profound attachment he has to his home, which for him replaces meaningful relationships with living beings. In this sense, WALL-E views his house as home and place, a centre of meaning and field of care.

This film presents many topical issues, including the way in which humans understand and conceive of house, home, place, and environmental sustainability, and the dire outcome when these are treated as discrete, rather than intimately connected, phenomena. These themes, and the relationships between them, are the focus of this study of sustainable Dwelling.

This introductory Chapter is divided into five sections. The first introduces the topic, and includes an outline of the dominant form of housing provision in Australia. This is followed by an overview of domestic architecture and key trends in the housing industry in Melbourne, within which there is an emerging sector that is sustainability-focused. As such, an attempt will be made to define this as sustainable domestic architecture. This section concludes with a brief overview of the origins of suburban development, and the current debates in Australia regarding the ongoing provision of new housing within low density residential developments.

The second section outlines the aim of the research, which is to gain a deeper understanding of the experience of house, home, place and sustainability, and the relationships between these, for people who have built houses based on sustainability principles. The third section outlines the significance of the study, which is founded on reframing environmental problems to environmental symptoms of a human problem. The dominant, technological approach to solving these environmental problems is subsequently reframed to enable a more useful exploration of these phenomena and associated issues. The final section outlines the thesis structure.

1.2 Statement of the Topic

1.2.1 Dominant Housing Paradigm in Australia

The dominant provision of new housing in Australia comprises low density suburban residential developments on the urban fringe. Various criticisms regarding this form of housing provision have been articulated, and in 2006 a movement against this form of housing was founded by John Brown, a Professor of Architecture at the University of Calgary. Inspired by the slow food movement, the Slow Home Movement draws parallels between fast food and mass produced housing in that they are standardised, homogenous, and wasteful. According to this movement, "cookie-cutter housing" has contributed to a fast life that has a negative impact on people, cities, and the environment, and it is devoted to raising awareness about the way in which good design can positively affect quality of life.

Not only is Australia continuing to produce cookie-cutter housing in increasing numbers, they have also been steadily increasing in size. These houses are now commonly described as McMansions, a reference to their prevalence, uniformity, and more recently, the "super-sizing" of these houses. The average house size (floor area) in Australia today is 240 square metres, compared with an average of 177 square metres in 1986, a 35% increase within 21 years (ABS 2008). Meanwhile, the average household size (people per dwelling) has been falling (Australian Bureau of Statistics 2007), which essentially means that less people are consuming more space (McPhail 2008). Frank Lanza, a proud home owner of a new two-storey 'castle' of 33 squares on a 1030 square metre block describes his experience:

> I prefer to have as much space as I possibly can, if you work hard enough, you should be able to have what you want in life, not to be restricted. I've seen how they live in high-rise apartments. Unfortunately, many people can't afford to move out, but I think if they had the opportunity they would jump at the chance to move to a house like this or even bigger (Lanza 2008, cited in Webb 2008).

While the trend towards larger houses has been facilitated by strong economic growth over the past twenty years, it may also be explained from two different, though complimentary, social perspectives. The first, articulated by Alain de Botton (2004, p. 3), is founded on philosophy and defined as 'status anxiety'. This affliction, according to de Botton (2004, p. 4), is the worry of failing to conform to the measures of success articulated by our society, and 'that we are currently occupying too modest a rung or about to fall to a lower one'. It is the result of the decline of a social system based on nobility, whereby one's social status was fixed at birth, and the rise of meritocracy, whereby one makes one's own luck. In a meritocracy, a higher status accords the individual various pleasant consequences, including 'resources, freedom, space, comfort, time and, as importantly perhaps, a sense of being cared for and thought valuable' (De Botton 2004, p. 3).

One of the most visible, and culturally acceptable, measures of success in Australia is the size (and, in some circumstances, the location) of one's house. As Ravetz (1995, p. 18) notes, despite the profound social and economic changes over the past century, the suburban home remains a 'signifier of an individual's status'. Furthermore, a high status is often accorded to people who have amassed many possessions, which may be coveted by others. As Hume (1984 (reprint), p. 425) noted:

> 'Tis worthy of observation concerning that envy, which arises from a superiority in others, that 'tis not the great disproportion betwixt ourself and another, which produces it; but on the contrary, our proximity.

The second perspective comes from Viktor Frankl (1984, p. 128), a Viennese psychiatrist, who defines this human condition as an 'existential vacuum'. The symptoms of this condition include depression, aggression and addiction (especially excessive consumerism); alternatively, the will to meaning in life is replaced by the will to power, the will to money, and the will to pleasure. These symptoms are also, according to authors such as Moore (1992), Hillman (1996; 2004), Tolle (2005), and Carroll (1998), a physical manifestation of a neglected soul.

The increasing desire for larger houses has been facilitated by economic conditions that have created a housing crisis in terms of both supply – there are not enough, and affordability – they are beyond the reach of the average Australian wage earner (Payne et al. 2008; Beer 2008). The economic drivers include fiscal policies that favour existing home owners rather than new home buyers (for example, stamp duty); fiscal policies that are directed towards the new home buyer (for example, the First Home Owner Grant), which have had the perverse effect of increasing house prices in accordance with the value of the grant; low interest rates; and sustained economic growth. The last three in particular created high consumer confidence, and, combined with easily available credit, have enabled home buyers to demand larger houses (Beer 2008). The house, therefore, is a useful mechanism through which to explore the deeper social conditions that created this situation.

1.2.2 Australian Domestic Architecture

Boyd (1968; 1970; 1972; 1979) was acutely critical of what he perceived as cultural and aesthetic failings of the architecture of many Australian houses, especially mass-produced, cookie-cutter houses in suburban developments. For Boyd, these houses lacked the architect's vision, a vital element that transforms a building into architecture. What is worse, however, is that the house is 'architecturally exceptional'; private houses have an essential 'emotional element' that may be designed in, but is frequently overlooked (Boyd 1970, p. 6).

While Drew (1985, p. 6) concedes that many of these failings in Australian domestic architecture remain unchanged today, he suggests that Glen Murcutt's domestic architecture offers an alternative vision, and a 'means of restoring our national self-respect'. Murcutt's architecture is deeply rooted in the Australian landscape, and attempts to 'convey something of the discrete character' of the Australian landscape in built form (Murcutt 1984, p. 7). Preferring small scale domestic work outside the confines of the city, Murcutt draws on the unique characteristics of the site:

> When I consider the magic of our landscape, I am continually struck by the *genius* of the place, the sunlight, shadows, wind, heat and cold, the scents from our flowering trees and plants, and, especially, the vastness to the island continent. All these factors go to make a land of incredible strength combined with an unimaginable delicacy (Murcutt 1984, p. 8).

While both Boyd and Murcutt are concerned primarily with Australian domestic architecture, Boyd's attention was focused on suburban residential development, whereas Murcutt chooses to work with clients who have unique rural or natural sites. Regardless of where the house is located, however, there remains a profound relationship between many Australians and their houses. Boyd (1970, p. 4) notes 'Where else can one start a word-association game with "architecture", assured that the response will be, not "building" or "city" or "monument", but "home"?'.

The unique situation in Australia is the result of a number of factors, probably the most important being the much higher proportion, relative to other developed countries, of house ownership or the aspiration to house ownership (Lewis 1999). Moreover, houses are unique among the material possessions of Australians, such as cars and furniture, because they are more intimately connected with the quality of living, rather than the 'quality of culture' (Boyd 1970, p. 5).

1.2.3 Sustainable Domestic Architecture

An increasing trend within domestic architecture and the housing industry in Melbourne is that of ecologically sustainable design (ESD). Where mass-produced housing is necessarily designed to be located on almost any generic block of land, ESD architecture specifically responds to the site to reduce reliance on artificial heating, cooling and lighting (among others), and to integrate the house with the unique features and orientation of the site.

This form of design is not new. The most consistent and comprehensive resource-efficient and energy-conserving design and building techniques are found in vernacular domestic architecture from around the world, especially prior to the industrial revolution (Gonzalo & Habermann 2006). Vernacular domestic architecture was specifically designed for the local climatic and site conditions, which was essential in extreme climates, and generally used locally abundant materials.

These traditional design and building techniques were passed down through generations until the industrial revolution, when, in the name of progress, they 'were no longer considered appropriate for the time' (Gonzalo & Habermann 2006, p. 11). Probably the final blow for vernacular architecture - in Western societies in particular - was the advent of mass-produced housing after the Second World War. Furthermore, the concurrent development of technology that artificially modified indoor air quality, especially heaters and air-conditioners, enabled houses to be designed and produced in large numbers, regardless of local climatic or site conditions.

While the resource-efficient and energy-conserving techniques used in vernacular domestic architecture were practical and necessity-driven, today the rationale for sustainable development is quite different. The aim, when this became an issue of worldwide concern in the 1980s, was to integrate broad environmental considerations into economic policy, and hence into mainstream social, political and economic spheres; to balance environmental concern with economic development, especially in developing countries (Dresner 2002).

As such, in 1983 the UN General Assembly created the World Commission on the Environment and Development (WCED). In 1987 the WCED published *Our Common Future* (commonly known as the Brundtland Report), which defined 'sustainable development' as 'development that meets the needs of the present without compromising the ability of future generations to meet their own needs' (*Our Common Future* 1987, p. 8). Within this context, the Australian Government launched the National Strategy for Ecologically Sustainable Development (NSESD) in 1992, which defined ESD as 'using, conserving and enhancing the community's resources so that ecological processes, on which life depends, are maintained, and the total quality of life, now and in the future, can be increased' (Australian Government: Department of the Environment 2007).

ESD is an increasing sector of the housing industry in Melbourne. This trend is due to a range of push and pull factors, including the establishment of legislation for minimum housing performance standards, which tend to focus on reasonably easily measurable outcomes such as water and energy use. At the other end of the spectrum, key stakeholders in the housing industry, including architects and home-owners, are voluntarily electing to pursue sustainable design and building techniques above and beyond the minimum requirements. Of those who are pursuing this approach, Glen Murcutt was one of the pioneers of a holistic approach to design based on the unique characteristics of the site and the principles of ESD (Williams 2007). ESD architecture, therefore, embodies qualities such as spontaneity and authenticity of the individual experience, social and environmental responsibility, celebration of the real things of everyday life, and expresses empathy and humility (Stansfield-Smith 1994, p. 326).

Within the context of this research, domestic architecture that is designed and built based on ESD principles will be referred to as sustainable domestic architecture (SDA). Furthermore, for the purposes of this study, the intent of the designer and client or occupier to achieve SDA, rather than the measurable outcomes of sustainability performance, is most important for selecting appropriate respondents and their houses.

1.2.4 Suburban Development in Australia

In the context of the roughly 9000-year history of urban settlements (Boyden 2004, p. 4), suburban development is a relatively new model of housing provision. First conceived and introduced just over a century ago, the theoretical origins of suburban development are embedded in the goal of achieving a balance between city and nature, which was a reaction to the urban impacts of the industrial revolution. The rapid increase in industrial activity encouraged rural-urban migration, and by the middle to late nineteenth century, large numbers of people lived in crowded urban centres which have been described as 'forerunners of late twentieth-century megacities' (Wheeler & Beatley 2004, p. 7). The myriad of problems associated with these urban centres included overcrowding, inadequate urban infrastructure and sanitation, and declining public health.

Furthermore, the rapid increase in the pollution and depletion of natural resources for the purposes of industrial activity were also clearly visible, and exacerbated the situation.

Within this context, the primary theme that emerged in urban planning during the 19th century was achieving a balance between city and nature, as described in Howard's *Garden Cities of To-morrow* (1898). This work, in addition to contributions from Geddes and Mumford, identified extreme overcrowding in early industrial cities as the primary urban problem, and advocated a balance between city and country as the solution. These garden cities were designed as a solution to the social and environmental *symptoms* of the industrial revolution. They laid the design foundations for garden suburbs, which have transformed into the residential suburbs prevalent today.

However, as Lewis (1999, p. 23) notes, the term suburb did not initially 'evoke a carpet of residential development, as it does today'. It is this carpet of residential development which is described by some critics as the central *problem* currently facing urban centres in Australia and the USA. The relevance of this form of residential development within the current social, economic, and environmental context is tenuous, yet the suburban ethos continues to dominate residential development in Australia. Moreover, Australians identify with suburban development to the extent that, as Davison (1997, p. 16) states, it is 'not just an unfortunate planning aberration. It is us'.

Advocates for suburban developments argue that they are simply providing housing to meet a strong market demand – that individuals and families who choose to live in outer urban residential developments enjoy all they have to offer (Stretton 1991; Troy 1996). Troy (1997, p. 25) is a vocal opponent to urban consolidation, which he describes as 'a policy designed to reduce general housing standards'. Furthermore, there are doubts about the overall benefits from urban consolidation and increasing urban density, especially the trade-off between the alleged saving in infrastructure cost, which comes 'at the cost to our way of life and the nature and character of our cities' (Troy 1997, p. 19).

However, there is a considerably more extensive body of literature demonstrating the problems resulting from ongoing suburban residential development and the associated urban sprawl specific to transport (Newman & Kenworthy 1999, 2000; Wheeler & Beatley 2004), land use and urban design (Calthorpe 1993; Jenks, Burton & Williams 1996, 2000; Katz 1994), energy use and environmental impacts (Beatley 1994; Girardet 1999; Newman & Kenworthy 2000), and social equity issues (Hayden 1984; Jenks, Burton & Williams 2000). There are also serious concerns regarding the ability of suburban residential developments to meet either local or international sustainability standards such as Agenda 21 (Wheeler & Beatley 2004). While there is relative agreement regarding the unsustainability of current forms of suburban residential estates, there is disagreement regarding the preferred alternative, including suggestions such as the compact city (Jenks, Burton & Williams 1996) and new urbanism (Katz 1994).

An attempt to address this issue was outlined in *Melbourne 2030*. This Victorian Government policy document, released in 2002, frames the strategic directions for urban development until 2030. A key initiative within this policy was the introduction of an urban growth boundary surrounding metropolitan Melbourne. As of 2 December 2008, this boundary is under review for possible extension, signalling a significant change in the Victorian Government's policy position and commitment to sustainable urban development in general (Moncrief 2008). Within days of these changes, the recently released *State of the Environment Victoria 2008* (McPhail) report criticised this decision, calling for widespread reform to the current patterns of urban development within Victoria, and metropolitan Melbourne in particular.

It is within this context that current debates about environmental sustainability and suburban development are located, and they remain focused on the physical manifestation of the problem. The sustainability measures currently being incorporated into houses in mainstream residential developments in Melbourne include a mandatory minimum 5 Star thermal efficiency rating, and the choice of either a water tank or a solar hot water system. These measures focus on re-specifications to existing generic floorplans, rather than design, attitudinal or behavioural changes. There is a lack of research focussed on understanding the underlying motivations of homemakers – the prevailing concepts of home have led to the current urban form of Melbourne. How do we seek to construct sustainable dwellings and what shapes individual's attempts to Dwell sustainably?

1.3 Research Aim

This study therefore seeks to explore the understanding and experience of house, home, place and sustainability from the perspective of the human psyche (soul). The purpose of this study is to gain a rich understanding of these phenomena, and the relationships between them, for people who have built houses based on sustainability principles. This is situated within the broader context of suburban sustainability. The study will explore the respondents' complex, multidimensional, lived experiences of house, home and place within a framework of experiential theories of place.

The first of these theories is Heidegger's concept of Being[1], especially Being-in-the-World, and the way in which this relates to the human experience of place. The second is the related concept of

---

[1] English translations of Heidegger's work usually capitalize Being, Dwelling, and Dasein (Frede 2006, p. 42), whereas commentary about Heidegger's work does not consistently follow this pattern. As such, quotes include the author's

Dwelling, which for Heidegger is the 'basic character of Being' and is intimately connected with building (Heidegger 1951, p. 362). The third perspective, articulated by Relph (1976), draws heavily on Heidegger's concepts of Being and Dwelling to define place as the experience of rootedness, authenticity, and insidedness, and the absence of these as placelessness. The fourth theory is the *genius loci*[2] of place, also referred to as the 'spirit of place'. Dwelling is the point of departure for this theory which discusses the way in which architecture concretises the spirit of place so place may be experienced as an integrated totality. The final theory, articulated by Bachelard (1994), discusses a phenomenological approach to place as memory, suggesting that this is the conflation of intimate experience, memory, and imagination. This perspective is explored through the experience of home, especially the childhood memories of home.

The physical, intellectual, and emotional boundaries between the experiences of house, home and place are imprecise, and inevitably an exploration of one of these perspectives leads to an exploration of the others. It is the intersections between these complementary threads that enable the synthesis of an intricate and holistic description of the lived experience of sustainable domestic architecture. The research questions that explore these phenomena are:

1. *How do people describe their understanding and experience of house, home, and place?*

2. *How do people describe their understanding and experience of the relationship between house, home, place and sustainability?*

3. *How do people describe the relationship between childhood memories and their understanding and experience of home?*

1.4 Significance of the Study

This study is unique in that it explores the multidimensional understanding and experience of house, home, place and sustainability, and the relationships between these, especially from the perspective of the human psyche. The data collection techniques include a combination of a cultural probe and in-depth interviews, which maximise the richness and depth of the interviewees' responses. The cultural probe is a purposefully designed mixed media package seeking to provoke inspirational, creative and emotional responses, and is a relatively new data collection technique for research of this nature. The selected research approach – phenomenography - complements this form of data,

---

original emphasis (either capitalisation or non-capitalisation), and the remainder of the text will use capitalisation for these terms.

[2] Norberg-Schulz (Norberg-Schulz 1980) italicises the term *genius loci*, and as such this precedent will be followed.

and enables the exploration of the differences, as well as similarities, between the respondents' understandings and experiences.

Furthermore, within this study the dominant understanding of environmental issues is reframed, which subsequently enables the approach to be reframed. In the context of the intersection of private property, public legislation, and environmental sustainability, problems are framed as environmental, and the legislative proposals to address these problems are frequently technology-based, producing reactive, tactical and end-of-pipe sustainability measures (Shellenberger & Nordhaus 2004). Reframing the issue from an environmental problem to an environmental symptom of a *human problem* creates an opportunity for viewing the situation from a perspective that has the potential to be more constructive.

Rather than placing blame on the environment, it shifts the focus from fixing the environment, to acknowledging the human role in creating the current situation, thus highlighting the human role in changing the outcome. This shift in focus is encouraged by Head, Trigger and Mulcock (2005), who argue for the importance of research into the ways in which cultural processes are central to environmental attitudes and behaviours, and the usefulness of qualitative research methods to understand these relationships in depth. They support the approach that conservation policies are inherently social phenomena, arguing that 'conservation interventions are the product of human decision-making processes and require changes in human behaviour to succeed' (Mascia et al. 2003, p. 649).

It is essential, therefore, to understand housing choices from a human perspective. What memories, assumptions, and understandings do people bring to the lived experience of domestic architecture, and of house as home? How do these influence the lived experience of domestic architecture? What is the relationship between house, home and place? And more specifically, in the context of suburban sustainability, what is the relationship between sustainable domestic architecture and all of these?

1.5 Thesis Structure

This thesis comprises ten chapters. This chapter has defined the topic and provided the context and rationale for the study, and outlined the purpose and significance of the study.

Chapter 2 provides a literature review of house and home, and defines the instances when house may be understood to be architecture. House is also the physical form within which home may be experienced, and as such an attempt is made to define home. This process highlights the insufficiency of literature discussing the human psyche's experience of house, home and place with respect to sustainable domestic architecture in Australia. Given that there are a number of place theories that explore the human experience of place, and home by definition may also be considered a place, then these theories provide a useful framework for exploring human-environment interactions.

Chapter 3 presents the theoretical framework which is developed from theories of place within humanistic geography and the philosophies of phenomenology and existentialism. These include Being-in-the-World, Dwelling, place and placelessness, *genius loci*, and place as memory. This framework will enable an exploration of people's understanding and experience of house, home and place unique to Australia, and how this is concretised in sustainable domestic architecture.

Chapter 4 outlines the research design, and includes an overview of phenomenography as a research approach. The data collection techniques – a cultural probe and in-depth interviews - are explained, and issues of trustworthiness and ethics are discussed. This chapter concludes with an overview of the conduct of the study.

Chapter 5 presents the results of the study regarding the qualitatively different ways the respondents described their understanding and experience of their house, and the relationship between house, home, and place. Four conceptual categories of description emerged from the data. In the first, the respondents described their house as an extension of themselves; in the second the interviewees described their house as an agora, a meeting place for family and friends. The respondents in the third category described their house as a refuge that provides respite from the world; and in the fourth they described their house simply as utilitarian shelter.

Chapter 6 presents the results of the study regarding the qualitatively different ways the respondents described their understanding and experience of their home, and the relationship between this and their childhood memories of home. Three conceptual categories of description emerged from the data. In the first, the respondents described their home as a harmonious synthesis of house and place; the interviewees in the second described home in terms of family and friends who share it; and those in the third category found it difficult to articulate what home means to them, suggesting a sense of homelessness.

Chapter 7 presents the results of the study regarding the qualitatively different ways the respondents described their understanding and experience of place. Four conceptual categories of description emerged from the data. In the first, the respondents described place as the area for which they held deep feelings of care and respect. The interviewees in the second described place in terms of the services and amenities they used in their local neighbourhood. The respondents in the third category described an increasing sense of alienation from place; and in the fourth they felt an immediate affinity with place.

Chapter 8 presents the results of the study regarding the relationship between the qualitatively different ways the respondents described their understanding and experience of their house, place and sustainability. Two conceptual categories of description emerged from the data. In the first, the respondents described sustainability as Being, as a holistic approach to the world and a mode of thinking and behaving that permeates their whole lives. The interviewees in the second described sustainability as doing, as a moral obligation to the greater good, and viewed conservation as something "out there".

Chapter 9 discusses the relationships between each of the categories of description for the four phenomena of house, home, place and sustainability (the outcome space), and provides a visual representation of these connections. The results are synthesised with the theoretical framework established in Chapter 3, the connections between the qualitatively different ways the respondents described their understanding and experience of house, home, place and sustainability are discussed, and the three research questions are answered.

Chapter 10 provides an overview of the results of the study and discusses their implications.

2 House and Home

To build a house is to create an area of peace, calm and security, a replica of our own mother's womb, where we can leave the world and listen to our own rhythm; it is to create a place of our very own, safe from danger. For once we have crossed the threshold and shut the door behind us, we can be at one with ourselves (Marc 1977, p. 14).

2.1 Introduction

It is widely accepted that the first human houses were caves (Gardiner 2002; Marc 1977). The transition from the house as a cave to the house as a human-made structure is believed to have coincided with the advent of agriculture about 10000 years ago; though it was probably a gradual process, these people developed from hunter to farmer, cave-dweller to home-owner (Boyden 2004; Daniel 2003; Eisler 1990; Gardiner 2002). These structures were designed and built based on local climatic conditions and the materials available, and were influenced by culture, customs, and religious beliefs (Gonzalo & Habermann 2006; Marc 1977). They were the first examples of vernacular domestic architecture, and also the first temple-house (Marc 1977). The first houses, therefore, provided more than the utilitarian function of shelter; they were physical expressions of the people who built them and the way in which these people viewed the world.

Where a house is the tangible physical shelter for people, a home is the intangible emotional shelter, a place of 'protected intimacy' (Bachelard 1994, p. 3). Home may have a multitude of meanings for different people, however the experience of home remains an essential human need (Relph 1976; Weil 1952). The affective ties people develop with significant physical environments from childhood remain an important aspect of human psychological development (Marcus 1995). Furthermore, a home may not necessarily be a house, it could be anywhere that people inhabit, for 'all really inhabited space bears the essence of the notion of home' (Bachelard 1994, p. 5).

The focus of the first section of this Chapter is the house, the physical form within which home may be experienced. Within this context, a number of definitions of architecture are provided. The second section focuses on the human experience of home. While there is an extensive body of literature discussing the home as a social or cultural construct (Blunt 2005; Blunt & Dowling 2006; Bourdieu 1990; Busch 1999; Dovey 1999; Dowling & Mee 2007; Feldman 1990; Rybczynski 1987; Shove 2003), there is a far more limited selection of literature discussing the human experience of home, especially from the perspective of the human psyche. Despite this, home remains a central concept in geography, and authors such as Tuan (1991), Relph (1976) and Seamon (1979) consider home to be a place, a centre of meaning and field of care. These perspectives are explored in detail.

The purpose of this Chapter is twofold. The first is to review the literature about the human experience of house and home, and the relationship between them. The second is to define key terms which will be used throughout this study.

2.2 House

A house is a building that provides shelter and protection for people and their belongings. It may be found or constructed; temporary or permanent. From caves to castles, the house may be constructed out of a range of materials and take a multitude of physical forms. It is generally purposefully designed for living, with varying degrees of success. Throughout time, however, the underlying purpose of the house has remained largely constant: to provide for the essentials of existence including shelter, cooking, and warmth (Gardiner 2002). Some authors argue that it provides for higher order needs as well, including safety and privacy, and more importantly, as a place for repose and reflection (Marcus 1995; Marc 1977).

2.2.1 House as Architecture

A house may be defined in two ways: first, as a building, and second, as architecture. Many architects will emphasise there is a profound difference between the two; to explain that difference is a more difficult task, and one that has been attempted for many years. In 1943, Pevsner's *Outline of European Architecture* contained what seemed to be a self-evident opening sentence: 'A bicycle shed is a building; Lincoln Cathedral is a piece of architecture'. While this statement caused controversy at the time, a definition such as this would not even be entertained today. Until the late twentieth century, architecture was often thought of as discrete buildings, monuments, and works of art; today it is generally nothing less than the totality of the built environment (Sutton 1999). This is exemplified by Reyner Banham's sweeping definition of architecture, from the perspective of critic and commentator, as '"that which changes land-use"' (Sutton 1999, p. 7).

In the Australian context, Robin Boyd is one of the most prolific writers, and critics, of Australian domestic architecture. Boyd wrote extensively from the 1940s through to the late 1970s about Australian architecture, and specifically the architecture of Australian houses. It is Boyd's definition of architecture, and in particular domestic architecture, that is arguably the most relevant to this research.

Prior to defining architecture, and in order to establish the social context, the primary criticisms of both architecture as a product, and architecture as a profession, will be addressed. In the *Ten Books on Architecture*, a seminal text and one of the most influential works of architectural history in the Western world, Vitruvius (1999, p. 21) devotes the first chapter in Book 1 to 'The Education of the Architect'. Though he is careful to point out that architectural expertise is the result of both practice and reasoning, he states that the education of the architect should include knowledge and training in the areas of letters, draftsmanship, geometry, arithmetic, history, philosophy, physiology, music, medicine, climate, law and astronomy:

> Therefore, because so great a profession must be adorned by and abundant in so many ways and such various types of expertise, I do not believe that architects can simply announce themselves as such, none but those who have climbed step by step, nurtured from an early age by education – in letters above all, and in the arts – to reach the loftiest sanctuary of Architecture (Vitruvius 1999, p. 23).

In the twenty centuries since this was first published, the perception and stature of architecture as a profession has, in some contexts, declined. Given the current social, political, and economic situation, in addition to the world's growing population, there is a pervasive belief that most important requirements are for practical shelter and buildings. Within this context, there is a perception that architecture is art and is therefore considered trivial and out of touch with reality (Boyd 1970).

Nevertheless, there remains a difference between the perception of that which is architecture and that which is a building. Buildings will always be required to provide shelter for a rapidly increasing population; but architecture is something more than simply building, 'more than a sequence of rooms, more than the sum of its parts' (Gardiner 2002, p. 222). Architecture is 'the creative activity aimed at producing a complete shelter that transcends mere usefulness into realms of pure delight. . .' (Boyd 1970, p. 7). Despite being able to define this elusive quality, or perhaps because of it, Boyd (1970, p. 8) concedes that a concise definition is impossible: 'There is a hoary saying that you cannot define architecture; you can only design it'.

The question remains: what is good architecture? Boyd (1970, p. 10) suggests that it is inspired by the living conditions which will be provided for its occupants, and 'above all, the emotive power of the spaces that will be created'. If we accept this, then the concept of good living conditions is translated into the physical building through the design process. Within this context, the critical element is the intangible quality that transforms a building into an expression of the human spirit, which Boyd (1970, p. 111) argues is the 'strength of the architect's vision'.

Thus the concept of good living conditions, combined with the architect's vision, is physically manifested through the unification of four qualities. The first is surface, the colour and texture of the materials. The second quality includes the internal spaces and external form. The third is the structure and the structural system. The final quality is spirit, which is evident in architecture when it has been designed with this vision and 'single-minded devotion', which then becomes the living psyche of the building (Boyd 1970, p. 16). Furthermore, this vision is unique to the architect. It is the combination of 'the architect's personality, his place and time . . . the site, and all the other conditions' (Boyd 1970, p. 111). The concept of the architect's vision is central to Boyd's definition of architecture, and as such this term will be explored in further detail.

The word vision implies an otherworldly quality, a metaphysical experience. Jung identified the word image with the human psyche; more accurately that the human psyche is constituted of images, and that 'the soul is primarily an imagining activity most natively and paradigmatically presented by the dream' (Hillman 2004, p. 19). Vision, therefore, is closely associated with the human psyche and soul. The word psyche comes from the Greek *psyche*, meaning breath or soul, which the dictionary defines as the 'human soul' or 'human mind' (Krebs 1981).

While the human psyche and soul remain elusive to define, they have been a pervasive theme in Western thought since Antiquity. In Plato's *Republic*, the 'Myth of Er' explicitly describes the human soul, arguing that at birth each soul is given its own daimon, a soul-companion, which has selected an 'image or pattern' for the life of the person and soul on earth; the daimon is also referred to as a person's calling, fate, destiny, or character (Hillman 1996, p. 8). Similarly, the word spirit comes from the Latin *spirare*, meaning to breathe.

The words psyche, soul, and spirit not only reference each other in their definitions (Krebs 2004), they converge on a number of shared meanings. The first, and most important in this context, is that these words refer to something that is not matter, a person's intangible being rather than their physical presence. The second meaning includes qualities such as feelings and emotions. The third meaning is thinking, or connected with the intellect and mind; and the final shared meaning is that these words refer to an essential part or quality, the real meaning, or the fundamental nature of anything (Krebs 1981). These convergences demonstrate that there is enough shared meaning between these terms that they may be used interchangeably, and will be used as such depending on the context. While the various meanings of psyche, soul, and spirit may lead to some confusion, Hillman (1996, p. 10) points out that numerous meanings of a term that is elusive to define may not necessarily 'tell us *what* "it" is, but they do confirm *that* it is.'

The understanding that a building may be considered architecture when it embodies the architect's vision is widely held within the architectural profession. Walter Gropius and Sigfried Giedion, two of the great architectural theorists of the early twentieth century, describe this vision as the result of an 'intuitive leap'; the creative step that an architect makes to reach an ideal solution to each unique brief or problem. Both creativity and genius are often attributed to intuition, and as such the idea of an intuitive leap and the resulting spiritual dimension within architecture is not new; it has been written about since the architecture of Classical Greece (Fletcher 1987). The word intuitive is the adjective of intuition, which in turn comes from two Latin words: '*in-*' meaning 'in', and '*tueri*', meaning 'to look at'; literally, to look within. It is a knowing of something without conscious reasoning (Krebs 1981).

Within the field of archetypal psychology, intuition means direct and unmediated knowledge which possesses a mythic quality, because when a myth reaches us, it seems true and gives sudden insight. The key characteristic of intuition, according to Hillman (1996, p. 98), is that it is not a gradual process of unravelling meaning; rather intuitions simply occur as a sudden idea, perceiving in complete form 'the image, the *paradeigma*, a whole gestalt'. Similarly, Jung (1959, p. 282) defines intuition as '"perception via the unconscious"', and cautions against assuming all intuitions are correct. While Jungian psychology identifies intuition as one of the four functions of consciousness, along with thinking, feeling and sensation, Jung emphasised the need for the four functions to be seen as a whole rather than in isolation (Hillman 1996, p. 99).

The definitions of architecture explored in this chapter all converge on the idea that it must include an intangible, spiritual dimension. For Boyd, in the context of domestic architecture in Melbourne, architecture may be defined as a building based on a concept of good living conditions, and an understanding of the emotive power of the spaces that will be created. This concept is physically manifested as architecture through the four qualities of surface, space, structure and spirit, the most important being the spirit, the living psyche of the architecture. These qualities are brought together in a cohesive manner through the architect's vision - the images of their psyche, and their 'intuitive leap'- direct and unmediated knowledge from within. The creation of architecture therefore is a creative experience that is by definition beyond rational thought; it is the tangible expression of the architect's intangible spirit. To return to Boyd (1970, p. 113):

> Can one explain the spirit of architecture in clear English? Only abstractly. For instance, it is there when an idea expressive of living, neither purely intellectual nor purely poetic, illuminates the building. Or you can say, as Le Corbusier did, that it is there when your heart is touched.

2.2.2 Architecture and the Human Psyche

If we accept the understanding that architecture is an expression of human creativity, a physical manifestation of the architect's spirit, then what is the relationship between the inhabitant's spirit and the architecture? Of the subject with the object? Within this limited body of literature there are two approaches to the representation of the human spirit in architecture, both based on Jungian psychology. The first argues that the human psyche's journey towards individuation, as defined by Jung, is expressed through housing choice, because of the need to externalize the internal journey of the human psyche (Edinger 1972; Marcus 1995). The second draws on Jung's seven archetypal signs, which summarise the human relationship with the universe, and explores the way in which architecture throughout the world is composed of these signs (Marc 1977).

Jung (1959, p. 275) defines the journey towards Individuation as the process by which people become '"in-dividual"', an 'indivisible unity or "whole"'. The journey towards individuation inevitably goes through cycles, during which either the ego-self is dominant, and expressed in external world, or the transpersonal Self is dominant, and expressed in the external world. Jungian analyst Edward Edinger (1972, p. 166) describes the ego as an entity which 'participates in the vicissitudes of time, space, and causality'; in contrast, the Self (the centre of the archetypal psyche) is in a world beyond consciousness. In this scenario 'the ego is the centre of subjective identity; the Self, the centre of objective identity' (Edinger 1972, p. 166).

According to Marcus (1995), the journey towards individuation tends to follow a cyclical pattern. Within this cycle, the ego-self tended to remain dominant while the individuals were involved with meeting the demands of family, marriage, child rearing, work, and society. It was not until these tasks were less prominent in their lives (for example, the children had left home), that they were able to turn inward to focus on the process of individuation. This process is described as '*inflation*, or too close an identification with the self, and *alienation*, or rupture in the ego-self connection' (Marcus 1995, p. 120).

If we accept the Jungian notion of individuation as a gradual but insistent striving toward the transpersonal Self or soul, and that this journey is externally manifested in the individual's surroundings, then houses provide a useful insight into this journey. As a physical manifestation of the psychological processes an individual is undergoing, housing choice may highlight a particular area of an individual's psyche that is seeking attention. Marcus (1995, p. 15) describes this process as placing the psyche '"out there" for us to contemplate, just as we need to view our physical body in a mirror'. The unconscious often chooses houses, buildings, and secret rooms as symbols: the basement is often a metaphor for the unconscious, of something hidden that needs to be explored, whereas the highest part of the house, the attic or roof, tends to reflect a desire to explore transpersonal realms or spiritual directions (Jung 1995).

Furthermore, when people think of their home, rather than their house, it tends to encompass far more than simply the building in which they reside; it is inextricably linked to the neighbourhood. If these surroundings fail to nurture and protect and create a sense of home, 'it matters little how beautiful or spacious our house is. Like any living being, humans need not only a nest or dwelling, but a whole ecological setting in which they can feel '"at home"' (Marcus 1995, p. 212).

For this reason, some individuals are unable to distinguish between the impact of the location from the impact of the house, thus dissatisfaction with one may spill over into dissatisfaction with the other; for others both of these are a conscious decision (Marcus 1995). Housing location appears to be equally as important as housing choice in the expression of either the ego-self, or the transpersonal Self, or degrees of both. An individual may place themself in a highly unsuitable location in order to force into consciousness a psychological problem which is symbolised by this dissonance, or a couple may separate because the chosen location reflects the inner needs of one but not the other (Marcus 1995).

2.2.3 House and the Human Psyche

Where Edinger (1972) and Marcus (1995) discuss the process of individuation as represented in the house, Marc (1977, p. 9) refers to the human psyche as the 'inner house', and that this inner house must exist prior to the manifestation of the 'exterior house'. The human psyche, as the inner house, is externalised and revealed through the archetypal signs, which are pre-existent to consciousness and represent the collective perception of '*a priori* structural forms' (Jung 1995, p. 380). They are an attribute of human instinct, and as such they 'possess a specific energy which causes or compels definite modes of behaviour or impulses' (Jung 1995, p. 380).

The relationship between the human psyche, the inner house, and the universe, is represented through specific combinations of archetypal signs. For example, the circle is the expression of a perfect, whole universe, and the cross is the expression of the human soul. When a cross is placed in a circle it is the representation of the relationship between the individual soul and the universe, the "original unity", and 'on ritual vestments it may be seen all over the world' (Marc 1977, p. 46).

In *The Psychology of the House,* Marc (1977) explores the relationship between the human psyche and the universe through archetypal signs. He argues that the use of Jung's archetypal signs in architecture suggests that it is in many ways a primal, and universal, experience. These seven archetypal signs 'enabled man to summarise the universe around him and his relations to it' (Marc 1977, p. 32). Moreover, four of these - the circle, the triangle, the square, and the cross - can be found in religious architecture throughout the world, including temples, Tibetan mandalas, Indian and Himalayan stupas and chortens, Sumerian ziggurats, Egyptian and American pyramids, the Ka'ba of Mecca (Marc 1977). These symbols contain 'such a wealth of meaning that they provided the basic texture of language and art. Organised in another way, they produced the house' (Marc 1977, p. 32).

In *Vers une architecture*, Le Corbusier also claimed that the primary geometric shapes, which include the archetypal signs of circle, triangle, square, and the cross that divides these, are essential to beauty in architecture (Hudnut 1949, p. 26). While these four signs are the product of human spirit, the three remaining signs – the spiral, the wave, and the dot – represent the universe itself, and the natural impulses that pass through humans and unite them to the cosmic order (Marc 1977). Moreover, the spiral contains within it the wave and the dot, and represents the principle of growth within the universe. These three signs appear throughout the world as complimentary elements of costumes, adornments, everyday artefacts and architecture (Marc 1977). However, they are not necessarily confined to being complementary elements in architecture; Frank Lloyd Wright's Guggenheim Museum in New York *is* a three dimensional spiral.

Marc (1977, p. 32) also suggests that these three signs 'manifested through man, without any interpretation on his part', they were instinctual, and 'consciousness seemed to withdraw itself before them as if better to allow the world of impulse its full force of expression.' Primitive humans used the spiral, wave and dot to express the 'strongest, deepest and richest elements in nature', to reconnect the bond with nature that was severed at birth, and to reassure themselves that 'nature and her laws' were still within them (Marc 1977, p. 40).

The relationship between the human psyche and the universe is represented through archetypal signs, and this spiritual journey is represented through the archetypal signs used in architecture, especially religious architecture. Moreover, there is a profound connection between religious architecture and the house because the house was the first temple, the first place of worship. The house was '"common ground", that is, it contained everything. It was the source of everything, and potentially could hold everything' (Marc 1977, p. 24).

The meaning of the house, therefore, has changed over time. While the functions of temple and house were originally contained in the same space, the division of these purposes was accompanied by the development of two distinct types of architecture, which are a reflection of the purposes. As the famous architect Louis Sullivan (1896) proclaimed, 'Form follows function' (although this was originally spoken by an American sculptor, Horatio Greenough). As such, in Western societies, the temple is generally recognisable by its cruciform design, which represents the interior path of the human spirit, whereas the house generally uses the four archetypal signs – the circle, square, triangle, and cross – and has come to be understood as the 'temporal nucleus where man asserts his earthly condition' (Marc 1977, p. 58). Despite this schism, there remain traces of the original spiritual dimensions of the house:

> To build a house is to create an area of peace, calm and security, a replica of our own mother's womb, where we can leave the world and listen to our own rhythm; it is to create a place of our very own, safe from danger. For once we have crossed the threshold and shut the door behind us, we can be at one with ourselves (Marc 1977, p. 14).

The house is a microcosm within the macrocosm; as domestic architecture it represents the opportunity for, and necessity of, creative expression. In this sense, for thousands of years architecture has been the richest mode of human expression and creativity, which is 'nothing less than the power of life, for life creates, and everything that lives creates. The need to create is innate in the human spirit' (Marc 1977, p. 79).

The house provides physical protection, and is the place from which all human activities have emerged. More importantly, it provides a secure 'base from which consciousness is formed, consolidated and expanded, and the self defined'; the house is the 'hearth, the common ground of the psyche's growth and transformation' (Marc 1977, p. 67). If we accept that the human psyche, throughout a lifetime, searches for the unity with the universe in order to reconnect the bonds that were severed at birth, then 'the house-temple represents the religious aspect of this search, the link with oneness, the rebinding inside the soul of the bonds which were torn asunder at birth' (Marc 1977, p. 69).

Further evidence for the belief that the first house and temple were one and the same is provided from an anthropological perspective of human history, which suggests that societies have previously been organised according to partnership principles, rather then the dominator principles widespread today (commonly referred to as patriarchy or matriarchy) (Eisler 1990). Partnership societies were prevalent until about 5000 B.C. and were societies where social relations were based on the principle of linking, rather than ranking, and difference was not equated with inferiority or superiority (Eisler 1990). These societies worshipped a mother-goddess as the representation of the universe as an all-giving life force; it would therefore be reasonable to surmise that these societies worshipped the mother-goddess at the hearth within the temple-house, the traditional place within the house that is associated with women, life, and regeneration:

> Later, when human consciousness began to evolve further, the functions of the temple and the dwelling became separate. The woman was at the hearth; the mother goddess was in the temple; the Holy Virgin was in the church. The home had a door, and so did the temple; but both were derived from the same primordial aperture (Marc 1977, p. 25).

The house, therefore, is one of the most profound and important examples of architecture, and a primal, but universal, expression of the human psyche. While the architectural expression of the house may be unique to a region, climate and culture, the purpose and meaning of the house to the human psyche transcends all of these. Moreover, the first temple was also the first house. While the original purpose of the house as a place of worship may have been eliminated with the physical separation of the two functions, and the development of distinctive architecture for each, the spiritual dimensions of the house have endured through domestic architecture.

2.3 Home

There is a tendency within Western culture to conceive of home as a physical structure - such as a house - where space and time are controlled. These houses are described by Blunt and Dowling (2006, p. 88) as '"ideal" or "homely"' homes, and within the context of western domesticity, they are usually considered to be a detached (or semi-detached) house located in a suburb on the fringe of the city. As noted earlier, the origins of this ideal is found in the post-Second World War suburban development, and the belief that work and home should be both physically and conceptually separate, as should public and private spheres. Within this context, the city, associated with industry and work, was not deemed suitable for raising children and creating a family, instead the countryside was the preferred location for these activities.

These "ideal" homes are associated with a heterosexual, nuclear family, are individually owned, and inextricably linked economic processes in Australia in a number of ways. Firstly, the prevailing cultural belief that a home should be a house, rather than an apartment, and that it should be owned rather than rented (Lewis 1999). Secondly, the house/home is a site of material consumption of goods, which continues to rise (Blunt & Dowling 2006). And finally, the house/home is the site of a significant contribution of unpaid domestic work such as cooking, cleaning and child-rearing. Moreover, this work is often un-recognised in national accounting systems. The Australian Bureau of Statistics records these activities in the category of "time use" rather than "work" (ABS 2002), and they are not included in the Gross Domestic Product. If included, the British government estimated the value of this work to 'more than double the size of the economy' in 1997 (McDowell 1999, p. 83). This is supported, and advanced, by some of these governments, who have promoted the 'conflation of house, home and family as part of a broader ideological agenda aimed at increasing economic efficiency and growth' (Mallett 2004, p. 66).

Despite the tendency to use these terms interchangeably, there are meaningful differences between these concepts. Furthermore, the relationships between the terms house and home are unique to particular cultural and historical contexts, and must be established and defined with reference to these (Blunt & Dowling 2006). Within the context of this research, house and home are treated as two distinct elements that *may* coalesce to create a single experience. As Blunt and Dowling (2006, p. 88) point out, 'imaginaries of home can be connected to numerous places at multiple geographical scales'. Not every house becomes a home, and a home may not necessarily be a house, it may be any physical environment with significance for a person or people. A task of this study, therefore, is to identify the connections between house and home, and how they are made.

2.3.1 Home Defined

As previously noted, a house is a physical structure that provides shelter for people. Its physicality and tangibility enable it to be reasonably easily defined. In contrast, home is a highly contested concept within academic literature and has been discussed from various perspectives, including as a socio-spatial entity, a psycho-spatial entity and an emotional 'warehouse' (Easthope 2004, p. 134). Within the field of geography, the term home is a broad concept, and holds a range of diverse and contradictory meanings (Blunt 2005; Mallett 2004). As such, home is now often understood to be a multidimensional concept requiring a multidisciplinary approach to fully understand its complexity.

The view of home as a social or cultural construct is widely held within the field of critical geography and has been is discussed from a number of perspectives (Blunt 2005; Blunt & Dowling 2006; Bourdieu 1990; Busch 1999; Dovey 1999; Dowling & Mee 2007; Mallett 2004; Rybczynski 1987; Shove 2003). While this research has identified some normative meanings of home, such as privacy, identity, family (Mallett 2004), and belonging and attachment (Blunt & Dowling 2006), it has also shown that these meanings may vary across social groups according to class, race, gender and sexuality, among others (McDowell 1999).

Some of the more recent literature has been increasingly exploring the gay and lesbian experience of home, especially from the perspective of identity-creation and home-making, within the context of the '"heterosexualised"' western home (Gorman-Murray 2007, p. 231). The home is a key site of identity-creation and stability (Blunt 2003), and research suggests this is no less important to gay men and lesbians. The gathering of material possessions over time enables the home to become a site of identity expression (Noble 2004), especially an expression of sexual identity free from self-censoring. In this context, the process of identity-creation resists heteronormativity and affirms sexual difference, thereby legitimising and normalising 'gay/lesbian sexuality as a "routine" or "everyday" expression of human sexuality' (Gorman-Murray 2007, p. 234). Therefore, research suggests that gay and lesbian meanings of home may be both congruent with, but also challenge, normative meanings of home (Pratt 1999; Gorman-Murray 2007).

Within the field of humanistic geography, the concept of home is closely associated with place. While there are a number of perspectives within this approach, the following authors define home in terms of emotional attachments and as profound centres of human existence. For these authors, home is somewhere a person has affective ties; a location of meaning and field of care.

Tuan (1991, p. 99) defines geography as 'the study of the earth as the home of people'; in this sense, home is the unifying concept for all the subdivisions of geography, because 'home, in the large sense, is physical, economic, psychological, and moral'. Home exists at a range of scales, from the whole earth to the corner of a room, and embodies notions of place, location and space, three key concepts in geography. Within this context, home as a concept is far more than a physical setting, it is a 'unit of space organised mentally and materially to satisfy people's real and perceived basic biosocial needs and, beyond that, their higher aesthetic-political aspirations' (Tuan 1991, p. 102).

Home may be viewed as profound centres of human existence (Relph 1976). Within this perspective, home is more than simply a house; it is an irreplaceable centre of significance that cannot be arbitrarily moved around. It is located and meaningful, and intimately associated with people's identity as individuals and part of a community (Relph 1976). Within this context, home is 'an exemplary kind of place where people feel a sense of attachment and rootedness' (Cresswell 2004, p. 24).

For Seamon (1979), home is the centre from which a person's world is experienced, a private place where a person may seek repose and relaxation, and have control over their surroundings. Furthermore, an attachment to home is associated with *at-homeness*, which is the 'taken-for-granted situation of being comfortable and familiar with the world in which one lives his or her day-to-day life' (Seamon 1979, p. 78). According to Seamon (1979), there are five characteristics of at-homeness: rootedness, appropriation, regeneration, at-easeness and warmth.

Bachelard (1994) uses the terms house and home interchangeably; the meaning he ascribes to them is essentially the same. From this perspective, the experience of home is both intimate and intense, and 'all really inhabited space bears the essence of the notion of home' (Bachelard 1969, p. 87). The experience and memories of childhood homes are particularly significant, as these homes comprise 'our first universe, a real cosmos in every sense of the word', and frame the way in which people go on to understand the world (Bachelard 1969, p. 86). These memories form the threads of narratives past that come 'to dwell in a new house' (Bachelard 1969, p. 87).

To live in a home is a uniquely human experience; animals inhabit, but they do not (as far as we know) have homes. There is even a particular name for people who do not have a home: "homeless". As Zaborowski (2005, p. 496) notes, the fact that the term "homeless", rather than "houseless", is used to describe the situation suggests that the issue is not so much about the lack of physical shelter, but the absence of the complex psychological and social phenomena associated with having a home. Furthermore, to be human means:

> ... to live somewhere, to be at home in a particular place, to be able to make a place for oneself, to set up one's own system of coordinates, to have one's own relations of near and far, familiarity and distance, or height and depth. Man dwells as long as he lives – and even longer (Zaborowski 2005, p. 496)..

The concept of home is implicit in Heidegger's notion of Dwelling, and both are intimately associated with a sense of orientation in the world. The fourfold - earth, sky, divinities, and mortals – provide a single reference point for human existence in the world, and therefore the opportunity for humans to reflect on, and appreciate, their location in the world. For Heidegger (1951), this process enabled people to Dwell, and thereby to feel at home.

The notion of Dwelling, and an accommodation with one's surroundings, is also an essential aspect of the concept of *genius loci* which describes the spirit of place as an integrated totality. The *genius loci* of a place may be concretised through architecture, which then becomes a representation of the human understanding of both the natural environment and the existential situation in general. The construction of human-made place, therefore, is a deliberate and conscious act which makes tangible the human understanding of natural phenomena:

> To dwell between heaven and earth means to "settle" in the "multifarious in-between", that is, to concretise the general situation as a man-made place. The word "settle" here does not mean a mere economical relationship; it is rather an existential concept which denotes the ability to symbolise *meanings*. When the man-made environment is meaningful, man is "at home" (Norberg-Schulz 1980, p. 50).

The relationship between the human psyche and the spirit of place is a profound dynamic that contributes to a sense of accommodation, Dwelling, and home.

2.3.2 Home as Place

From all of these perspectives, home is by definition a place. Within this context, the distinction between house and home is similar to the difference between space or landscape and place. The house is a physical structure, and it becomes a home for a person when they experience it as meaningful, develop affective ties with it, and view it as a field of care. While homes may be located, it is not the house, nor the neighbourhood, that make a home. Rather 'homes can be understood as "places" that hold considerable social, psychological and emotive meaning for individuals and for groups' (Easthope 2004, p. 135). From this perspective, house as home and place are inextricable: 'For a man with deep roots in a place, climate, home and the self make a single whole' (Marc 1977, p. 60).

2.3.3 House and Home

A house is a physical, tangible structure within which a person may live and store their material possessions; a home is an intangible concept, an emotional feeling and attachment, where people store their memories, emotions, and experiences. Implicit in this definition is that a house becomes a home through a positive experience. Given that feelings are the language of the soul (Moore 1992), this suggests that an emotional attachment would not be possible unless there is also a spiritual experience of home, and that the two are inextricably linked. In this way, then, a home nourishes the soul. This also suggests that that a house is more likely to become a home when it is 'architecture'.

2.4 Conclusion

While architects agree that there is a difference between a building and architecture, the articulation of this difference is more elusive. The various interpretations and definitions of architecture converge on a number of essential elements: the design must contain creativity, vision, and intuition, all of which are expressions of aspects of the human spirit, psyche, or soul. These qualities form the living psyche of the house, which exists when the occupier experiences the emotive power of the architecture, pure delight, and, according to Le Corbusier, 'it is there when your heart is touched' (Boyd 1970, p. 113). These qualities are necessary for a house to be experienced as a home, for there is a direct link between the expression of the human spirit in domestic architecture, and the development of affective ties, which are essential to the experience of home as a centre of meaning and field of care.

The literature drawing on Jungian psychology attempts to explain the way in which the human psyche may be physically represented in domestic architecture. However, this study is focusing on the human psyche's *experience* of the house as home and place, rather than the *representation* of the human psyche in architecture, and as such this literature does not provide a conceptual framework for the research design of this study. Given that there are a number of place theories that explore the human experience of place, and home by definition may also be considered a place, then these theories provide a useful framework for exploring these human-environment interactions (Easthope 2004). Place theories will therefore be reviewed in the following chapter with the aim of constructing a theoretical framework that will be used to explore the human psyche's experience of house as home and place.

3 Theories of Place

The essence of place lies in the largely unselfconscious intentionality that defines places as profound centres of human existence (Relph 1976, p. 43).

3.1 Introduction

The concept of "place" is highly contested across a number of academic disciplines, including geography, philosophy, planning, architecture, and ecology. Place theories, therefore, are an important intersection between these diverse, but related, professional fields of enquiry, and provide a lens through which interdisciplinary research may be viewed. Within geography in particular, place studies tend to focus on the "how" and "why" places are created and experienced. While the phenomenon is global – places may be created and experienced anywhere on earth that humans have ventured - the meaning of place is generally local[1]. The concept remains fundamental to human existence, and the study of place has been one of the 'particular concerns' of geography since Strabo wrote about it in the first century AD (Relph 1976, p. 1).

Place has always been central to geography, however the approach to, and definition of, place has changed over time. Geographers originally conceived of place in a relatively narrow context – that of describing regions - a theme which remains current today, although the focus is now on the human activities that produce regions, rather than describing regions that already exist (Cresswell 2004). One of the first modern attempts to define place was undertaken by Lukerman in the 1960s. He suggested that 'Geography is the knowledge of the world as it exists in places' (1964, p. 167). From this perspective, places are dynamic and unique, and include the components of a location - integrations of nature and culture - which are connected to other places through the movement of goods and people (Lukerman 1964; Relph 1976). Despite this initial work, the concept remained relatively undeveloped until the 1970s. Since then, two dominant approaches have been articulated.

The first was a result of the emergence of humanistic geography, a stream of geography founded on the philosophies of phenomenology and existentialism, and the principles of humanism[2]. From this perspective, Relph (1977, p. 178) suggests that a humanistic geographer is one who 'conducts his life and studies humanistically, who is tolerant of the views of others yet constantly questions dogma and prejudice, and who always considers the human implications of his own decisions and actions'. This approach to place theories deliberately rejects the scientific procedures which view the lifeworld - 'the culturally defined spatiotemporal setting or horizon of everyday life' (Buttimer 1976, p. 277) - through dualistic terms, separating subject/object, thought/action, and people/environment.

---

[1] Authors such as Relph (1976), Tuan (1977), and Auge (1995) nevertheless have lamented increasing globalisation and tourism which contributes to the prevalence of non-places and placelessness.
[2] For debates regarding the nuances within this approach refer to (Relph, Tuan & Buttimer 1977).

According to authors such as Relph (1976; 1979), and Tuan (1975; 1977), a dualistic approach is inadequate to investigate the complexities of place as an element of the lifeworld; in contrast, a phenomenological approach aims to allow the essence of place to reveal itself on its own terms. Within this approach, place is viewed as a centre of meaning and field of care, an essential component of human life that forms the basis for human interaction (Malpas 1999; Sack 1997). In this context, Tuan (1975, p. 152) defines place as a 'centre of meaning constructed by experience'. This approach tends to focus on understanding and describing the essence of the human experience of place in detail, and has been adopted by humanistic geographers, neo-humanists and phenomenological philosophers.

The second approach, that of critical geography, was developed in part as a reaction to humanistic geography. Rather than drawing on the philosophies of phenomenology and existentialism, critical geography was developed from social theories including Marxism, feminism, and cultural studies. From this perspective, authors such as Anderson (1991), Clayton (2000), and Till (1993), argue that places are the product of social processes. Within this context, Cresswell (2004, p. 17) defines place, at a 'basic level' as 'space invested with meaning in the context of power'. The focus of this approach is on explaining why places operate as human social constructs, and the way in which wider social and institutional factors and processes contribute to the creation of place. The authors who take this view are particularly interested in how place is a product of unequal power relations, and how places represent 'instances of more general underlying social processes' (Cresswell 2004, p. 51).

Within this context, the literature will be reviewed with two purposes. The first is to develop a theoretical framework for answering the research questions:

1. *How do people describe their understanding and experience of house, home, and place?*

2. *How do people describe their understanding and experience of the relationship between house, home, place and sustainability?*

3. *How do people describe the relationship between childhood memories and their understanding and experience of home?*

The experiential nature of the research questions immediately discounts the approach to theories of place taken by critical geographers. As such, the following theories from within humanistic geography provide a framework for exploring and answering the research questions. These are place as Being[3], place as Dwelling, place and placelessness, place as *genius loci*, and place as memory. The second purpose of this review is to identify criticisms and weaknesses in the selected theories with the aim of addressing them, where possible, in the subsequent design of the study. The scope of this section is limited to theories of place as experience, specifically the experience of the human psyche, as described in the previous chapter. These theories will necessarily be founded on phenomenology and existentialism.

This chapter contains two sections. The first includes a definition of the concept of place, especially from the perspective of humanistic geography. Within this, place is articulated with reference to the closely related concepts of space and landscape, and as a way of understanding the world. The second section contains a review of five relevant place theories, and an overview of the primary criticisms of these theories.

The first of these theories is Heidegger's concept of Being, especially Being-in-the-world, and the way in which this relates to the human experience of place. The second is Heidegger's concept of Dwelling, which, for Heidegger, is the 'basic character of Being' (Heidegger 1951, p. 362). Dwelling is intimately connected with building, and is concerned with the way in which Dwelling is a spiritual experience that 'unites the natural and human worlds' (Cresswell 2004, p. 22). The third perspective, articulated by Relph (1976), draws heavily on Heidegger's concepts of Being and Dwelling to define place as the experience of rootedness, authenticity, and insidedness, and the absence of these as placelessness. The Norwegian architect, Christian Norberg-Schulz (1971; 1975; 1980; 1985), is one of the key authors who has developed the concept of *genius loci*, also referred to as the 'spirit of place'. This is the fourth theory to be reviewed. Norberg-Schulz uses Heidegger's concept of Dwelling as the point of departure to discuss the way in which architecture concretises the phenomena of a site, especially the phenomena of natural place, so place may be experienced as an integrated totality. The final theory, articulated by Bachelard (1994), discusses a phenomenological approach to place as memory, suggesting that poetic images are located in the soul and are the conflation of intimate experience, memory, and imagination. This perspective, defined by Bachelard (1994) as topoanalysis, is explored through the experience of home, especially the memories of home.

---

[3] English translations of Heidegger's work usually capitalize Being, Dwelling, and Dasein (Frede 2006, p. 42), whereas commentary about Heidegger's work does not consistently follow this pattern. As such, quotes include the author's original emphasis (either capitalisation or non-capitalisation), and the remainder of the text will use capitalisation for these terms.

Hence, the purpose of this Chapter is to present a review of relevant literature regarding these theories of place, and identify and define foundational concepts and themes within each theory that are relevant to the understanding and experience of home as place.

3.2 Definition of Place

The distinctions between the definitions of place, space, and landscape are highly contested yet meaningful and necessary. Precisely because places are everywhere, people tend to have commonsense ideas about what places are. However these tend to be confined to viewing place at the scale of a village or town, and are often 'quite vague when subjected to critical reflection' (Cresswell 2004, p. 11). A more detailed definition has been offered by Agnew (1987b), who claims there are three key aspects required in order to define somewhere as a "place". The first is that a place must be located; it must exist as a physical location. However this does not need to be stationary, or even on land. For example, a ship may hold meaning for some people, even though it is changing location; the Aborigines in New South Wales named the parts of the ocean along the coastline that held meaning for them (Read 2000). The second aspect is that a place must provide a physical setting for social relations, a locale, within which a person experiences place. The third aspect is a 'sense of place', which Cresswell (2004, p. 7) describes as the 'subjective and emotional attachment people have to place'.

For humanistic geographers, place is a deeper, richer, and more profound human experience than is adequately explained within spatial science or social constructions of place. Humanistic approaches emphasise subjectivity and experience. Tuan (1974, p. 246) explains that 'the humanist begins with a deep commitment to the understanding of human nature in all its intricacy'. From this perspective, humanistic geographers tend to view place as an 'integral part of psychological and social well-being' (Seamon 1993, p. 2).

Within humanistic geography, place is commonly defined as space invested with meaning, somewhere people have affective ties which are developed through experience. While place is related to space and landscape, 'its experiential dimension is qualitatively different' because places are 'constructed in our memories and affections through repeated encounter and complex associations place experiences are necessarily time-deepened and memory-qualified' (Relph 1985, p. 26).

Similarly, for Heidegger, a location, or building, may be understood as a place primarily through use and experience (Sharr 2007, p. 52). Using the example of a bridge, Heidegger claims that the place wasn't there before the bridge was; rather, the bridge and the area around it (what it "gathers") are 'understood differently once the bridge was built. It became in peoples' minds the place of the bridge' (Sharr 2007, p. 52). For Heidegger, the act of building is 'less about abstract objects than located individuals', especially locating individuals in place (Sharr 2007, p. 10).

Another method for thinking about place is the aspect of scale. Place may be thought of as a product of a 'pause' and a chance of attachment (Tuan 1977, p. 149). From this perspective, it exists at many scales, from the whole earth at one extreme to a corner of a room at the other. The problem, for Tuan (1974), is that geographers tend to think of place at the scale of a settlement, rather than a house or a chair.

Place may also be defined by what it is *not* in relation to two other concepts from geography which are often substituted for place – space and landscape.

3.2.1 Place and Space

The concept of space within geography gained credence and popularity during the 1970s. It was developed from a nomothetic approach, and, drawing from scientific approaches, the aim was to generate laws that could be applicable anywhere. Space, therefore, is a more abstract concept than place; it is empty and unembodied. As Escobar (2001, p. 143) notes, 'Since Plato, Western philosophy – often with the help of theology and physics – has enshrined space as the absolute, unlimited and universal, while banning place to the realm of the particular, the limited, the local and the bound'.

Although there are two distinct approaches to place within geography, both tend to identify a difference between abstract space - what Lefebvre (1991) calls absolute space - and meaningful, inhabited space. This meaningful, inhabited space is generally defined within humanistic geography as place, and within critical geography as either social space, socially produced space, or place.

From the perspective of humanistic geography, both Tuan (1977) and Relph (1976) conceptualise space and place as diametrically opposed, with abstraction at one end and experience at the other; space may become place only when it becomes meaningful to humans and affective ties are developed. However each of these authors has a slightly different characterisation of space with reference to place. Tuan (1977) argues that the concepts of "space" and "place" require each other for definition. From this perspective, Tuan (1977, p. 6) defines place, in relation to space, as the pauses between movement; each of the pauses enables 'location to be transformed into place'.

However, Relph (1976) focuses on space as an abstract concept, juxtaposed against place as a lived reality. From this perspective, space is intangible and cannot be described, yet 'however we feel or explain space, there is nearly always some associated sense or concept of place' (Relph 1976, p. 8). In this sense, space and place are inextricable; space provides the context for place, yet it is also meaningless without place.

More recent literature within geography explores the relationship between space and place (and time) within the context of the increasing internationalisation of capital, expressed as the increasing movements of people, goods, and capital around the globe (Agnew 1987a; Cresswell 1996, 2004; Harvey 1989, 1996; Massey 1994; Oakes & Minca 2006; Sibley 1999). One of the central themes is the phenomenon of "time-space compression", and what Massey (1994) describes as the stretching out of different kinds of social relationships. The result is a perception of disorientation, uncertainty about the meaning of place, and the accelerating erosion of place (Cresswell 2004).

The underlying tension between time-space compression, and place, is the perception of the 'fixity' of place, which is in opposition to the fluidity of the global economy (Massey 1994, p. 151). In this context '"time" is equated with movement and progress, "space"/ "place" is equated with stasis and reaction' (Massey 1994, p. 151). Within this context of change and uncertainty, Harvey (1989) argues that people are increasingly looking to a sense of place for stability. One of the expressions of this is the increasing attempts to define and delineate the boundaries of place. The result of this, however, is the increasing "transgression" of these boundaries.

When people turn to a sense of place for a feeling of stability, it is often associated with the construction of 'tightly bounded place-identities' (Massey 1994, p. 162). Agnew (1987a) describes these as the territorial identity of sense of place. These identities, by their nature, define themselves in opposition to an "other", and this 'denial of difference' contributes to resistance against these forces (Sibley 1999). Gated communities are an increasingly common, reactionary and defensive response to the movement of people and the construction of a place-identity. It creates a physical and spatial separation from "others" and the various perceived maladies these people bring (Sibley 1999). While Pratt (1999) argues that boundary construction is an effort to organise space, Harvey (1989) claims that it has a political dimension, defining areas of local government and social power. In this scenario, the residents are protecting their "fixity" of place, securing it against the 'uncontrolled vectors of spatiality' (Harvey 1996, p. 292).

In contrast, Massey (1994, p. 147) argues for a sense of place that is 'adequate to this era of time-space compression'. The internationalisation of capital is changing the role of geographical places within the broader context, and in this process 'their boundaries dissolve as they are increasingly crossed by everything from investment flows, to cultural influences, to satellite TV networks' (Massey 1994, p. 161). Therefore, a 'global sense of place' that is 'progressive; not self-enclosing and defensive, but outward-looking' is the most appropriate for this era of time-space compression (Massey 1994, p. 147).

Yet another, though less commonly used, definition of space and place is offered by de Certeau (1984), who defines space and place in reverse; place is a meaningless empty grid, the site for practice, whereas space is given meaning through practice.

3.2.2 Place and Landscape

Landscape as a concept dates back to the Renaissance and refers to the material topography of the earth's surface, which may be altered, to varying degrees, by humans; it specifically refers to the 'portion of the earth's surface that can be viewed from one spot' (Cresswell 2004, p. 11). Landscape is therefore a predominantly visual data which, from the perspective of the humanistic geographer, is 'seen more as objects for interpretation than as contexts of experience' (Relph 1985, p. 23).

Embodied in the concept of landscape is not only that which can be seen, but also the way it is seen, and the way in which the scene is framed. The important distinction between landscape and place within humanistic geography is the position of the viewer; generally the viewer of a landscape is *outside* of it, whereas for humanistic geographers, place by definition means the person must experience it from the *inside*. In this sense, landscape is the antithesis of place.

3.2.3 Place as a Way of Understanding

Place may also be defined as a way of understanding the world in which we live. There is a general acknowledgement by humanistic geographers who argue for theories of place as experience, that to be human is to be "in place" (Relph 1976). As these theories of place are founded on Husserl's philosophy of phenomenology, then the primary concerns of this philosophy are also important aspects of these theories. One of these concerns is the idea of "intentionality", which is the "aboutness" of human consciousness. Husserl (1931) argues that humans cannot be conscious without being conscious of something, which then constructs a relationship between the self and the world.

For Relph (1976, p. 42), this consciousness is intimately connected with being in place. From this perspective, places are the 'basic elements in the ordering of our experiences of the world'; the "something" that humans are conscious of is something in its place (Relph 1976, p. 43). The meaning and essence of place 'lies in the largely unselfconscious intentionality that defines places as profound centres of human existence' (Relph 1976, p. 43). When the world is viewed as a dynamic system of places, as a 'rich and complicated interplay of people and the environment' then the attachments between people and place are highlighted (Cresswell 2004, p. 11). Place as experience, therefore, is not simply something a person experiences as a physical thing, it can also be a way of seeing, knowing and understanding the world.

3.3 Place as Being-in-the-World

The question of "Being" has been a central thread of philosophical discussion since Plato and Aristotle. For Aristotle, the question '*ti to on*, What is being?', has been, and will always remain, a 'matter of perplexity', and as such it constituted an essential component of his work (Krell, D. F. 1993, p. 4). Like Aristotle before him, for Heidegger the question of Being was the core element that pervaded all his life's work (Frede 2006; Glendinning 1998; Sharr 2007). Heidegger argued that an exploration and understanding of Being should start from the 'condition of being', which he defined in relation to its opposite, nothing (Sharr 2007, p. 28). Thus, in *Being and Time*, Heidegger (1962, p. 21) states that "Being" is simultaneously the most universal and the emptiest of concepts that does not require any definition, 'for everyone uses it constantly and already understands what he means by it'.

Within this framework, existence was explored in relation to non-existence, human presence in relation to its absence, and life in relation to death. In particular, this approach to philosophy began with the 'remarkable but often overlooked fact that human life exists' (Sharr 2007, p. 28). It is this wonder about life – and an appreciation for the reminders of this - that provides an appropriate perspective from which to contemplate it. When we remember to notice our own being, we find respite that 'allow people to locate themselves in a bigger picture, in a time span much longer than a life' (Sharr 2007, p. 8).

For Heidegger, the framework provided by contemporary philosophy was 'riven by inherited conceptual distortions' because 'modern philosophy operates with an objectifying conception of what it is to be human' (Glendinning 1998, p. 44). It is this distortion that Heidegger was attempting to rectify with his definition of Being (Glendinning 1998, p. 44). From this perspective, the primary barrier to properly understanding the question of Being is the 'orientation' influenced by the anthropology and anthropocentrism of Christianity, and compounded by the ancient Greek conception of man as the *animal rationale* (Glendinning 1998, p. 45). In this context, Heidegger characterises humanist anthropology as a tradition which defines 'man' as an entity among others, but separate from them in the sense that humans are 'endowed with the power of reason or language' (Glendinning 1998, p. 45).

Heidegger's definition of Being, therefore, begins with a rejection of this conception of what it is to be human, and the idea that it is merely an accident that humans are located in a world. To further emphasise this point, Heidegger uses the compound expression "Being-in-the-world", 'stressing thereby that the "in the world" aspect of our existence is not an added extra but an essential and irreducible feature of it' (Glendinning 1998, p. 46).

In rejecting the dominant modes of philosophy of his time, Heidegger (1962, p. 29) proposed that inherent in the question of Being is the 'considerations required for working it out', which he suggested should be treated phenomenologically. From Heidegger's (Heidegger 1962, p. 50) perspective, phenomenology 'expresses a maxim which can be formulated as "To the things themselves!"', which is essentially the process of allowing things to manifest themselves. It is a way of thinking that enables people to see things clearly, especially, for Heidegger, the true essence and character of Being (Frede 2006).

The question of Being, therefore, is fundamentally a question of truth as disclosure and unconcealment (Krell, David Farrell 1991, p. 129). The "thing" that is disclosed in this process, the true essence and character of Being, Heidegger referred to by the traditional German term for existence: "Dasein". In making this connection, Heidegger provides further insight into the condition of Being. Within this context, Dasein is not a synonym for human being or person, 'but re-inscribes within an ontologically appropriate setting what is named by, but misconceived in, the discourses with those other names' (Glendinning 1998, p. 47). Being-in-the-World, therefore, is the basic state of Dasein, and is enabled and facilitated by place: "Dasein" names that which should first be experience, and thence properly thought of, as Place – that is, the locale of the truth of Being (Heidegger 1949 p. 202, cited in Fell 1979, p. 47).

The basic conditions of the world that Heidegger's Being inhabits are the earth, sky, divinities and mortals, which he refers to as the fourfold (Heidegger 1962). The fourfold are 'installed' through 'construction' (such as building) (Sharr 2007, p. 55). By gathering the fourfold 'around it for reflection', a building gives the fourfold presence and plays a critical role in mediating this relationship (Sharr 2007, p. 34). Sharr (Sharr 2007, p. 52) notes that when Heidegger refers to '"gathering", it might also be translated to English as "placing"'. As such, when a building gathers the fourfold, and it is experienced as gathering, place is created.

Heidegger's concept of Being heavily influenced the phenomenological approach to place theories within the field of geography. For these theorists, 'Place is the phenomenal particularization of "being-in-the-world"' (Casey 1993, p. xv). Starting from the premise that 'Being-in-the-world is the basic state of human existence' (Relph 1985, p. 17), this approach focuses on understanding the relationship between human beings and the world with reference to geographical concepts, especially place. Moreover, Being-in-the-world acknowledges the fact that there is already 'an environment for each of us before we become curious about the earth and the location and character of its different places' (Relph 1985, p. 19).

This thread of philosophical thought has been the basis on which philosophers of place, such as Sack (1997), Malpas (1999), and Casey (1993; 1997), have developed their theories. In the past decade these authors have argued for a more fundamental role for place in human life, and that 'there is no possibility of understanding human existence – and especially human thought and experience – other than through an understanding of place and locality' (Malpas 1999, p. 16).

Place as Being-in-the-World may be viewed as encompassing social activities and institutions that both determine and express the structure of a place (Malpas 1999). While a particular place may be ordered in terms of space and time, according to the social ordering, Malpas (1999) argues that this does not does not legitimate the claim that place, space or time are merely social constructions. Moreover, social activities do not exist except within the context of place; it is only 'within the structure of place that the very possibility of the social arises' (Malpas 1999, p. 36).

While this approach draws heavily on an experiential perspective, both Malpas (1999) and Sack (1997) embrace the notion that places are the products of human society and culture. However, they argue that there are deeper, more fundamental components to place than simply the interaction of social forces, and that 'society itself is inconceivable without place – that the social (and the cultural) is geographically constructed' (Cresswell 2004, p. 31). Furthermore, Malpas (1999) and Sack (1997) claim that humans must be in place before they can construct social and cultural meanings; that being in place is the experience of Being-in-the-World.

3.4 Place as Dwelling

Heidegger developed the concept of Dwelling as a way of exploring the character of Being. These concepts, then, are intimately connected in the sense that Dwelling is *'the basic character* of Being' (Heidegger 1951, p. 362). When individuals reflect on the fourfold and appreciate their 'location in the world and circumstances they find themselves in', they reach a peaceful accommodation with their surroundings (Sharr 2007, p. 32). This accommodation between individuals and the world facilitates Dwelling.

As previously established, the fourfold are 'installed' through building (Sharr 2007, p. 55). As such, Heidegger explored the connection between Dwelling and building through etymology, the history of the meaning of words. In this context, Heidegger searched for connections through the multiple meanings of the verb "to build". The Old German word for building, *buan*, means to Dwell, which signifies to remain, to stay in place (Heidegger 1951, p. 348). Heidegger believed the fact that building and Dwelling share the same root in old German was 'no coincidence', for 'It indicated that 'building' and 'Dwelling' were previously understood as one and the same activity' (Sharr 2007, p. 39).

Furthermore, *bauen* is related to the German words *buan*, *bhu*, *beo* and *bin*; *bin* is the conjugated form of the verb *bis*, meaning "to be", which Heidegger claims provides an indication of *'how far the essence of dwelling reaches'* (Heidegger 1951, p. 349). In this sense, the conjugated forms of the verb - I am, you are - really mean 'I dwell, you dwell'; that 'man *is* insofar as he *dwells*' (Heidegger 1951, p. 349). This suggested to Heidegger that 'building and dwelling were once at the core of any affirmation of being' (Sharr 2007, p. 40).

Furthermore, the old word *bauen*, like the Old Saxon word *wuon*, and the Gothic *wunian*, also mean to remain, or to stay in place (Heidegger 1951, pp. 350-1). However, the Gothic *wunian* provides an indication of how this remaining is experienced; *wunian* means to be at peace, to be brought to peace, or to remain at peace (Heidegger 1951, p. 351). The German word for peace, *Friede*, means the free, das *Frye*, and *fry* means preserved from harm and danger, preserved from something, or safeguarded (Heidegger 1951, p. 351). Thus, to free essentially means 'to spare' (Heidegger 1951, p. 351). However, sparing is more than simply not harming the one whom we spare, it is 'something *positive* and takes place when we leave something beforehand in its own essence, when we return it specifically to its essential being' (Heidegger 1951, p. 351). Thus to Dwell means to be set at peace and remain at peace within the free, which in turn 'safeguards each thing in its essence'; for Heidegger (1951, p. 351) *'The fundamental character of dwelling is this sparing'*.

Further meanings of the word *bauen* include to cherish and protect, to preserve and care for, and especially to till the soil, to cultivate the vine (Heidegger 1951, p. 349). Within these meanings, Heidegger articulates the distinction between two forms of building. The first is building that does not actually make anything, but preserves, nurtures, and cultivates (Latin *colere*, *cultura*); 'such building only takes care – it tends the growth that ripens into its fruit of its own accord' (Heidegger 1951, p. 349). The second form of building is the construction of physical forms, such as temples and houses; this is building 'as the rising up of edifices, *aedificare*' (Heidegger 1951, p. 349). Dwelling, however, encompasses both forms of building.

In this context, the essence of building is a 'producing that brings something forth' (Heidegger 1951, p. 361). The Greek for 'to bring forth or to produce', *tikto*, shares its root, *tec*, with *techne*, meaning technique, 'to make something appear, within what is present, as this or that, in this way or that way' (Heidegger 1951, p. 361). Thus *techne* was understood by the Greeks in terms of 'letting appear', which Heidegger claims has been 'concealed in the tectonics of architecture since ancient times' (Heidegger 1951, p. 361). In this sense the word *techne* is a mode of knowing, which *brings forth* what is present: '*techne* never signifies the action of making' (Heidegger 1956, p. 184).

The critical link between building and Dwelling is twofold. First, buildings are essential to facilitating Dwelling; and second, building has Dwelling as its goal (Heidegger 1951, p. 347). The sole reason for building is to provide an existential foothold to enable Dwelling. However, there is a clear distinction between buildings that simply 'house' people, and those in which Dwelling occurs; houses in themselves do not necessarily 'hold any guarantee that *dwelling* occurs in them' (Heidegger 1951, p. 348). In this sense, Dwelling 'implies something more than "shelter"' (Norberg-Schulz 1980, p. 5). The example of a building that enables Dwelling is a farmhouse in the Black Forest:

> The essence of building is letting dwell. Building accomplishes its essential process in the raising of locales by the joining of their spaces. *Only if we are capable of dwelling, only then can we build*. Let us think for a while of a farmhouse in the Black Forest, which was built some two hundred years ago by the dwelling of peasants. Here the self-sufficiency of the power to let earth and sky, divinities and mortals enter *in simple oneness* into things ordered the house. It placed the farm on the wind-sheltered mountain slope, looking south, among the meadows close to the spring. It gave it the wide overhanging shingle roof whose proper slope bears up under the burden of snow, and that, reaching deep down, shields the chambers against the storms of the long winter nights. It did not forget the altar corner behind the community table; it made room in its chamber for the hallowed places of childbed and the "tree of the dead" – for that is what they call a coffin there: the *Totenbaum* – and in this way it designed for the different generations under one roof the character of their journey through time. A craft that, itself sprung from dwelling, still uses its tools and its gear as things, built the farmhouse (Heidegger 1951, pp. 361-2).

From Heidegger's perspective, building and Dwelling, are essentially the same and are 'vitally connected with human presence in the world' (Sharr 2007, p. 46). In this context, Dwelling gave rise to the configuration of the farmhouse by gathering the fourfold (Sharr 2007, p. 68). As such, the building of the farmhouse is the result of a dynamic relationship between Dwelling and the fourfold. The farmhouse was built 'according to the needs of dwelling and dwelt according to configurations of building', and was the means by which people could understand their surroundings (Sharr 2007, p. 69).

The theme of vernacular architecture, especially domestic architecture, as an exemplary form of architecture that enables Dwelling, has been examined by a number of authors (Harries 1983; Norberg-Schulz 1965; Rykwert 1972; Zaborowski 2005). Harries (1983) suggests that the primitive hut is to architectural theory what the social contract is to political theory. For Laugier (1755, cited in Harries 1983, p. 49) the first hut is the paradigmatic building, as it is the first attempt to reconcile the human needs of cave and forest, neither of which were adequate on their own. The first house, then, expresses both the image of the cave and the image of the forest (Norberg-Schulz 1965, p. 125). The primitive hut, and the farmhouse in the Black Forest, are both examples of architecture that provides an existential foothold, a concretisation of 'man's existential space' (Norberg-Schulz 1971, p. 12). They are completely integrated with the fourfold, a relationship that is critical to enable Dwelling.

Humans Dwell when they can orientate themselves within, and identify with, an environment, and when they experience the environment as meaningful (Norberg-Schulz 1980). Drawing explicitly on these concepts, and providing an analysis of Dwelling that is relevant to the various forms of human settlements today, Norberg-Schultz (1985, p. 7) defines multiple modes of Dwelling. These include collective, public and private Dwelling, and each of these modes requires a different setting. Collective Dwelling is undertaken in the settlement and its urban spaces; public Dwelling is enacted in institutions or public buildings, which are the 'embodiment of public dwelling'; and private Dwelling is reserved for the house, the 'private retreat where the individual could prosper' (Norberg-Schulz 1985, p. 13). In these contexts, the built environment is always related to the landscape within which it sits, and therefore 'gathers' (Heidegger 1951, p. 347).

Dwelling, therefore, is foundational to the concept of place as experience. From this perspective, place as Dwelling is 'a spiritual and philosophical endeavour that unites the natural and human worlds' (Cresswell 2004, p. 22). This is a profound relationship that is concerned with ideas of rootedness and authenticity. However there are increasing concerns that the ability to Dwell is being compromised by increasing separation from 'both the earth and our own human being' (Seamon & Mugerauer 1985, p. 1). As the human domination of the earth increases, so does our homelessness.

From a philosophical perspective, the fact that Heidegger is considered *the* thinker on Dwelling suggests that it had not previously been the philosophical problem that it appears to be today

(Zaborowski 2005, p. 500). Heidegger observed that in the post-war era the Western world was becoming increasingly dominated by technology and economics rather than human experience. He argued that people understand their world through their surroundings, and their emotional attachments and responses to them. Buildings, therefore, remain central to people's understanding of their world, and as such 'the primary trade of architects is arguably in human experience' (Sharr 2007, p. 2).

Moreover, if philosophy is concerned with ideas that are important at that point in time, then the fact that the concept of Dwelling has emerged as a theme in twentieth-century philosophy suggests a direct relationship between the possibility of Dwelling and the current state of the world:

> Dwelling itself has become a question and a problem. This state of affairs says something about man's place in the world. More precisely: about the loss of place, man's homelessness in the modern world, which has often been a theme of discussion. Man has lost his home, he has lost the place that belongs to him. "In truth," says Theodor W. Adorno so significantly, "it is no longer possible to dwell." (Zaborowski 2005, p. 501)

While Adorno claims it is no longer possible to Dwell (Zaborowski 2005, p. 501), Relph (1976) discusses these ideas in terms of place and placelessness, which will be explored in the following section.

3.5 Place and Placelessness

Relph (1976) developed his theory of place and placelessness in response to the discussion around environmental issues at the time. His explicit aim was to contribute to the development of an alternative approach to understanding the environment, and, in direct opposition to the prevailing scientific approach at the time, to present a theory of place that identified the variety of ways in which places are experienced. Within this context four themes were explored. The first is the relationship between space and place; the second is the way in which places vary with respect to components and intensity of experience; the third is 'the nature of the identity *of* places and the identity of people *with* places'; and the fourth is 'the ways in which sense of place and attachment to place are manifest in the making of places and landscapes are illustrated' (Relph 1976, p. i).

This approach draws on Heidegger's (1958, p. 19) perspective of place, which suggests that '"place" places man in such a way that it reveals the external bonds of his existence and at the same time the depths of freedom and reality'. From this perspective, there is a 'deeply felt involvement' and 'profound psychological links' between people and the places in which they live and experience

(Relph 1976, p. i). Relph (1976, p. 1) therefore surmises that place 'is a profound and complex aspect of man's experience of the world'. Moreover, he argues that it is an important human need to have ties with places, and that a profound attachment to place is as necessary and significant as meaningful relationships with other people. In this sense, to be human 'is to live in a world that is filled with significant places: to be human is to have and know your place' (Relph 1976, p. 1). There are three aspects to this approach to place and placelessness that are particularly relevant to this study: rootedness, insideness and authenticity.

3.5.1 Rootedness

A sense of rootedness comes from a deep attachment to a place, a familiarity that is part of 'knowing and being known' in a particular place (Relph 1976, p. 37). Beyond knowing, a sense of rootedness is commensurate with a 'sense of deep care and concern for that place' (Relph 1976, p. 37). This relationship transcends the physical, and is one of the most important, yet least recognised, needs of the human soul (Weil 1952). While it is one of the hardest to define, Weil (Weil 1952, p. 43) suggests that a person has 'roots by virtue of his real, active and natural participation in the life of the community, which preserves in living shape certain particular expectations for the future'.

Moreover, to have roots and to feel a sense of rootednesss, is a 'necessary precondition for the other "needs of the soul"' (Relph 1976, p. 38). It is intimately associated with a sense of belonging, and provides a 'secure point from which to look out on the world' (Relph 1976, p. 38). When a person feels a sense of rootedness, they have a 'significant spiritual and psychological attachment to somewhere in particular' (Relph 1976, p. 38). The places where people feel a sense of rootedness and belonging become a 'field of care', a physical environment in which people have had 'a multiplicity of experiences and which call forth an entire complex of affections and responses' (Relph 1976, p. 38). Associated with the experience of place as a field of care is a sense of respect, responsibility, and commitment to that place. This is an approach to place that Heidegger referred to as sparing, which is 'a willingness to leave places alone and not to change them casually or arbitrarily, and not to exploit them' (Relph 1976, pp. 38-9). This sense of sparing and rootedness is essential for a sense of home to be properly realised. Moreover, to have and experience a sense of home is also to Dwell.

3.5.2 Insideness

The extremes of this experience of the essence of place are insideness and outsideness. A sense of insideness is experienced when people belong to, and identify with, a place. Moreover, Norberg-

Schulz (1971) suggests that the entire concept of place is formed around the goal of a sense of insideness. In this context, defining what is inside and what is outside, and the attachment to inside, is critical to dwelling. Through this attachment, 'man's experiences and memories are located, and the inside of space becomes an expression of the "inside" of personality. "Identity", thus, is closely connected with the experience of place' (Norberg-Schulz 1971, p. 25).

This sense is a feeling of knowing who you are. It is a sense of safety and enclosure, a sense of being simultaneously surrounded by it and a part of it. A sense of insideness is not necessarily fixed and rigid. Instead it is fluid, and the boundaries between inside and outside are in a state of flux depending on people's intentions. As such, there are many possible levels of insideness. However, Relph (1976) notes three primary levels. The first is behavioural insideness, which is simply a physical presence in a place. The second is empathetic insideness, whereby there is an emotional connection with a place. The third is existential insideness, which involves complete and unselfconscious commitment to a place. These experiences are immediate and direct; conversely, vicarious insideness is less immediate, and describes the secondhand experience of place through various media including art and novels.

In contrast, a sense of outsideness generally results from little or no emotional attachment to a place. There are three ways of experiencing outsideness. The first is incidental outsideness, where places are merely backgrounds for other activities. The second is objective outsideness, a situation where places are treated as concepts and locations. The third is existential outsideness, and involves a profound alienation from all places (Relph 1976, p. 50).

3.5.3 Authenticity

These notions of insideness and outsideness correspond to the concepts, developed from Heidegger (1962), of authentic and inauthentic attitudes to place. In this context, authenticity 'connotes that which is genuine, unadulterated, without hypocrisy, and honest to itself, not just in terms of superficial characteristics, but at depth' (Relph 1976, p. 64). This mode of being is congruent with Dasein. An authentic attitude to place is understood to be a direct and genuine experience of place, of a sense of insideness and belonging, and importantly, of these experiences being unreflected and unselfconscious. It just is. As such, an authentic attitude to place is generally expressed by an existential insider.

Conversely, an inauthentic attitude to place is characterised by 'no sense of place' and no understanding of the profound significance of place (Relph 1976, p. 82). It is this condition of inauthenticity that is 'the prevalent mode of existence in industrialised and mass societies', and that

Relph (1976, p. 81) refers to as 'placelessness'. However, it was Heidegger (1951) who first claimed that distances were shrinking in the post-war world due to travel and the mass media, and that simultaneously the distance between humans and their own existence was increasing. Relph (1976) is also highly critical of shrinking distances and the homogenisation of the world, which prevents people from developing a sense of insideness and authentic relationships with place.

From this perspective, tourism is cited as one of the most prevalent homogenising influences, which results in the 'disneyfication', 'museumization', and 'futurization' of places (Relph 1976, p. 93). Similarly, he is especially critical of 'other-directed architecture', which is designed for spectators as consumers, and does not represent the people living and working in them (Relph 1976, p. 93).

One of the most important factors contributing to a sense of placelessness, however, is increasing housing mobility. This degree of movement is a relatively new phenomenon in the history of housing, and is due to a range of factors including the degree of private and public investment in housing, tenure arrangements, and the prevailing economic and social context. In Australia in particular, investment in housing is increasingly viewed as an opportunity for wealth creation and as a signifier of social status (Blunt & Dowling 2006). This mobility has significantly changed the way western societies view purchasing and inhabiting houses, and has diminished attachment to place. In contrast, for primitive and vernacular cultures both practical and religious feelings about place are interwoven, 'and there is a deep and multi-faceted attachment to a single, clearly defined home area' (Relph 1976, p. 83). The current attitudes towards the interchangeability of house and home not only reduce the significance of home in a spiritual sense, but also the significance of home-in-place.

3.6 Place as *Genius Loci*

Heidegger's concept of Dwelling is the point of departure for an approach to place that views it as an integrated totality. The Latin term for spirit of place, *genius loci*[4], describes the essence of this integrated totality (Rigby 2004). While the spirit of a place includes the topography, appearance, and social activities and functions, it is more than the sum of these, for it can persist despite major changes in any of these components. The concept of *genius loci* is intimately connected with Heidegger's (1951; 1978) notions of building and Dwelling to the extent that '"Existential foothold" and "dwelling" are synonyms, and "dwelling", in an existential sense, is the purpose of architecture' (Norberg-Schulz 1980, p. 5).

---

[4] Norberg-Schulz (Norberg-Schulz 1980) italicises the term *genius loci*, and as such this precedent will be followed.

Moreover, humans dwell when they experience an environment as meaningful. Dwelling, therefore, 'implies something more than "shelter". It implies that the spaces where life occurs are *places*, in the true sense of the word. A place is a space which has a distinct character' (Norberg-Schulz 1980, p. 5). Architecture provides the means by which humans identify with and orientate themselves in their environment. It concretises and visualises the *genius loci*, thereby enabling humans to Dwell. In the context of the *genius loci* of place, the existential meanings of places are beyond the social and are determined by 'the structures of our *being-in-the-world*' (Norberg-Schulz 1980, p. 6).

The *genius loci* of place is articulated through four distinct, but essential, aspects: the phenomena of natural place, the spirit of natural place, the phenomena of human-made place, and the spirit of human-made place. The first aspect, the phenomena of natural place, is something that humans have always comprehended as having structure and embodying meaning (Norberg-Schulz 1980, p. 23). When these meanings are experienced, two things happen. Firstly, humans come to understand (existentially) heaven and earth, and their intersection, which is essential in order to Dwell; and secondly, humans feel 'at home' (Norberg-Schulz 1980, p. 23). This understanding of the natural environment developed 'out of a primeval experience of nature as a multitude of living "forces". The world is experienced as a "Thou" rather than an "it"' (Norberg-Schulz 1975, p. 428).

Primeval humans were both embedded in nature, and critically dependent on these natural forces. This understanding of the natural world as having a life force is a significant factor in shaping an individual's understanding of, and relationship with, the natural environment (Eliade 1963). The primary mode of understanding these natural phenomena, and making sense of the world, are mythologies (cosmogonies and cosmologies) which have formed the basis of Dwelling. Norberg-Schultz (Norberg-Schulz 1980) therefore suggests that a phenomenology of natural place should take mythologies as its point of departure.

The interaction of the earth and sky is the basis of the spirit of natural place, which is the second aspect of *genius loci*. The dynamics of this relationship vary with distinctive geographic regions. While there is interaction between the earth and sky everywhere, there are some regions where the balance between the two creates a 'harmonious whole of medium scale which allows for relatively easy and complete identification' (Norberg-Schulz 1980, p. 42). Within this context, it is a common understanding that landscape determines fundamental existential meanings or contents – people describe a sense of feeling "lost" when they move to an unfamiliar landscape (Norberg-Schulz 1980, p. 47). This is because landscape functions as an extended ground to the human-made places, and as '"preparation"' for the human-made places, landscapes provide 'natural insides' (Norberg-Schulz 1980, p. 48).

The third aspect of *genius loci* is the phenomena of human-made place. This aspect is concerned with the way in which humans express and concretise the essence of a place through physical means. While this may include any structure, temporary or permanent, architecture is generally the most prolific means of doing so. From this perspective, the human-made environment has structure and embodies meaning, and thereby facilitates Dwelling.

The construction of human-made place, therefore, is a deliberate and conscious act which makes tangible the human understanding of natural phenomena. This understanding of natural phenomena does not necessarily precede building - the act of building may become a means to this understanding, and that in fact there exists a 'reciprocal relationship between the natural and man-made place' (Norberg-Schulz 1980, p. 52). The phenomena of human-made place, therefore, are a physical manifestation of the existential situation. For example, primeval humans experienced natural place and the phenomena within it as alive, and this magical life force, or 'mana', was also embodied in buildings and artefacts (Norberg-Schulz 1980, p. 50).

The fourth aspect of *genius loci* is the spirit of human-made place, which is the *genius loci* of the integrated totality (Norberg-Schulz 1980). The specific *genius loci* of human-made place is determined by what is visualised, complemented, symbolised or gathered. In this context, the term "gather" is used in the sense defined by Heidegger (Heidegger 1978). Inherent in the act of gathering is place identification, which can occur at a range of scales from the house to the city. The *genius loci* of a site emerges when the building and the site create an integrated totality, and therefore place. From this perspective, there is a clear distinction between vernacular architecture and urban architecture. The essence of place expressed by vernacular architecture is crystallised from the natural place, drawing on the variety and mystery of natural forces. In contrast, urban architecture is more comprehensive and eclectic, and draws on the 'spirit of the locality to get "roots"' (Norberg-Schulz 1980, p. 58).

3.7 Place as Memory

In *The Poetics of Space*, Gaston Bachelard outlined a particular phenomenological approach to memory explored through the experience of home, especially the memories of home. Bachelard's (1969) central idea was the way in which self may be understood through an investigation of the places it inhabits. This approach was primarily concerned with the 'placiality of the psyche', suggesting that the soul provides a place for images, especially poetic images (Casey 1997, p. 288). In this sense, he set out to 'affirm the soul as a place or set of places'; from this perspective, 'place can be non-physical and yet still count fully as place' (Casey 1997, p. 288).

This approach is similar in a number of ways to both Freud and Jung in their interest in the 'localisation of our memories' (Bachelard 1969, p. 89). However, Bachelard's (1969, p. 89) area of research is essentially the convergence of descriptive psychology, depth psychology, psychoanalysis and phenomenology, which he defined as 'topoanalysis . . . the systematic psychological study of the sites of our intimate lives'. Casey (1997, p. 288) describes this as 'Less a method than an attitude', which focuses on the 'placial properties of certain images'. From this perspective, these images are divided into 'the places they offer for their own content' (Casey 1997, p. 289).

The poetic image Bachelard was particularly interested in was the house, for 'the house image would appear to have become the topography of our intimate being' (Bachelard 1994, p. xxxvi). Where Heidegger considered the world as a house for mortals, Bachelard considered the house to be a world, 'a place-world, a world of places' (Casey 1997, p. 291). Within this context, the house is a 'privileged entity for a phenomenological study of the intimate values of inside space' (Bachelard 1969, p. 86). For Bachelard, the importance of the house cannot be overstated, for it is 'body and soul. It is the human being's first world' (Bachelard 1969, p. 88).

Moreover, Bachelard (1969, p. 87) suggests that 'all really inhabited space bears the essence of the notion of home'. From this perspective, the experience of home is both intimate and intense, for our house is 'our corner of the world . . . our first universe, a real cosmos in every sense of the word' (Bachelard 1969, p. 86). As such, it is important to properly understand and engage with the initial experience of the house, as our first universe and cosmos, before attempting to understand the wider universe. Bachelard explains this in terms of the 'I and the non-I', and argues that the beginning of images start with the home, 'the non-I that protects the I' (Bachelard 1969, p. 87). The experience and memories of childhood homes are particularly significant, because, as our first universe, they frame later understandings about the world. These memories form the threads of narratives past that come 'to dwell in a new house' (Bachelard 1969, p. 87). From this perspective, the home is fundamental to all future experiences.

Despite the importance placed on childhood memories, there is an acceptance that the images and memories are unlikely to be accurate. While the poetic images of home are really a conflation of experience and memory, and are therefore probably inaccurate, the 'imagined/remembered' house 'is highly structured and knows its own limits' (Casey 1997, p. 292). In this sense, the imaginary space holds great value for Casey (1997) who argues that it is consistent, specific and highly detailed. However, Bachelard (1969, p. 87) suggests that it is through 'poems, perhaps more than through recollections, we touch the ultimate poetic depth of the space of the house'.

3.8 Criticisms of Theories of Place as Experience

Humanistic geographers have relied heavily on the philosophies of phenomenology and existentialism to develop their theories of place. Due to this, a number of valid criticisms have been directed towards these theories. One of the broadest comes from Pred (1984, p. 279), who argues that within the context of humanistic geography place is conceived of as 'an inert, experienced scene', rather than a dynamic site of social change and process. This criticism probably stems from a clash of perspectives; humanistic geographers emphasise the holistic experience of place, and as such the environment in which place is experienced is as important as the person experiencing it. The focus in this context is, from a phenomenological perspective, on the individual's connection with, and experience of, place. For critical geographers, however, the social processes are more important than the environment in which they take place. As social processes are dynamic, and are generally able to respond more quickly to changing conditions than the built or natural environments, it follows that the understanding of place provided by humanistic geographers may be considered static by critical geographers.

At a more specific level, there are a range of criticisms of Heidegger's concepts of Being, Dwelling, and authenticity, which impact on the validity of the subsequent place theories that incorporate these concepts. One of the most prevalent and substantiated criticisms of Heidegger's concept of Being, and the subsequent approach to place as Being-in-the-World, is that it tends to remain in the realm of philosophy rather than applied to real situations (Cresswell 2004). Philosophers of place such as Sack (1997), Malpas (1999), and Casey (1997) tend to discuss place in general or use idealised examples, as Heidegger did with the cabin in the Black Forest. As such, the concept of Being tends to remain a philosophical notion that informs place theory, rather than an explanatory theory of place. A task of this study, therefore, is to explore this within an Australian context.

Similar criticisms are directed towards Heidegger's concept of Dwelling, and its relation to place; there is a dearth of examples demonstrating this concept, especially current examples. Heidegger's example of a fictional farmhouse in the Black Forest is relatively straightforward to portray as sparing and preserving its surroundings, being embedded in its location, and gathering the multifarious in-between. This romanticised example is not transferable to an urbanised environment. However, Heidegger (1951) himself conceded that the social, political, economic, and even environmental circumstances in which the fictional farmhouse would have been built have fundamentally changed. Instead, the farmhouse was used to demonstrate the 'ethos that Heidegger advocated' in terms of building and dwelling (Sharr 2007, p. 71).

Now that the majority of the world's population of 6.6 billion people live in urban rather than rural areas, there are a range of issues emerging that have never before been experienced at this scale. These include increasing rates of migration (especially rural – urban), displacement, and refugees in developing countries; expanding urban sprawl in developed countries; and the emergence of mega cities in both (Carnevale et al. 2007). It is, perhaps, more critical than ever before for the inhabitants of earth to achieve a 'peaceful accommodation between individuals and the world' (Sharr 2007, p. 37). It follows that there is a need to explore how this may be accomplished in the world today.

Given that the concepts of Being and Dwelling are foundational to both Relph's theory of place and placelessness (and the associated notions of rootedness, insideness and authenticity), and Norberg-Schulz's theory of *genius loci*, these tend to suffer similar criticisms. There are also criticisms specific to each theory. For place and placelessness, it is directed towards Heidegger's (1962) notion of authenticity:

> Such claims admit two sorts: the knowing *cognoscenti*, Heideggerians who appreciate clues of being; and those who do not know, or have not been taught, how to see. For Adorno and others, authenticity is dangerous because it is divisive and potentially exclusive (Sharr 2007, p. 13).

The approach to place as *genius loci* is vulnerable to criticisms regarding the examples used to demonstrate this theory. Like Heidegger's farmhouse in the Black Forest, Norberg-Schulz (1980, p. 30) tends to rely on exemplary architecture from Classical Greece (for example, the tholos of Athena, and the theatre and temple of Apollo, all at Delphi) to demonstrate the way in which the 'individual and intelligible' character of particular sites were concretised in architecture, thus achieving a '"reconciliation" of man and nature'. These examples tend to be in Europe, the Middle-East, and Northern Africa, all of which have distinctive vernacular architectural heritage that is essentially akin to Heidegger's farmhouse. However, the landscapes, mythologies, and the architecture of these regions are not directly transferable to the distinctive conditions in Australia, which has its own indigenous heritage. While there is an increasing body of literature focusing on this in an Australian context (for example Cameron 2003; Rigby 2003; Tacey 2003), this study will explore and articulate a *genius loci* of place unique to Australia.

The primary criticism of Bachelard's approach to the experience and memories of home is that it considers "ideal", rather than "real", homes. These critics argue that Bachelard's descriptions focus 'on nostalgic or romantic notions of home' (Mallett 2004, p. 69). Furthermore, critics of the ideal home 'reject exclusively positive descriptions and assessments of home as naïve expressions of false consciousness' as these descriptions do not reflect the diverse experiences and understandings of home (Mallett 2004, p. 69).

Similar criticisms have emerged from within the field of critical geography, where feminist critiques of the experience of home argue that many women do not hold this 'rosy view of home/place that humanistic geographers tend to place at the center of the discipline' (Cresswell 2004, p. 25). Authors such as Friedan (1963), Hayden (1984), McDowell (1999), Pratt (1999), and Rose (1993) argue that for many women the home is the private site of abuse, neglect, drudgery, isolation, and domestic slavery.

In fact, Rose (1993, p. 35) argues that the home is 'the central site of the oppression of women', and that from this perspective there is limited evidence to support the humanistic geographers' claim that home provides the ultimate sense of place. Furthermore, the quest to uncover the essence of the experience of place, and thereby articulate a universal experience, fails to acknowledge that many experiences are possible. This failing is addressed in this study through a research approach (phenomenography) that seeks to articulate the qualitatively different ways people describe their understanding and experience of house, home and place.

3.9 Conclusion

The theories of place as experience that have been reviewed share a foundation in the philosophies of phenomenology and existentialism, and the principles of humanism. This approach aims to allow the essence of place to reveal itself in its own terms. Within each of these theories there is an acknowledgement that the human connection with place transcends the physical, and it is because of this that place may be experienced, and thus created. From this perspective, place is viewed as a centre of meaning and a field of care that is constructed through experience. However, place is more than experience; it is also a way of seeing, knowing and understanding the world. While the theories reviewed are intimately connected, each explores a different aspect of the human psyche's experience of place.

The first theory, place as Being-in-the-World provides a philosophical framework for understanding human existence – thought and experience – through place and locality. From this perspective, Being-in-the-World, as the basic state of Dasein, is given expression and existence through place. The second theory, place as Dwelling, provides another philosophical framework within which to explore the experience of Dwelling as the basic character of Being. Dwelling, as a peaceful accommodation between the fourfold, is facilitated by building, especially building that spares and preserves. The third theory, place and placelessness, explores the ideas of rootedness, insideness, and authenticity, all of which may be experienced as part of a deep attachment, care, and concern for a place. It is suggested that this profound relationship between a person and place is as important to human wellbeing and sense of self as interpersonal relationships.

The fourth theory, the concept of *genius loci*, or spirit of place, focuses on the way in which architecture concretises the spirit of a place, and in so doing provides an existential foothold for humans to orient themselves in the world. When this occurs, humans experience the environment as meaningful, which in turn facilitates Dwelling. The final theory, place as memory, provides a philosophical framework for understanding how the experience and memories of home as place conflate to create poetic images that are located in the soul. This approach emphasises the importance of childhood homes, as the first universe, in framing the way people go on the think about and experience the world.

These theories, and the themes articulated within them, will inform the subsequent design of this study, and will be drawn upon to create the conceptual framework to explore how people describe their understanding and experience of house, home, place and sustainability, and the relationships between these.

4 Research Design

Writing is a representation – we make choices, and what we choose is a situated approximation (Kamler 2008).

4.1 Introduction

The review of the literature in Chapter 2 provides the context for this study. The meaning and experience of house and home for the human psyche were discussed, and the significant gaps in the existing literature concerning the human psyche's experience of house as home and place were revealed. The qualitative research that was undertaken in order to address this gap, and contribute to the existing body of knowledge, is outlined in this chapter.

The first section provides an outline of the research questions and the nature of the research. This is followed by an overview of phenomenography as the selected approach and the major assumptions associated with this. The data collection techniques include a cultural probe and in-depth interviews, and the rationale for the selection of these is discussed, in addition to specific guidelines for their use. Issues related to the trustworthiness of the research design and conduct, and the associated ethics are discussed. The chapter concludes with an outline of the conduct of the study and a detailed discussion of the four phases: initiating the study; data collection; data analysis; and theorising from the study.

4.2 Research Questions

The aim of this project is to describe the way in which people understand and experience house, home, place and sustainability, and the relationship between these, by answering the following research questions:

1. *How do people describe their understanding and experience of house, home, and place?*

2. *How do people describe their understanding and experience of the relationship between house, home, place and sustainability?*

3. *How do people describe the relationship between childhood memories and their understanding and experience of home?*

The research questions seek to explore the intimate relationships between people and their house, home and place, and the way in which their understanding of sustainability influences these experiences. They also focus on the respondents' memories of childhood experiences of home, and the way in which this framed the way they went on to conceptualise and experience home as an adult. Due to the qualitative nature of this study, the data collected are well grounded in rich descriptions and explanations. Within this context, the aim of the study and the review of the literature suggest a particular research approach and techniques that are most suitable for answering the research questions.

4.3 Research Approach

Phenomenography is the research approach used to undertake this study. It is a research approach that specifically seeks to explore respondents' conceptions and experience of aspects of the world, which is the aim of this study. A central assumption within phenomenography is that there is variation in the way people experience the same phenomena. The results of this research approach are rich descriptions that are distilled to generate categories of description for each phenomena, which in this study are house, home, place and sustainability. While this research approach has traditionally been used within education research, it is increasingly being applied to a wider context (Bowden 2000), including the study of sustainability practices. For example, a recent PhD thesis authored by Gooch (2003) used phenomenography to explore the experiences of sustainability and resilience for catchment volunteers in the east coast of Queensland, Australia.

4.3.1 Phenomenography

Phenomenography was developed in the 1970s within the field of education research to better understand students' experience of learning. It was not until the early 1980s that Ference Marton (1981) defined this approach as phenomenography and proposed that it should be a research specialisation in its own right.

Since then, three streams of phenomenography have emerged (Marton 1988). The first stream is content-related, and seeks to identify the relationship between the differences in students' learning outcomes to the differences in their learning approaches. The second stream is focused on the examination of learning in different educational realms, such as physics or maths. These two streams are often referred to as developmental phenomenography (Bowden 2000). The third stream is interested in how people experience aspects of the world around them, for example politics, social security or taxes (Dall'Alba 2000; Marton 1986, 1988). This stream is considered to be "pure" phenomenography as it considers the full spectrum of lived experiences with the aim of developing rich descriptions of the range of experiences of a particular phenomenon (Bowden 2000). This stream is also described as discursive phenomenography by Hasselgren and Beach (1997).

Marton and Booth (1997) define phenomenography as a "research specialisation", rather than a research method or a theory of experience. While Svensson (1997) supports this position that phenomenography is not a research method or theory, he further defines phenomenography as a research orientation, composed of two aspects. The first is phenomenography as a research tool, which uses descriptions of conceptions to study various phenomena. The second is phenomenography as a research program, in which the focus is the aim of research in terms of what should be investigated, and how it creates a field of research and a field of knowledge. However, Svensson (1997, p. 162) notes that phenomenography also 'includes characteristics of method of a general kind intimately related to the orientation', and can therefore be viewed as a research approach.

As a research approach, phenomenography is concerned with human-world relations and interactions, and therefore places equal emphasis on the phenomena being experienced and thought about, and the person who is experiencing and thinking about the phenomena (Marton 1986; Svensson 1997). In this study, the phenomena are house, home, place and sustainability. Phenomenography is defined by Marton (1986, p. 31) as:

> . . . a research method for mapping the qualitatively different ways in which people experience, conceptualise, perceive, and understand various aspects of, and phenomena in, the world around them.

A significant foundational assumption of phenomenography is that for each phenomena, concept, or principle there are a limited number of qualitatively different ways of understanding them.

Phenomenography is closely related to both Gestalt psychology and phenomenology, however it differs from them in important ways. Gestalt psychology is interested in *how* people perceive and conceptualise the world. The focus is generally on the act of perception and conceptualisation, with the aim of characterising this *process* in general terms, and deriving overarching laws of thought and perception that can be applied to any situation or subject matter. In contrast, within phenomenography:

> . . . thinking is described in terms of what is perceived and thought about; the research is never separated from the object of perception or the content of thought (Marton 1986, p. 32).

The aim is to elicit all the qualitatively different ways people understand specific phenomena and sort them into conceptual categories. The point of departure is the focus on the *relationship* between the individual and the phenomenon. Phenomenographic research adopts an experiential, or second-order perspective, where participants are asked to consciously reflect on the meaning of the phenomenon being studied (Hasselgren & Beach 1997). In contrast, a first-order approach encourages participants to describe the phenomenon itself, rather than the experience of that phenomenon. Thus, phenomenographers do not aim to make statements about the world as such, but about people's conceptions of the world (Hasselgren & Beach 1997; Svensson 1997).

Phenomenography shares some fundamental similarities with phenomenology. However, phenomenography was not developed from phenomenological philosophy. As such, Svensson (1997, p. 164) suggests it is inappropriate to include phenomenography within this philosophical tradition. While both use hermeneutic processes, Marton (1986) defines three main points of divergence between phenomenography and phenomenology. The first is that Husserl's phenomenology takes a first-person perspective. The second is that phenomenology explores lived experiences in order to arrive at the *essence of the meaning* of the phenomenon (Husserl 1931). Conversely, phenomenography seeks to identify the *variations* between the limited number of qualitatively different ways people understand a particular phenomenon. The third difference is that, within Husserl's phenomenology, the distinction between experience and conceptual thought is emphasised, whereas the focus for phenomenography is the relationship between the individual and the world or phenomenon, regardless of whether these relationships are manifested in the forms of immediate experience, conceptual thought, or physical behaviour.

4.3.2 Research Paradigm

As an empirical research tradition, phenomenography is not derived from a philosophical tradition defining metaphysical beliefs about the nature of reality and the nature of knowledge. There is no direct relationship between this research approach and ontological and epistemological assumptions (Svensson 1997). Conversely, research paradigms such as constructivism, positivism, post-positivism, and critical theory, are characterised by ontological, epistemological, and methodological assumptions (Lincoln and Guba 2000).

4.3.3 Ontological Assumptions

Ontological assumptions are concerned with the nature of the "knowable", and the nature of reality (Bryman 2004). Two of the general metaphysical positions concerning the nature of reality are materialism and idealism. It is possible for phenomenographic research to encompass any of these positions. Phenomenographic research makes assumptions about the nature of the objects or phenomenon of study, rather than the nature of reality. These assumptions, therefore, concern the nature of conceptions, which are intimately related to the nature of knowledge. In this context, knowledge is assumed to be based on thinking, and is dependent on the external reality towards which the thinking is directed. Therefore, conceptions within phenomenography are 'dependent both on human activity and the world or reality external to any individual' (Svensson 1997, p. 165).

4.3.4 Epistemological Assumptions

Epistemological considerations are concerned with what is regarded as acceptable knowledge (Bryman 2004). More specifically, it describes the nature of the relationship between the knower (the inquirer) and the known (or knowable). The ontological assumptions in phenomenography concern the nature of conceptions, which also have the character of knowledge. In this sense, ontological assumptions also become epistemological. However, the research results of phenomenographic enquiry have specific epistemological assumptions.

The first is the emphasis on description, which assumes an acceptance of 'knowledge as a matter of meaning and similarities and differences in meaning' (Svensson 1997, p. 167). In contrast with other research approaches that pre-determine categories of meaning (implying a generality of meanings), a phenomenographic approach seeks to empirically explore the various meanings. The second is the assumption that description is useful for exploring the nature of conceptions, which 'form the results of and conditions for human activity' (Svensson 1997, p. 167). Descriptions are abstracted to form categories of description.

4.3.5 Methodological Assumptions

Methodological considerations are concerned with the way in which the researcher should elicit knowledge. The methodological approach that is consistent with phenomenography is both hermeneutic and dialectic. The purpose of the hermeneutic component is to identify the multiple constructions and describe them as accurately as possible; the purpose of the dialectic component is to compare and contrast these constructions, and to refine them[1].

4.3.6 Assumptions within Phenomenography

Both qualitative and quantitative research adheres to general assumptions that are made while working with data which ensure the data is meaningful, and should be made explicit (Miles & Huberman 1994). The following assumptions are applicable to phenomenography in guiding the collection and analysis of the data, and are adhered to throughout this project.

---

[1] Within the dialectic aspect of this methodology, these constructions are compared and contrasted so that each respondent confronts, and accepts, the constructions of others. Phenomenography as a research approach is congruent with this methodology in the hermeneutic aspect and thus the elicitation and description of multiple constructs. However it diverges within the dialectic component as it does not force respondents to confront and accept the constructs of others with the aim of generating substantial consensus.

4.3.6.1 Willingness to Participate

One of the most important assumptions within qualitative research of this nature is the willingness of the respondents to participate, and their commitment to honest reflection and truthfulness about their experiences and understanding of the phenomena in question. Furthermore, the data collection techniques require significant time commitments. This study was complicated by the fact that the phenomena explored are very personal, and a number of participants describe distressing experiences of home as both children and adults. Despite this, all participants demonstrated a willingness to fully participate due to their self-identification with, and stated commitment to, sustainability in general.

4.3.6.2 Bracketing/Epoche

Bracketing, also known as Epoche, was described by Husserl (1970, p. 577) as the freedom from suppositions:

> We must exclude all empirical interpretations and existential affirmations, we must take what is inwardly experienced or otherwise inwardly intuited (e.g., in pure fancy) as pure experience, as our exemplary basis for acts of Ideation. . . We thus achieve insights in pure phenomenology which is here oriented to *real (reellen)* constituents, whose descriptions are in every way "ideal" and free from . . . presupposition of real existence.

Bracketing is a technique whereby the researcher sets aside all their prejudgments, biases and preconceived ideas about things, previous knowledge, and experience. The purpose of this is to enable the "truth" to emerge from the data on its own terms. The researcher must set aside all existing knowledge and thoughts about the phenomenon under study to enable it to be 'gazed upon, to be known naively and freshly through a "purified" consciousness' (Moustakas 1994, p. 85). Bracketing was employed at all times when dealing with the data.

4.3.6.3 Nature of Conceptions

The nature of conceptions is closely related to the assumptions about the nature of knowledge and thinking. People's conceptions are based on both human activity and thinking, and the external world or phenomenon being thought about. Within phenomenography, there is an understanding that knowledge is 'relational, not only empirical or rational, but created through thinking about external reality (Svensson 1997, p. 165). A phenomenographic approach does not make statements about "reality"; rather, this approach attempts to uncover the various ways the respondents describe conceptions of the world around them. In this thesis, the conceptions explored are the various ways respondents describe their understanding and experience of house, home, place and sustainability.

4.3.6.4 Relation Between Subject and Object

The focus of phenomenographic research is on the relationship between the subject and object, the individual and the phenomenon. The individual does not exist independently of the phenomenon, and as such this research approach is nondualistic (Marton & Booth 1997). Phenomenographic research adopts a second-order perspective, where participants are asked to consciously reflect on the meaning of the phenomenon being studied (Hasselgren & Beach 1997).

4.3.6.5 Categories of Description

The conceptual categories of description are the results of phenomenographic research (Marton 1981). These categories are created by an iterative and interactive process of classifying the respondents' descriptions of their experience of the phenomenon. Whereas in traditional content analysis these categories are predetermined and imposed on the data, a phenomenographic analysis allows the categories to emerge from an iterative process of comparisons conducted within the data (Marton & Saljo 1984). This process involves two aspects. The first is identifying the most distinctive characteristics that appear in the data; and the second is identifying the structurally significant differences that clarify the various experiences of the relationship between the individual and the phenomenon (Marton 1986).

For each of the conceptual categories of description, there exists an internal horizon and an external horizon which are defined by the participant. The internal horizon or internal boundary describes the delimitation of parts of the phenomenon (Marton 1994). The delimitation from, and relation to the context, is the external horizon or external boundary of the phenomenon. The combination of the two horizons forms the structural aspect of the experience.

While the categories of description originated from a contextual understanding, the resulting categories of description are therefore decontextualised, and may be applied to other situations. Each of these categories is also part of an overarching structure within which all the categories are related - the outcome space - which is the goal of phenomenographic research.

4.3.6.6 Variation

A significant difference between phenomenography and other qualitative research approaches is that a phenomenographic approach seeks to identify variation, rather than uniformity, in the categorisation of the respondents' experiences of particular phenomena. Within this study, all the respondents' experiences are gathered and the limited number of conceptual categories of description are identified.

4.3.6.7 Outcome Space

The outcome space represents the hierarchical structure of the relationships between the categories of description, and is generally a visual representation of this relationship (Hasselgren & Beach 1997, p. 196).

4.4 Research Techniques

The nature of the research is highly personal, and as such it benefits from a rigorous consideration of how to properly engage with participants, particularly engaging with empathy. Ashworth and Lucas (2000, p. 300) outline a number of practical guidelines for the conduct of phenomenographic research with this in mind. These were used as the basis for developing the following guidelines for this study:

- The broad objectives of the research study are tentatively identified (the phenomena under investigation), recognising that the meaning of this may be quite different for the research participant.

- The selection of participants should aim to avoid presuppositions about the nature of the phenomenon or the nature of conceptions likely to be held by particular individuals.

- The most appropriate means of obtaining descriptions from respondents should be identified. In this study they are a cultural probe and in-depth interview. The aim is to allow maximum freedom for the research participant to describe their experience.

- The process of obtaining descriptions from respondents should enable the respondent to reflect on their experience, and the questions posed should not be based on researcher presumptions about the phenomena but emerge during the interview.

- Interviewing skills should be subject to ongoing review and refinement.

- The transcriptions of the interviews should be verbatim and aim to reflect the emotions and emphasis of the respondent.

- Data analysis should be undertaken using bracketing and empathetic understanding.

- The process of analysis should be sufficiently clearly described to allow the reader to evaluate the attempt to achieve bracketing and empathy and trace the process by which findings have emerged.

4.4.1 Data Collection

These guidelines provided the framework for selecting the most appropriate research techniques. As noted, the selected data collection techniques include a cultural probe and in-depth interview. The aim of combining these two techniques is to enable the participant to reflect on the meaning of their experience (which they may not previously have done), and to allow greatest freedom for the participant to describe their experiences.

4.4.1.1 Cultural Probe

Cultural probes are a relatively new method of data collection that were initially used by Gaver, Dunne and Pancetti (1999) as part of a community consultation process, and have since been used extensively in design-based research. A cultural probe is a purposefully designed mixed-media package (which may include notebooks, postcards, and disposable cameras) given to respondents to complete in their daily environment away from the gaze of the researcher. They are designed to be playful, creative, and 'provoke inspirational responses' about respondents' feelings, emotions, and experiences (Gaver, Dunne & Pacenti 1999, p. 22).

Cultural probes should be valued for their obliqueness rather than their comprehensibility; they are able to create 'intimate distance', and provide a 'feel for people, mingling observable facts with emotional reactions' (Gaver et al. 2004, p. 55). The fragmentary data collected from the cultural probes have traditionally been used by designers in order to assess and understand the needs of a group or community, and facilitate discussions with the respondents towards unexpected ideas, without focusing on the 'needs and desires they already understood' (Gaver, Dunne & Pacenti 1999, p. 22). Within the context of this study, the intention of the cultural probe exercises is to support and enrich the interview process, rather than act as results in their own right to be individually analysed. Therefore, the practical purposes of a cultural probe in this study are threefold.

The exercise of completing the cultural probe both prompts, and enables, the respondents to reflect on their experience of house, home, place and sustainability away from the gaze of the researcher. The aim of this process is to elicit responses that are well considered, thoughtful, and are a more accurate representation of the respondents' experiences. Furthermore, given the personal nature of the phenomena being studied, it enables the respondent to decide which aspects of their experiences they would like to share, and those aspects that they choose not to share.

The process of reviewing the completed cultural probe package will provide a level of understanding of how people interact with the environment of their day-to-day lives, the lived experience of their environment, and help to build empathy with the respondent prior to the interview. During the interview, the cultural probe data provide prompts, and facilitate threads of discussion that may not have otherwise been created, particularly emotional responses to house, home, place and sustainability.

Finally, the data from the cultural probes necessitate co-creating the data on two levels - the content and the context. The content of the image is the internal narrative, the story the image communicates, which is not necessarily what the image-maker (in this case, the respondents) had intended (Banks 2001). There may be multiple readings of the same image, hence the value in discussing the respondent's meaning of the content of the image during the interview, and ultimately co-creating the final understanding. The context for the image is linked to, but analytically separate from, the external narrative, and provides the social context for the image.

4.4.1.2 *In-depth Interviews*

The second data collection technique selected for this study is personal, semi-structured, in-depth interviews because, as Marton (1986) notes, personal interviews about specific phenomena enable a significant amount of rich data to be obtained. This type of interview is appropriate for phenomnographic interviews as it enables respondents to fully explore and reflect on their experiences. Rather than preparing a set of questions for the interviews, the cultural probe exercises provide prompts for discussion and the framework through which to explore respondents' experiences.

There are two advantages associated with this approach to interviewing respondents. The first is that it enables flexibility in the structure of the interview, a desirable quality for phenomenographic interviews. As noted, the cultural probe exercises have the potential to open a thread of discussion that may not otherwise have been possible with prepared questions. The second advantage is that it provides the respondent with the flexibility to discuss the cultural probe exercises in the order in which they feel most comfortable, which is generally more conducive to facilitating more detailed discussion and deeper insights.

It is acknowledged that conducting phenomenographic interviews is a difficult process. They have been viewed from a number of perspectives, including facilitating the thematisation of aspects of the interviewee's experience, and as the opportunity to bring the interviewee to a state of "meta-awareness", thereby creating a quasi-therapeutic interview situation (Marton & Booth 1997). However, Richardson (1999) notes there are political and ethical problems that may arise from treating the interview as a psychotherapeutic experience. Furthermore, the interviewer should be cognisant of the distribution of power within the interview context (Gubrium & Silverman 1989), which may be further exacerbated by approaching the interview as a psychotherapeutic experience. A more realistic approach is offered by Richardson (1999, p. 70), who suggests:

> To guard against such problems, what is needed is a reflexive approach that takes into account the social relationship between researchers and their informants and the constructed nature of the research interview.

Interviewer conduct, therefore, is an important issue. There are two key elements of interviewer conduct: rapport and neutrality (Rapley 2004). Rapport is something interviewers must work to establish through creating a relaxed and encouraging relationship, communicating trust and reassurance. Neutrality is a far more contested concept, with some authors arguing for this as essential practice (Ackroyd & Hughes 1992; Weiss 1994), and others claiming it creates a 'hierarchical, asymmetrical (and patriarchal) relationship in which the interviewee is treated as a research "object"' (Rapley 2004, p. 19).

Within the scope of non-neutral interviewing, Rapley (2004) defines three broad approaches. The first involves gently nudging without bias, during which the interviewer is neutral about the topic while displaying interest, and facilitates the interview without overly directing the responses. The second is interviewers as 'persons', which involves interviewer self-disclosure. Within this approach, the interviewer is a vocal collaborator in the interaction, and may redirect or reposition an issue based on the interviewee's response. The third approach includes working with intimate reciprocity, a dynamic in which the interviewer offers complementary reciprocity in order to build a mutual sense of cooperative self-disclosure.

The following interview guidelines, suggested by Ashworth and Lucas (2000, pp. 302-3), are appropriate for this study:

- use of prepared questions should be minimised;
- use open-ended questions;
- engage in empathetic listening to hear meanings, interpretations and understandings;

- use bracketing - consciously silence preoccupations and judgements; and
- use prompts to pursue and clarify the participant's own line of reflection and allow the participant to elaborate, provide examples and to discuss events at length.

The most appropriate interview method for this study is a combination of the first two techniques. The act of bracketing while interviewing lends itself to the first technique. However, as noted previously, the cultural probe exercises produce images that require discussion for the respondents' true intention to be conveyed, and as such the interviewer is required to collaborate in the creation of the meaning of the image to some extent. In this context, however, there is no need for interviewer self-disclosure.

4.5   Issues of Trustworthiness

The evaluation of qualitative social research remains a highly contested, and unresolved, issue. In response, LeCompte and Goetz (1982) sought to apply the concepts of reliability and validity to qualitative research. However, others suggest that because these criteria were developed for quantitative research they are not appropriate for qualitative research (Bryman 2004). In contrast, Lincoln and Guba (1985) propose two criteria for assessing qualitative research: trustworthiness and authenticity. There are four aspects of trustworthiness which parallel the quantitative research criteria: credibility, transferability, dependability, and confirmability.

4.5.1   Credibility

Credibility parallels internal validity, and requires that the research is undertaken according to good practice (Lincoln & Guba 1985). This includes respondent validation, a process whereby the researcher submits portions of the research, such as the interview transcript or the research findings, to the people who were studied for confirmation that the researcher has correctly understood their social world. An alternative method is triangulation, which may be used within and across research strategies, and involves using multiple sources of data (among other techniques) which are cross-checked to improve confidence in the findings (Bryman 2004).

4.5.2   Transferability

Transferability parallels external validity. As qualitative findings tend to be oriented to the particular social context of the phenomena being studied, they are unlikely to hold in some other context, or even in the same context at another time. Rather, qualitative researchers are encouraged to produce rich descriptions, which provide a database for making judgements about the possible transferability of findings (Lincoln & Guba 1985).

However, phenomenographic research differs from other qualitative research in this regard. As noted, the process of defining conceptual categories of description involves two steps. The first aspect is identifying the most distinctive characteristics that appear in the data; and the second is identifying the structurally significant differences that clarify the various experiences of the relationship between the individual and the phenomenon. Therefore, while the categories of description originated from a contextual understanding, the resulting categories are decontextualised, and may be applied to other situations (Marton 1986).

4.5.3 Dependability

Dependability parallels reliability. This aspect is concerned with establishing the merit of the research, and as such qualitative researchers should maintain complete, detailed records of all phases of the research process to demonstrate that proper procedures have been followed. If necessary, peers may audit these records, although Bryman (2004, p. 275) notes that this has not 'become a popular approach to enhancing the dependability of qualitative research.'

In contrast, the question of reliability in phenomenographic research is addressed by Marton (1986) in terms of reliability as replicability. There are two issues embodied in the replicability of phenomenographic results. The first is the original researcher's identification of conceptual categories of description, and whether other researchers working independently would identify the same categories. The second issue is whether peers could recognise the conceptions identified by the original researcher based on their categories. Marton (1986, p. 35) suggests that it is reasonable to expect replicability in the second case for the following reason:

> The original finding of the categories of description is a form of discovery, and discoveries do not have to be replicable. On the other hand, once the categories have been found, it must be possible to reach a high degree of intersubjective agreement concerning their presence or absence if other researchers are to be able to use them.

A common method for demonstrating reliability as replicability is using an inter-judge panel (Marton 1986; Sandbergh 1997). This process requires a panel of co-judges to read the data with reference to the categories of description that have been identified by the researcher, and to organise the data according to the categories of description. The intention is to identify to what extent others can see the same differences in the material, and the process provides a measurement of this. The greater the correlation between the researcher's categories of description and the inter-judge panel, the more reliable the results are considered to be (Marton 1986).

4.5.4 Confirmability

Confirmability parallels objectivity. While complete objectivity is not possible, the researcher should be able to demonstrate that they have not overtly allowed personal values or theoretical inclinations to influence the conduct of the research and the findings deriving from it. Within phenomenographical research, this is also associated with bracketing presuppositions (Ashworth & Lucas 2000; Sandbergh 1997).

4.5.5 Authenticity

The second aspect of qualitative research evaluation, proposed by Lincoln and Guba (1985), is authenticity. This aspect includes the following five criteria: fairness, ontological authenticity, educative authenticity, catalytic authenticity, tactical authenticity. The emphasis on practical outcomes is similar to the aims of action research, and differentiates it from other social research (Bryman 2004). However, these criteria have not been widely adopted within qualitative research, and as such they will not be used to asses this study.

4.6 Issues of Ethics

The issue of ethics in social research is important, and tends to be associated with four main aspects. These include whether there is harm to participants; whether there is a lack of informed consent; whether there is an invasion of privacy; and whether deception is involved. These issues are addressed by adhering to the following procedures which are adapted from Bryman (2004, pp. 309-14) for phenomenographic research:

The researcher should ensure they minimise disturbance to both the respondent, and to the respondent's relationship to their environment.

- The researcher should ensure confidentiality and secure storage of the interview data.

- Prospective respondents should be given enough information to make an informed decision about whether to participate.

- The notion of respondent privacy is closely linked with informed consent, to the extent that if the respondent agrees to participate in the study, they are effectively surrendering their right to privacy for that limited domain. Given the nature of this study, however, significant efforts are made to ensure the respondent is comfortable with the degree of disclosure at all times during the cultural probe exercises and the interview.

- Ensuring privacy is also dependent on the anonymity of the respondents, and confidentiality in the research process.

- Deception occurs when a researcher represents their research as something other than it is. Within this study there is no reason or advantage to misrepresent the nature of the study, and as such the respondents should be provided with detailed information.

4.7 Conduct of the Study

This study consists of four phases. The first is the initiation of the study, and includes identifying the field and scope of the research, reviewing the literature, developing a theoretical framework, and refining the research questions. The second phase is the data collection, during which the data collection techniques were identified and the tools developed, pilot studies were undertaken to test these tools, and potential respondents were identified, contacted, and interviewed. The third phase is data analysis, during which the data were sorted into the four phenomena (house, home, place and sustainability), categories of description were developed for each, and the themes within each category were identified. From this the outcome space was identified. The final phase involved relating the outcome space to the theoretical framework developed in the first phase.

4.7.1 Phase 1: Initiating the Study

The first phase included all the activities undertaken in order to initiate the study. The topic of interest was identified as the human psyche's experience of domestic architecture, From this, research questions were articulated which explored conceptions of house, home, place and sustainability. A literature review was undertaken to critically review the existing literature discussing the human psyche and domestic architecture, and conceptions of home and place. It highlighted that the literature tends to focus on the way in which the human psyche is represented or externally manifested in domestic architecture, rather than the experience of domestic architecture. This process identified the significant gap in the existing literature, and that a theoretical framework was required for framing the study. This review also identified a body of literature that views house as home, and home as place. As such, the theoretical framework was derived from place theories that discuss the human psyche's experience of place, and especially home as place. This suggested a particular approach to the design of the study in terms of the research paradigm, approach and techniques.

4.7.2 Phase 2: Data Collection

The second phase included the steps taken to collect the data. A number of activities were undertaken simultaneously in this phase. The first was identifying suitable respondents. Given the focus of the study is the understanding and experience of house, home, place and sustainability, and the relationships between these, the respondents selected all lived in houses designed based on sustainability principles, or intended to renovate their house in this manner in the future. Some of the respondents had literally built their house themselves, whereas others had renovated an existing house. The respondents selected represented a cross-section of locations and neighbourhood types, including alternative communities, inner city and suburban, and coastal semi-rural locations. The potential respondents were identified through networks the researcher had developed, and contacts through colleagues.

The second activity was gaining ethical clearance from RMIT University regarding the conduct of the study. After this was approved, contact was made with potential respondents by both e-mail and telephone conversations. During these, the aim of the project and the desired outcomes were explained, in addition to the interview process and likely timelines and time commitments required from the respondents. The potential respondents were then invited to participate in the study.

The third activity within this phase was identifying appropriate data collection tools, which include a cultural probe and in-depth interviews. After the initial cultural probe was designed, a pilot study of three respondents was conducted. The aim was to test the effectiveness of this as a tool for interviewing respondents in terms of:

- the appropriateness of the activities included in the cultural probe;

- the capacity for these exercises to inspire emotional, thoughtful, reflective responses;

- the capacity for these exercises to act as prompts during the interview;

- the logistics involved with making the cultural probes;

- the logistics involved with delivering the cultural probes to the respondents, explaining the exercises and how these relate to the research, and collecting the completed cultural probes prior to the interview; and

- the respondents reaction to the cultural probes, and the way in which they completed the exercises.

The exercises in the cultural probe were inspired by various sources, including a number of drawing exercises outlined in Marcus (1995, pp. 42, 75-6). Based on the results of these pilot interviews, the cultural probe exercises were refined and the logistics of delivering and collecting them altered. The final cultural probe included the following exercises:

Notebook – which included the following prompts:

- Answering from your perspective: House, I chose you because . . .
- Answering from your perspective: House, the way I feel about you is . . .
- Answering from your perspective: House, what do you communicate about me?
- Answering from the house's perspective: Who are you? Do you have a name? Do you like being in this location?
- Answering from the house's perspective: How do you feel about me living in you? Do you feel loved?
- Answering from the house's perspective: What is it that you can give to me? Is there something I can do for you?

Maps – which included the following prompts:

- Please draw a map of your house and garden.
- Please draw a map of your neighbourhood.

Camera – which asked respondents to take photos that represent:

Somewhere you feel comfortable; Somewhere you feel uncomfortable; Something that represents nature to you; Where you spend most of your time; Where you relax; Something you identify with; Something that reminds you of your childhood; Somewhere you enjoy going and/or being; Something that represents 'home' to you.

Drawings – Places of Childhood, which included the following prompts:

- As a child, my experience of home was . . .

- As a child, my experience of neighbourhood was . . .
- As a child, my experience of nature was . . .

Drawing – which included the following prompt:

- What Home Really Means to You . . .

Drawing – which included the following prompt:

- For me, sustainability means . . .

The following images display the exercises included in the final cultural probe.

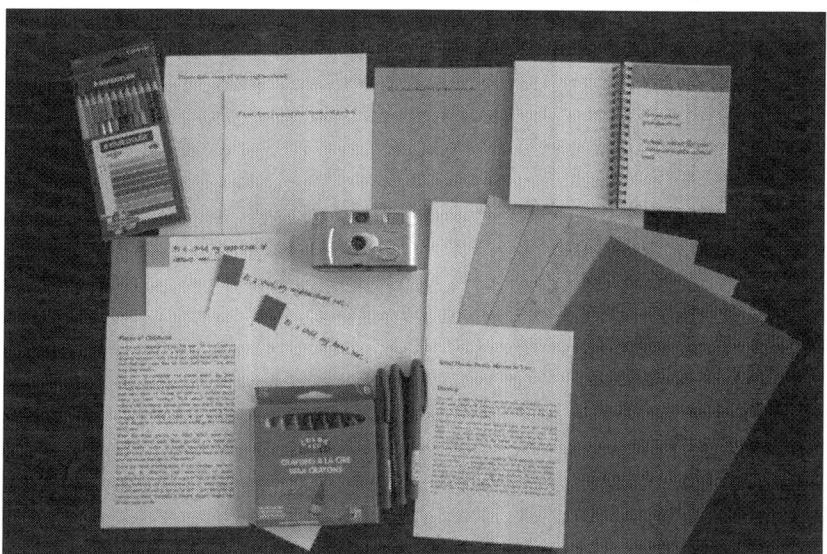

Figure 1: Cultural probe

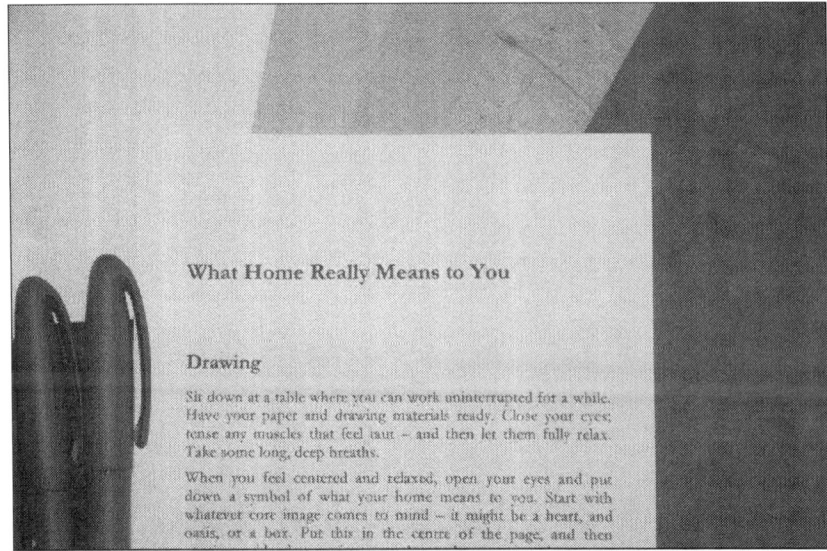

Figure 2: Cultural probe exercise: What Home Really Means To You . . .

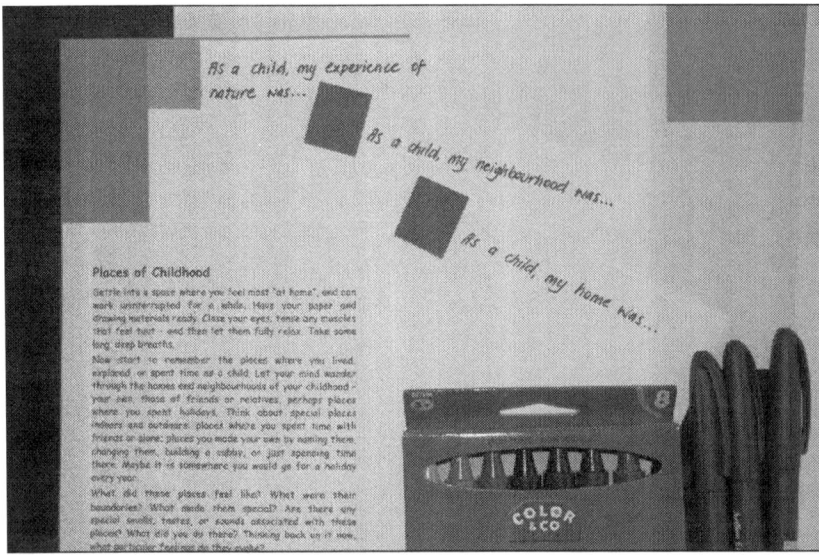

Figure 3: Cultural probe exercise: Places of Childhood

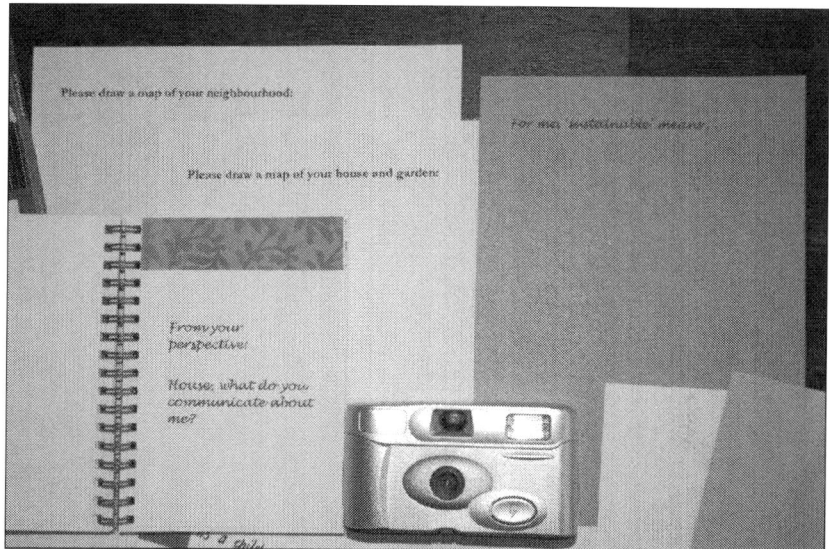
Figure 4: Cultural probe exercises: For me, 'sustainable' means . . . , notebook, camera and maps

Once these three activities were completed, the interviewing process began. In total, seventeen personal in-depth interviews were completed. The number of participants was determined by the new information being offered by the respondent - once 'saturation point' was reached, no further interviews were conducted. The respondents are listed below.

Respondent Number	Domestic Architecture	Location
Respondent 1	Whole house; built themselves.	Rural Conservation Co-op.
Respondent 2	Whole house, built themselves.	Rural Conservation Co-op.
Respondent 3	Whole house, built themselves.	Rural Conservation Co-op.
Respondent 4	Communal.	Rural Conservation Co-op.

Respondent 5	Communal, renovation.	Urban Eco Village.
Respondent 6	Communal, renovation.	Urban Eco Village.
Respondent 7	Whole house, renovation.	Coastal.
Respondent 8	Renovation.	Inner city.
Respondent 9	Renovation.	Inner city.
Respondent 10	Renovation.	Inner city.
Respondent 11	New house.	Coastal.
Respondent 12 – Pilot	Intention to renovate.	Master Planned Community, moved to inner city.
Respondent 13 – Pilot	Intention to renovate.	Master Planned Community, moved to inner city.
Respondent 14	New house.	Coastal.
Respondent 15	Whole house, renovation.	Coastal.
Respondent 16	Whole house, renovation.	Coastal.
Respondent 17 – Pilot	ESD, new	Suburban.

The interview process included three steps, each of which was conducted at a time and location that suited the participants. With the exception of one meeting with one respondent, all meetings and interviews were conducted at the respondents' houses. The first was the initial meeting with the participant to give them the cultural probe, provide an overview of the project, explain the interview process, and ask them to sign the ethics form prior to completing the cultural probe. The second step involved collecting the camera (and in some cases the cultural probe) and developing the photographs. The third step was the interview itself. During this meeting, it was explained that the cultural probe exercises would be used as prompts for discussion during the interview, and that they could determine the order of this. The participants were also asked if the interview could be recorded for transcription purposes (all agreed). While the participants were encouraged to speak freely, they were reassured that the level of disclosure was entirely within their control, and that at any time they could stop the interview if they were feeling uncomfortable. At the conclusion of the interviews, each participant was sent a hand-made card thanking them for their participation in the research.

The interviews were transcribed verbatim as soon as practicable after the interview. Approximately half were transcribed by the researcher in order to develop familiarity with the themes and the emotional nuances of the interviews. The remainder were transcribed by an assistant. These transcriptions were stored electronically, and electronic back-ups and a hard copy were stored separately. The interview transcripts were returned to the interviewees for their review and confirmation. Thirteen of the seventeen responses were used for data analysis, as four of the interviews were judged unsuitable for analysis within the context of this study. These include Respondents 15 and 16, children who were interviewed at their parent's request, and with appropriate ethics clearance; Respondent 14, who does not yet live in a house constructed based on sustainability principles, and who made it clear that he has no connection or interest in the house; and Respondent 17, which is a pilot interview.

4.7.3 Phase 3: Data Analysis

The third phase was the three-step data analysis. The first step involved sorting the data into the four phenomena - house, home, place and sustainability - followed by familiarisation with the data. Each recording was listened to immediately after the interview, and then again after they were transcribed to check the transcriptions were an accurate representation of the interview. The verbatim transcripts were read, and the recordings listened to, several times.

During this process, the researcher made notes about the various themes emerging within each phenomenon, and highlighted key quotes and phrases that supported these themes. Over time, recurring views and descriptions became apparent, and meanings were ascribed to these. Throughout this process, the researcher used bracketing by asking questions such as:

- What is this person really trying to say?

- What common ideas, views and themes are being expressed?

After these themes were condensed and key words ascribed to them, the researcher looked for the similarities and differences with a view to grouping similar statements for each phenomenon.

The second step required reviewing groupings of similar themes and statements for consistency and accuracy, and an overall phrase was identified which captured the essence of the group of themes, and therefore described the category. Eventually four categories of description were defined for house, three for home, four for place, and two for sustainability. These themes were tested through an inter-judge process, whereby a selection of the categories of description and associated quotations from each of the four phenomena was given to the co-judges. The descriptions were separated from the quotations, and the co-judges were instructed to decide which quotations best fitted into each of the categories of description. Although there were minor discrepancies in the choices made, an overall consensus emerged. This process of inter-judge reliability was an important step in minimising the potential for researcher biases to influence the results.

The third and final step included comparing each of the categories of description across the four phenomena, and defining the internal and external horizons of each. From this the outcome space was defined, and the links between the categories across the phenomena were represented diagrammatically. This process highlighted relationships between and within the categories of description, and enabled more profound insights into the meanings of the categories. As a visual representation of the results of the study, the outcome space condensed large amounts of data into a simple model.

4.7.4 Phase 4: Theorising From the Study

The final phase involved relating the outcome space to the theoretical framework developed in the first phase. The two categories of description of sustainability – Sustainability as Being, and Sustainability as Doing - represent the two qualitatively different ways the respondents described their understanding and experience of sustainability with respect to house, home, and place. These two categories were discussed with respect to the place theories outlined in the theoretical framework: place as 'Being-in-the-World', place as Dwelling, place and placelessness, place as *genius loci*, and place as memory. The purpose of this was to theorise from this study about the way in which the experiences and connections the human psyche has with house, home, and place may impact on people's understanding and experience of sustainability.

5 House

You are my sanctuary, my place of peace, comfort, warmth, rest and quiet bliss. You are my escape from the pressures of work, my favourite eating place and the place where I sleep in peace and absolute quiet. You are a holiday house in your own right, scenic, with a direct link to the wilderness of the real Australia, with genuine original unspoiled flora and fauna. I can simply sit and look out of your windows and be instantly transfixed by the raw beauty that surrounds me. Each time I do this I tune again in to the ongoing story of a world in balance, a world that sustains itself (Respondent 1).

5.1 Introduction

This chapter explores the qualitatively different ways the respondents described their understanding and experience of their house, and the relationship between house, home, and place. Four conceptual categories of description emerged from the data. In the first, the respondents described their house as an extension of themselves; in the second the interviewees described their house as an agora, a meeting place for family and friends. The respondents in the third category described their house as a refuge that provides respite from the world; and in the fourth they described their house simply as utilitarian shelter. Within the four categories, four themes were explored. These include: the respondents' description of the relationship between house, home and place; the connection to their house; how the respondents feel about their house; and what the house communicates about the respondents.

Each of the four categories directly corresponds to the four qualitatively different ways the respondents described their understanding and experience of place. While this relationship appears reasonably straightforward, the relationship between house, home and place is more complex. As such, the categories of description of house and place do not directly correspond to categories of description of home. This complex relationship is explored in the following chapter. However, the relationship between house, home and place is briefly outlined at the beginning of each category of description in this chapter in order to frame the exploration of the themes.

This chapter contributes to answering the first research question:

1. *How do people describe their understanding and experience of house, home, and place?*
2. *How do people describe their understanding and experience of the relationship between house, home, place and sustainability?*
3. *How do people describe the relationship between childhood memories and their understanding and experience of home?*

While there is significant overlap between the themes that have determined the categories of description, the categories bear the title of the respondents' strongest overall descriptions of their understanding and experience of their house. The four categories outlined in this chapter contribute to the overall outcome space within this study.

5.2 Category of Description 1: House as Self

The first category of description of house is defined by respondents who describe their house as an extension of Self. These respondents were all intimately involved with the design of their house, and some were also involved with the construction process. As a result, they all describe a profound connection with the physical structure of the house. These respondents describe their house as a peaceful place that communicates something very personal about them.

5.2.1 Theme 1: Holistic Relationship Between House, Home and Place

The respondents in this category describe a holistic perspective of their understanding and experience of house, home and place, and as such the distinction between these phenomena is blurred to the extent that they are inseparable. These respondents use the terms house, home, and place interchangeably. As each of these phenomena clearly informed their experience and understanding of the others, they have a profound connection to all three:

> *[Responding from the house's perspective]* **Well really I'm just a house, although some call me Home and Home Sweet Home.** *I've been referred to as our little mud hut.* **I see myself as a rearrangement of the soil that covers this land, taller now, home for many creatures.** *Humans, tuans, ringtail possums. . . I'm visited by uncountable other ranging from the large to the small. The carnivorous to the vegetarian. Underground to over ground.* **I'm just part of the scenery here, not threatening, enticing because of the promise of shelter, warmth and food.** *I neither enjoy or despair, I just am. I am useful.* **I slowly yield to the weather and age. I will return from whence I came just like everything else** *(Respondent 1).*

5.2.2 Theme 2: Profound Connection to House

These respondents have a profound connection with the physical structure of the building, and view it as a physical manifestation and extension of themselves. While all the respondents in this category had an intimate role in the design phase, they can be further divided into two groups: those who physically built their house, and those who acted as very involved clients. The following respondents are from the group who physically built their house:

> *Because I have been there from the start in your creation and through the building process* **I also feel you are an extension of me.** *There is not a part of you*

> *that I cannot think back and remember the process that created you (Respondent 1).*
>
> **Over a period of five years we worked on you on weekends, school holidays, and in spare moments.** *It took a while but we were able to shape you in a way that traditional houses could not grow and develop.* **We made all your mud bricks, doors, and the windows. We adzed your red gum posts, built and hand-brushed your walls, and slowly and painstakingly finished off a myriad of individual features.** *We chose your fittings and your furnishings.* **We now feel that we know you very intimately** *(Respondent 2).*

In Jungian terms, a house is a physical expression of an individual's journey from the ego-self towards the transpersonal Self or soul (Jung 1959; Edinger 1972). The ego-self of these respondents is expressed in the physical structure of the house, however their close involvement in both the design and construction suggest that there is also an aspect of the transpersonal Self or soul in the physical manifestation of the house. Respondent 1 alludes to this when he says the house feels like an extension of himself.

Where Marcus (1995) suggests the journey towards individuation is cyclical between the ego-self and transpersonal Self or soul, and that an individual's choice of houses provides insight into this journey, these respondents indicate that this house is an expression of their soul more than their ego. This suggests that the process of designing and building their house was an integral part of the journey towards individuation, but also that they are near the end of their journey of individuation and that their dominant mode of expression in the world is their transpersonal Self or soul rather than their ego-self.

The following respondents were thoroughly involved in the design and construction process, though did not physically build their houses themselves. The experience of participating in the design process is described in terms of creating something meaningful and bringing it to life. These respondents describe a detailed level of intimacy with their house and a heightened level of care for the house:

> *I did,* **I highlighted my own personal spaces***, so study, living space, courtyard, kitchen, laundry/ bathroom. And I just outlined what's the outline of my daily tramp, if you like. But I just didn't put it down with the same clarity but it's all there.* **All those spaces are absolutely intimate to me because I've been totally involved in all the design processes and I've been in them on a daily basis.** *But*

we're now into the relinquishing phase of others living in them. So they're going into their own territory, as it were, their own new journey. Um, my role there is diminished (Respondent 6).

I found having built a house, I am more careful with not denting it, and making a mark on the walls or something. *And whilst I think those things are part of normal wear and tear,* **I think I'm a little bit more careful than I would have been before.** *And I've asked the kids to be a bit more careful. . . So, I think,* **just caring for it more**, *because it's new and we've sort of put a lot of thought and effort and money into it, and all that sort of thing (Respondent 7).*

In *The Psychology of the House*, Marc (1977) refers to the human psyche as the "inner house" that must exist prior to the manifestation of the "external house". In viewing the house as an extension of themselves, these respondents indicate that their house is in fact an external representation of their "inner house" or psyche. In accordance with this, they describe a deep emotional connection to the physical structure of their house. Furthermore, these respondents describe a shared history between themselves and their houses, and because of this the house is often considered a member of the family:

You have now been a part of my family for nearly thirty years and this makes you the most important building in my life. *There may be other buildings but there will never be anything else like you. You were there when we were young and now you watch us grow old. I only hope you will find someone who feels as strongly about you as I do.* **Lately you have provided a cocoon that has sheltered me through my hours of pain and sickness. You have contributed in making the last few years more bearable** *(Respondent 1).*

Now, together with [partner] and [daughter], I have been involved with you for over a quarter of a century. **We have lived in you for longer than any other house**. *We have enjoyed watching and contributing to the creative experience of your design. We've worked hard together to help you rise and to make you into our home.* **You feature highly in many special memories and experiences we've had as a family, so it's sort of, it's a place that has special memories for me**. *Of course nothing is totally perfect all the time. We've had our down moments. . . However these fade into the background* **when I consider the very many special, unforgettable and irreplaceable things that crowd my memory** *(Respondent 2).*

5.2.3 Theme 3: House is a Place of Peace

These respondents describe intense feelings about their house. They experience it as a place of peace, a refuge, and a place where they can leave the world and be at one with themselves. These houses have captured the essence of what Marc (1977) describes as the original temple-house. For these respondents, the house is understood to provide far more than simply physical shelter and protection:

> *You are my sanctuary, my place of peace, comfort, warmth, rest and quiet bliss. You are my escape from the pressures of work, my favourite eating place and the place where I sleep in peace and absolute quiet. You are a holiday house in your own right, scenic, with a direct link to the wilderness of the real Australia, with genuine original unspoiled flora and fauna. I can simply sit and look out of your windows and be instantly transfixed by the raw beauty that surrounds me.* ***Each time I do this I tune again into the ongoing story of a world in balance, a world that sustains itself*** *(Respondent 1).*

> *So, the way I feel about you is a mixture of satisfaction, contentment nostalgia and frustration.* ***Um, you are my refuge. A place I can truly enjoy, relax and regenerate in*** *(Respondent 2).*

Respondents 1 and 2 share a house that they built together in a conservation area on the fringe of Melbourne. They laid the brick floor together which is in the shape of a spiral, beginning at the centre of the kitchen and dining area, and radiating out towards the hearth and living area. In Jungian terms, the spiral is one of the seven archetypal signs. It represents the universe itself and the natural impulses that pass through human and unite them to the cosmic order. The spiral also contains both the wave and the dot, which represent the principle of growth in the universe. Marc (1977) suggests that the manifestation of the spiral is instinctual and was used to both expresses the strongest elements of nature, and to represent a reconnection with nature. Whether consciously or unconsciously, these respondents have created a temple-house in a conservation area that symbolically expresses their desire to reconnect with nature.

The respondents below describe their temple-house as somewhere private and safe where they can leave the world and listen to their own rhythm:

> *So the way I feel about you is, I remember the first thought I had about this house - I think I put it onto one of the other cards -* ***that it would be a good place to be, that it was OK. It was safe. . . It felt good, yeah*** *(Respondent 6).*

> *House, the way I feel about you is: comfort, warmth, good for the planet, private, my space, our space, easy, rest.* So I guess when I imagine coming home, I don't probably ever do it, but when I imagine coming home, ***I think of just being able to be at peace.*** But I don't know that it often happens!! Just to sit in one spot for a while. But you know, probably it does sometimes happen *(Respondent 7).*

5.2.4 Theme 4: House Communicates Themselves

These respondents describe their house as an expression of their creativity, which is innate in the human spirit (Marc 1977). It is an external manifestation of who these people think they are and how they choose to be in the world. Their responses are a very personal comment about their values and what is important to them:

> ***I suppose that the form and the function of a house says a lot about its builders and its occupants.*** Given that I'm not the sole builder and occupier, it must say something about [partner] and [daughter] as well. ***Even though [daughter] has not lived in it for many years, her sweet and subtle presence is still felt. For the most part it says quite a bit about [partner] and myself.*** [Partner's] hard work and painstaking efforts are evident throughout the interior and exterior of the house. He did so much of the really hard backbreaking work in putting up the house. He is also responsible for the many refinements in the fittings and the fixtures. ***The house communicates his strength, perseverance, sensitivity, and amazing skills.*** I love the pantry and the cellar which he built single-handedly. His distinctive mark is everywhere in the house. . . ***The house communicates something about my aesthetic preferences, interest in art books and music, and my particular style of doing things, and my need for smooth function and order.*** But ah, you know, I think he did, you know, the really important um hard work *(Respondent 2).*

> I suppose I do feel a bit the mother earth here, which I haven't put down. I don't want to be the mother in any way, but um ***I do play quite a strong role in the, you know, the importance of all those basic elements of nurturing*** and um, I think yeah nurturing and um healthy stuff. ***Whether for the environment, or the food we eat, I feel quite strongly committed to all that, and to setting up systems.*** . . So rituals of um, you know, life rituals, um are very much based around home, carrying home into a bigger environment *(Respondent 6).*

> *House, what do you communicate about me?* **Colourful, alive, friendly, welcoming, harmonious**... *I think in terms of things fitting in, fitting in together, that sort of thing...* **I think, I think about living harmoniously, and living harmoniously sort of means, in relation to people, but also in relation to the space, perhaps**. *... It fits together perhaps (Respondent 7).*

In these responses, the interviewees explicitly describe how they view their house as a manifestation of themselves. Their house is a physical expression of their "inner house", and in a shared house it is the expression of multiple "inner houses". However the multiple "inner houses" obviously share some core traits as the houses are cohesive expressions of their personality, their values and their place in the world.

5.2.5 Summary: House as Self

Themes	Defining characteristics
Theme 1: Holistic Relationship Between House, Home and Place	Holistic perspective of house, home, and place. The distinction between these phenomena is blurred to the extent that they are inseparable. The terms house, home and place are interchangeable. Profound connection to all three.
Theme 2: Profound Connection to House	Profound connection with the physical structure of the building. View the house as a physical manifestation and extension of themselves. Shared history between the respondents and their house. House is often considered a member of the family.
Theme 3: House is a Place of Peace	Experience their house as a place of peace, comfort and warmth. Describe intense feelings about their house.
Theme 4: House Communicates Themselves	House communicates something very personal about them. House is a reflection of their values and creativity.

5.3 Category of Description 2: House as an Agora

The second category of description of house includes respondents who consider their house as primarily a meeting place and gathering place, an agora. The focus is on bringing people together, especially family and friends. For these respondents, the neighbourhood has meaning through their connections with people, services and amenities. Their house reflects their family values and is a material depository for family memories.

5.3.1 Theme 1: Anthropocentric Relationship Between House, Home and Place

These respondents describe an anthropocentric understanding and experience of both house and place, and all of these respondents live in an inner urban area. House, home and place are defined by the human connections between them, and these respondents describe a strong connection to all three:

> *From the house's perspective, who are you?* ***I provide a home for a family.* . . . *There are always lots of people in me. Some coming and some going. I like having lots of space to fit them all in.*** *I like where I'm located, there's lots of activity going on around me. There's lots of children walking to school, mums and dads with prams. Dogs on their morning and evening walk.* ***I like being in an active place where I can see and hear people and I feel like our neighbourhood is alive*** *(Respondent 8).*

> ***And even though it's inner city, it's really like living in a country town. Because you go down the street and say hi to people that you know all the time****, the shopkeepers know you, women in prams stop and have chats even though they don't know each other.* ***It's really, really friendly.*** *. . . And the community network that we became part of was really nice. . . .* ***Looking at the map of the neighbourhood, it's really important to us that our neighbours are our friends*** *(Respondent 10).*

The community networks these respondents describe are generally built up over time. Both respondents have lived in these houses for roughly five years, but have been familiar with the area for far longer. These respondents derive enjoyment from being surrounded by a community they consider to be their friends. Furthermore, they describe a sense of familiarity and predictability in terms of the people who comprise the community, and also the physical structure of the neighbourhood. This clearly important to them, and is an example of what Sibley (1999) describes as a desire to live in a place that is stable and orderly, and there is a measure of predictability.

5.3.2 Theme 2: Family Connection to House

These respondents describe a strong emotional connection to the house, which is bound up with their feelings for their family and community. Emotions play an important role in the production of social space, and Sibley (1999) argues that the material relationships between people and places can be depositories of feelings such as anxiety or pleasure. Houses, for these respondents, have been designed to facilitate family and friends gathering together in a bright, inviting space, thus creating feelings of pleasure. In this sense, their houses are the depositories of positive feelings about their family:

> *House I chose you because: you're a place of people and ideas and fine foods and wine (Respondent 5).*

> *This is our house. Our house, when we did renovate it, it was about um, the main thing that **I really wanted in the house was a big space that people could gather in** which is this space that we're in at the moment. **And a space that's light and bright**. The older part of the house is obviously quite dark and colder. This part of the house is north facing so it has lots of light coming in, even in winter. **I guess from an inside point of view this is the most important part of our house. We don't have particularly big bedrooms, we don't have an en suite or anything like that because we invested our money in making the biggest space possible for living**, I guess, rather than for those private activities, sleeping (Respondent 8, see Figure 5).*

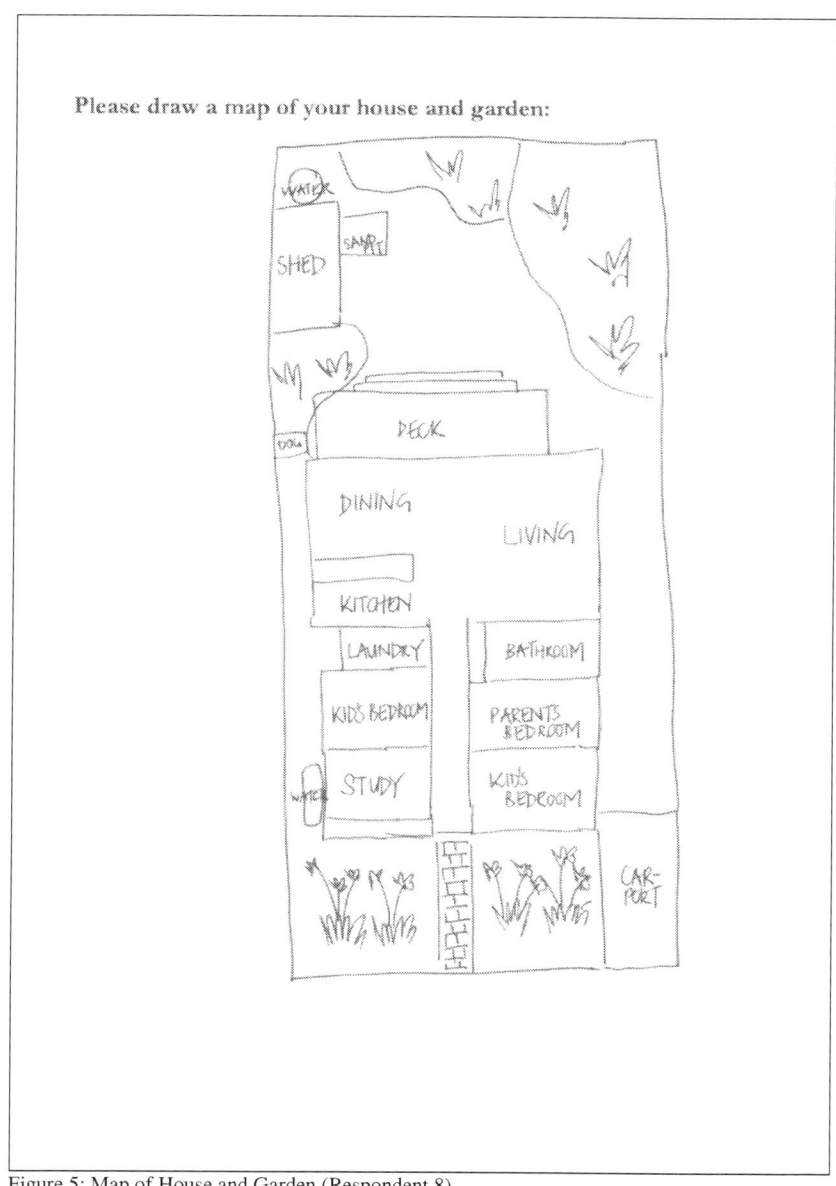

Figure 5: Map of House and Garden (Respondent 8)

5.3.3 Theme 3: House Evokes Sentimental Feelings

These respondents describe in further detail their emotional attachment to their house. While their strong sentimental attachment to their house is largely due to their involvement in the design and renovation phases, their feelings of pleasure, happiness, and commitment to the house reflect their underlying material relationship with the house. They feel their house is inviting and warm for both family and visitors, and they convey a sense of material and emotional generosity in their desire to share their house, as a depository of positive emotions, with others. Their feelings towards their house are entwined with their feelings for their family:

> ***House, the way I feel about you is: attached and committed to the house, like we've got a value now that's emotional and reflecting you***, *and a family and all those sort of things.* ***Inviting, I appreciate or connect with the warmth and light that comes out of the house as it's structured now****. I feel that it's integrated into its environment a bit more, and the area and that sense. And has a really strong foundation, it's been here for a while, just sort of making it better or fitting it in more.* ***I represent the family and provide a healthy happy space to live in*** *(Respondent 9).*

The following respondent describes in detail the various levels of meaning their house holds for the family. The first is the connection, through mentoring, between three generations of architects specialising in sustainable domestic architecture, one of whom is this respondent's husband. The second is the name, Will, which the two mentees have named their sons, after the original mentor Will Wainwright. The third is that the respondent and her family now live in a house that Will Wainwright previously owned, and used as a demonstration of sustainable domestic architecture. Similarly, the respondent's husband renovated the house and uses it as a current example of sustainable domestic architecture. This respondent shares a sense of intimacy with the house and a profound emotional connection with that goes beyond a sense of home and place:

> ***And then I wrote the story of Will****. . . . Now what happened, when we bought this house, or prior to that, [partner], when he started as an architect, one of his mentors was Peter Lockyear. You probably don't know him but he was a lefty pinko architect who, was really involved in sustainability, and sustainable architecture. And he was [partner's] mentor, and we're very good family friends. And about thirteen years ago they had a little boy and they called him Will. And that's fine.* ***And we went to his birthing day, his naming day, and Peter talked about how he'd named his son Will after his mentor, his architecture mentor, who is Will Wainwright...***
>
> *And that was fine and then six weeks later we bought this house.* ***And then we were going through the titles, and [partner] goes, 'Oh my god.' And I said***

> *what? And he goes 'Will Wainwright owned this house, it was Will's house.' And Will had actually, he was part of the town planning for Geelong West, and part of council and things, and basically, back in the early 80's I think they wanted to demolish a lot of the houses around Geelong West.*
>
> *So we, Will Wainwright, who we never met, he died before we sort of became friends with Peter, and he had renovated,* **bought this house, because he was saving it from being demolished, and he renovated it to show that you can modernise these old houses, and they can be useful, and you can let light in it, and you know they can be better than what they were, and adaptable to modern life in the late 70's and early 80's. And he actually had people through and showed them. And it did change Geelong West's town planning at the time because they stopped demolishing everything, all the old houses, then. And then just by chance we ended up buying it and now [partner] shows people through all the time as a display home of what you can do in the 21st Century with sustainability...** *I think that's really kind of special (Respondent 10).*

5.3.4   Theme 4: House Communicates a Simple Lifestyle

For these respondents, their house primarily communicates their commitment to a simple lifestyle, and that they are a member of a family and community. In Jungian terms, these respondents are acutely aware that their houses are representations of themselves. They convey a sense of holding a clear vision of what their "exterior house" was designed to represent, which also suggests that their "inner house" was clearly understood prior to undertaking this task. These respondents describe their house as light and warm, a place that reflects their family values and holds family memories:

> ***Right-oh, so you speak of my commitment to sustainable living.*** *So that's a statement. In other words* ***we don't exude um opulence and wastefulness and luxury*** *and we're trying to um, trying to preserve what's here and to use it, to put it to good effect. And um, and* ***I'm proud of the building because - and the way it's evolving – because um ah it's a statement about ah our sense of design***, *our sense of... I mean the building had always been beautiful to me, um, but it's now starting to look beautiful in quite a different way (Respondent 5).*
>
> ***We've tried to make it as simple as possible so that it's not particularly complicated, that the spaces are really very simple****, easy to live in, easy to maintain type of thing.* ***I think that's something that drove the design of the***

renovation. From a personal point of view a house, a home, it's constant that it's there for you. It's a base for you to operate from that's safe and warm. **Light is obviously a big thing for us in that you can be in the space for the majority of the day and not have to have lights on. That it's restful. It's important that our house reflects who we are. And I guess at the moment it reflects that we've got a young family. That we like our life to be relatively simple.** *And that the house is alive and it's living. So it's not a monument, it gets messy, it's to be lived in and it's to represent us (Respondent 8).*

From your perspective house, what do you communicate about me? **I think that combination of simplicity and functionality**. . . *A connection to the environment, and earthy sort of nature. . . Sustainable features in the extension I think reflect that knowledge and understanding of that, and the garden is important, and that sort of indoor/outdoor connection.* **And a place for memories, it features things from my family home now so that's good** *(Respondent 9).*

House what do you communicate about me? **That I like natural things, light and warmth**. . . *That I'm not fussy or the best housekeeper or gardener,* **but people are welcome**. *And that my husband worked on the house and had a large input, it's mainly him I suppose. . .* **The things like the fire and the bench and the northern light. It's very similar to the house I grew up in** *(Respondent 10).*

5.3.5 Summary: House as an Agora

Themes	Defining characteristics
Theme 1: Anthropocentric Relationship Between House, Home and Place	House is a meeting place and gathering place, an Agora. Neighbourhood has meaning through their connections with people, services and amenities. House, home and place are defined by the human connections between them.
Theme 2: Connection to the House Through Family	Focus of the house is on bringing people together, especially family and friends. Strong emotional connection to the house, which is bound up with their feelings for their family and community.
Theme 3: House Evokes Sentimental Feelings	Sentimental attachment to their house. House is inviting and warm for both family and visitors. Feelings for their house are entwined with their feelings for their family.
Theme 4: House Communicates a Simple Lifestyle	House communicates their commitment to a simple lifestyle. Describe their house as light and warm. House reflects their family values and holds family memories.

5.4 Category of Description 3: House as a Refuge

The respondents who comprise the third category of description consider their house to be a refuge. For these respondents, there is an intense sense of alienation from the community and neighbourhood, and therefore place. The house provides safety and a retreat from this perceived threat of the community and neighbourhood, and the house and home compensate for the acceptance that is lacking from the neighbourhood by being welcoming, warm and safe.

5.4.1 Theme 1: Conflicted Relationship Between House, Home and Place

These respondents suggest they experience a conflicted relationship between house, home and place. They convey a strong sense of alienation from the community, and in contrast an intense attachment to the house and home as a retreat from the world. As Marcus (1995) notes, a sense of home is inextricably linked to the neighbourhood, and individuals require a whole ecological setting in which they can feel at home. When part of this is absent, the sense of home is directly affected.

For these respondents, the intense alienation they feel from the community, neighbourhood and place is compensated for by their house as home. Therefore, the emphasis for these respondents is on their house and home rather than place:

> *[Partner] is the one who, when we decided to split up, [partner] is the one who moved down to the city, or she already had a place down there.* ***So she's the one who's now off the mountain. But I still sometimes have the feeling that she's the one that they would all rather have here.*** *So you know. But that's me, that's really got nothing to do with the house or whatever, but it's an interesting aspect of, of being here, that um, and about me I guess, that I have those feelings...* ***So to a certain extent, the sense that the house is a bit of a cave and a refuge is sometimes from the rest of the cluster as well*** *(Respondent 3).*

5.4.2 Theme 2: Intense Connection to the House

For these respondents, their material connection with the community is the depository of negative feelings, whereas their house is the depository of positive feelings (Sibley 1999). Their intense connection with their house is in contrast to, and compensates for, their sense of alienation from the community. This is clearly demonstrated by Respondents 12 and 13, who are living together in a lesbian relationship in a suburban housing estate that expresses and reinforces the heteronormative ideals of home and a heterosexual, nuclear family.

Their sense of alienation is largely due to the feeling that they have to hide their relationship from the broader community. In contrast, they consider their house as somewhere they can fully express themselves free from self-censoring. While the home is a key site of identity-creation for everyone (Blunt 2003), it is especially important for this couple. The process of identity-creation for this couple resists heteronormativity and affirms sexual difference, thereby legitimising and normalising their sexuality (Gorman-Murray 2007). These respondents, therefore, describe their house as providing safety and a retreat, and as a place of freedom and happiness:

> ***My house is a place of happiness. I am proud of my house because I was the one who built her (not literally).*** *I chose the block, the design, the colours, the garden. I have put my blood, sweat and tears into her. While my house is plain and simple, she is developing her own character.* ***I love her garden as this is something that I built from the ground up.*** *Looking back on the photos from her early days I can see how she has grown and developed.* ***For me it is now time to leave and I feel sad about that but it's not my house that I am leaving, it's the location.*** *I wish I could take her with me. I am proud of my house as she has been*

through a lot with me over the past seven years. Love, death, separation, new love, parties, study, footy grand finals, family, puppies . . . She has seen it all. ***I will miss her*** *(Respondent 12).*

5.4.3 Theme 3: People Oriented Feelings about House

While these respondents described a range of feelings, the critical factor in determining whether the feelings were positive or negative was the relationships with the people with whom they lived. If there were positive memories and experiences, then the respondent described an intimate and positive connection with, and love for, their house:

> **Oh, I was crying doing this. . . I feel that my house, like it's warm, it's safe, it's secure, it's peaceful, it's inviting, it's strong, it's welcoming, it's comfortable, it's open, it's love.** *All those things (Respondent 12).*

For this respondent, her feelings of love and respect for her partner influenced her feelings for the house they now share, which was originally her partner's:

> **Welcoming**: *Beginning with the thickness and smell of the rosemary bush as I walk towards the front door. I know whenever I open the front door I feel home.*
>
> **Happy**: *I think you look good and have been well looked after.* **Most of all because you're [partner's] house!**
>
> **Secure**: *the alarm system has a lot to do with this! House you look secure – there are no 'sideways' for people to walk down. . . the dog is a good warning system.*
>
> **Loved: I know you mean a lot to [partner] and she has put much of herself into you. I love [partner] and house you're a reflection of her in so many ways.**
>
> **Freedom**: *House you allow me to be completely free in my relationship with [partner]. You provide no barriers to what [partner] and I can do or say or dream.*
>
> **Care**: *it is important I look after you not only because you mean a lot to [partner] but also you have welcomed me (Respondent 13).*

The following respondent has a complex emotional relationship with both the house and his ex-partner, and has not yet untangled these feelings. There are obviously lingering conflicted feelings about the breakdown of his marriage, and the role the house may have played in this. In Jungian terms, the "exterior house" that this couple built together not longer is a reflection of this respondent's "inner house". Furthermore, the house, as a depository of these feelings, is now a constant reminder of the marriage breakdown for two reasons: firstly, they built the house together, and secondly, the house now feels cavernous and empty without other people living in it:

> *Look I don't know. I think um . . . that probably living in this house, or growing up with this house,* **building this house and so on was probably incredibly tied up with my relationship with my ex-partner.** *And um,* **I think that the project of building this house was probably very important for that relationship, in the sense that it um, it probably gave us a focus for a long while about doing things together.** *. . . I think that there was a, there was a dynamic between myself, my ex-partner, and this house that I haven't figured out. . .* **At some stage or other building the house became a source of friction, rather than, than um, than pleasure for us.** *. .*

> *So you know I haven't figured out any, managed to figure out any causal relationships in that. But, and what I mean by that in a sense was that um,* **the speed at which building progressed probably got slower and slower, and that became a source of friction. But I'm not sure whether, whether it got slower and slower because it was a source of friction, or it became a source of friction, so there was that sort of dynamic going on. . . probably its size probably emphasises its emptiness nowadays** *(Respondent 3).*

5.4.4 Theme 4: House Communicates Their Values

These respondents, like those in the other categories of description, believe the house reflects them in some way. However, for these respondents the focus is not on sustainability, which suggests that their understanding and experience of sustainability is not as integrated into their lifestyles as those of the respondents in the first two categories:

> *House, what does the house communicate about me?* **I think, I'm conservative. I'm pretty simple, traditional, even though my lifestyle doesn't suggest that.** *I've said that there, yeah. I really like having people over for dinner, and that kind of stuff, entertaining (Respondent 12).*

*Openness. You may be in an unknown area of the Western suburbs but at the moment that doesn't worry me. **I am not concerned about what others may think of you or your location because you have provided for me at this stage of my life** (Respondent 13).*

5.4.5   Summary: House as Refuge

Themes	Defining characteristics
Theme 1: Conflicted Relationship Between House, Home and Place	Intense sense of alienation from the community, neighbourhood and place. House is viewed as a safe haven. Emphasis for these respondents is on their house and home rather than place.
Theme 2: Intense Connection to the House	House compensates for the acceptance that is lacking. from the neighbourhood by being welcoming, warm and safe. House provides safety and a retreat.
Theme 3: Feelings About the House Entwined with People	Critical factor in determining whether feelings for their house were positive or negative was the relationships with the people they shared the house with.
Theme 4: House Communicates Their Values	House reflects them in some way. Focus is not on sustainability. Sustainability is not integrated into their lifestyle.

5.5   Category of Description 4: House as Shelter

The respondents in the final category of description consider the house as simply utilitarian shelter. They generally have a transient housing history, and have consciously chosen to remain emotionally detached from the house, thereby ensuring it does not become a home. They suggest that their house is a commodity, and their aspirations towards a sustainable lifestyle are expressed through their housing choice, either currently or in the future.

5.5.1   Theme 1: Disjointed Relationship Between House, Home and Place

For these respondents, the distinction between house and home is very clear, and these people are aware of having a house with the aim of creating a home in the future. They feel a strong connection with place rather than the house, and purchased or moved into the house with the intention of either significantly changing it, or building a new one, in order to make a home:

> *And you're not loved. And because, and it's partly because I probably . . . that particular house, which you would have seen, I never particularly wanted to become attached to it, nor did I become attached to it. . . It was the area.* It was the closeness to the water and um, the surroundings and things. . .*I feel an affinity with [the location]* yeah, yeah I do. *I feel good when I go down there, and it was that feeling that made me buy the place,* and decide that I wanted to put my own stamp on it I suppose *(Respondent 11).*

> Like because I stayed in a caravan before, when I first moved here, for about a year and *it was like really important to me to just put my roots down. And have like a roof over my head and that's why I sort of did up the hut, was to feel like I could really connect with the place and make it my own (Respondent 4).*

5.5.2 Theme 2: No Connection to House

These respondents have little or no connection to their current house. They tend to have lived in houses that were temporary - either rental properties or houses they intended to demolish. These respondents indicated that they consciously chose not to become attached to the house because they were either planning to move in a short period of time, or were going to build a new house to replace the existing one:

> *House I chose you because . . . I can knock you down without feeling anything (Respondent 11).*

> And one thing I really disliked about living in the city is um renting – I've only ever stayed in places for like one year at a time, and had to um - **basically the houses I've chosen have been ones that are about to be demolished or something, just basically to have a roof over my head and pay as little as possible, and so they get knocked down and I'm out again, and I only have a year there. And so I've never been able to make my mark. Like plant trees, or paint things, or connect with the place.** So here I've been able to do that. So I've done it pretty loudly and really made a mark *(Respondent 4).*

5.5.3 Theme 3: House is a Commodity

These respondents have lived in numerous houses and appear to be quite mobile and flexible with their living conditions. For these respondents, houses are essentially commodities that become meaningful only when they are inhabited:

> *From the house's perspective, how do you feel about me living in you? Do you feel loved?* **I like being lived in and cared for.** *I feel a little sorry for the other huts nearby. I hope they can be jazzed up and lived in too. I have a youthful energy surrounding me. I'm left alone for long periods of time, which is OK, I'm used to it.* **But it's nice to be lived in, it gives me purpose and meaning.** *I feel loved, but I could be loved more (Respondent 4).*

> *I'm looking forward to it,* **but I don't really feel anything for it yet, because its not, its not there. . . Yes, it's not tangible** *(Respondent 11).*

While this respondent has a history of housing transience, his current residence, a hut in an alternative community, provides a site for identity-creation and expression. The hut, echoing the temple-house, creates a space where he can leave the world and listen to his own rhythm (Marc 1977). It provides and the privacy and space to be himself:

> *From your perspective, the way I feel about you is:* **I feel I can be me in you.** *I can feel comfortable but sometimes a little chilly. . .* **I feel proud of you,** *I feel like I don't need much, but that which I do need I want with an* **air of quality and care.** *I have that with you. I would like to spend more time with you but just knowing that you are there for me is enough. I'm grateful (Respondent 4).*

5.5.4 Theme 4: House Communicates their Commitment to Sustainable Living

The house provides an opportunity for these respondents to express themselves and their creativity, an important human need (Marc 1977). In Jungian terms, these houses are a physical manifestation of their journey towards individuation. Their houses convey their ideas about, and commitment to, sustainable living:

> *From your perspective, house, what do you communicate about me?* **You communicate my choice for a simple life, my desire to connect with nature, my willingness to be loud with colour, my attention to detail, my ability to build on what exists and show what I can do, that I can do things well. You show that you don't need big, new expensive things to be happy** *(Respondent 4).*

So I'm hoping that it will communicate about me, um my sort of thoughts about protecting the environment but also the fact that I like to be a bit different (Respondent 11).

5.5.5 Summary: House as Shelter

Themes	Defining characteristics
Theme 1: Disjointed Relationship Between House, Home and Place	House is considered simply as utilitarian shelter. Distinction between house and home is very clear. Aware of having a house with the aim of creating a home in the future. Feel a strong connection with place rather than the house.
Theme 2: No Connection to the House	Little or no connection the house. Transient housing history. Consciously chose not to become attached to the house because they were either planning to move in a short period of time, or were going to build a new house.
Theme 3: House is a Commodity	Lived in numerous houses and appear to be quite mobile and flexible with their living conditions. Houses are essentially commodities that become meaningful only when they are inhabited.
Theme 4: House Communicates their Commitment to Sustainable Living	House expresses themselves and their creativity. House demonstrates their commitment to sustainable living.

5.6 Structural Aspect: House

The structural aspect of the experience of the phenomenon is made up of the internal and external horizons of the categories of description. In this case it is the way in which the respondents describe their understanding and experience of house. The internal horizon of the categories of description includes the aspects that make up the experience of the phenomenon. Within the context of house, these aspects include the way in which the respondents describe their understanding and experience of the relationship between house, home, and place; their connection to their house; the way they feel about their house; and what the respondents believe the house communicates about them.

The external horizon is the external boundary of the phenomenon, which is defined by the delimitation of the phenomenon to the context, and the relation of the phenomenon to the context. Within the context of house, these boundaries are represented by the categories of description, and therefore include four ways of viewing the house in its context. The first is as a physical extension of the respondents; within the second perspective, the house is an agora or meeting place; the third viewpoint describes house as a refuge that provides respite from the world; and the fourth is that it is utilitarian shelter. These internal and external horizons make up the structural aspect of the respondents' understanding and experience of house in this study.

6 Home

So I think, when I thought of what does home mean to you, I guess I thought that fundamentally it's the people... And then I think I started to think about the environments that I think of as home. And I guess when I looked back at what I'd done, I thought, well this is really the planet that I'm thinking about, because home is the planet (Respondent 7).

6.1 Introduction

The qualitatively different ways the respondents described their understanding and experience of their home, and the relationship between this and their childhood memories, are explored in this chapter. Three conceptual categories of description emerged from the data. In the first, the respondents described their home as a harmonious synthesis of house and place; the interviewees in the second described home in terms of family and friends who share it; and those in the third category found it difficult to articulate what the concept means to them, suggesting a sense of homelessness. Within the three categories, two themes were explored. The first is an exploration of what home really means, and the second is an exploration of childhood memories of their experience and understanding of home.

As noted in the previous chapter, the four categories of description of house directly correspond to the four qualitatively different ways the respondents described their understanding and experience of place. While this appears reasonably straightforward, the relationship between house, home and place is more complex. Home is the emotional construct that emerges in part from the dynamic between house and place, but also from previous experiences of home, memories that form the threads of narratives past that come 'to dwell in a new house' (Bachelard 1969, p. 87). As such, the categories of description of house and place do not directly correspond to categories of description of home.

This chapter contributes to answering the first and third of the following three research questions:

1. *How do people describe their understanding and experience of house, home, and place?*
2. *How do people describe their understanding and experience of the relationship between house, home, place and sustainability?*
3. *How do people describe the relationship between childhood memories and their understanding and experience of home?*

While there is significant overlap between the themes that have determined the categories of description, the categories bear the title of the respondents' strongest overall descriptions of their understanding and experience of home. The three categories outlined in this chapter contribute to the overall outcome space within this study.

6.2 Category of Description 1: Home as Symbiosis

For the respondents in this category, home is the synthesis of house and place. They have an expansive sense of home that extends beyond the threshold of their house, and consider their homes to be a place of sanctuary, peace, comfort and relaxation. In contrast to their experiences as adults, most of these respondents experienced a profound sense of displacement as children after migrating to Australia.

6.2.1 Theme 1: Home Means Symbiosis

These respondents discuss home in the context of the natural environment within which it sits, as the symbiosis of house and place. They suggest that their house is essentially a concretisation of place, and as such the location is an inextricable element of transforming their house into a home. Perhaps because of this they describe it as being expansive, extending beyond the walls of their house and the boundary of their property. For one respondent, home is boundless, suggesting, as Heidegger (1962) did, that the world may be considered our home. These homes are experienced as a microcosm intimately linked to the macrocosm, and provide the opportunity for creative expression for these respondents (Marc 1977):

> *And then I think I started to think about the environments that I think of as home. And I guess when I looked back at what I'd done, I thought,* **well this is really the planet that I'm thinking about, because home is the planet. And one of the first things I did was this wetland, and the hills. Then I put trees on the hills, and then sand dunes, and then ocean.** *And the colours were to represent, the nature is the green and the brown and the yellow, and all those natural colours. In a way, those colours were the,* **symbolic of all the things we create around us that create our comfortable home.** *So they're like 'pillows'. Something like that. But they just represent, I think the colour of the things that we've created and synthesised within our natural environment.* **And then the sun came in, and I guess the sun had to touch on everything** *(Respondent 7, see Figure 6).*

Figure 6: What Home Really Means . . . (Respondent 7)

The following two respondents share a house in a conservation cooperative, and both describe the location of the house as and important element of transforming the house into a home:

> *Um, and I respond: you can continue to provide me with warmth and protection from the elements and a place to enjoy and sustain the lifestyle that I have become so accustomed to.* **You can continue to be my haven in a location that I love, a place where I can observe and be part of the natural environment. You can**

continue to be my special living and breathing space, one which makes a minimal impact on the bush and gives credence to the philosophy of sustainable living. You can continue to be a place that inspires me to practice my art and to keep learning more about nature and my environment. You can continue to provide me with the tranquil, stimulating and uplifting environment which I need to continue my reading and my learning experiences (Respondent 2).

*And then, **through the window all the time no matter where I am I've got the animal life and the trees and the hills** (Respondent 1, see Figure 7).*

Figure 7: Home (Respondent 1)

For these respondents, home is associated with the people who share it, their family and friends. The home provides a place for gathering these people together and entertaining, and this is symbolized by the kitchen, cooking, wine and food:

*It's the **kitchen, the wine, um cooking**, which I get involved in too. Um, and my favourite chair, if times are tough and I've got to relax, sleeping, sharing (Respondent 1).*

*I like **entertaining at home with my friends and family**, and um I'd have to do another one with food and stuff in it I think (Respondent 2).*

> And then I suppose **I thought well sitting round tables was very much part of home, wherever you are.** And conversations and discussions and um yeah lots of issues of the day and things... **So there was a lot of ritual. I didn't write the word ritual down, I probably should have.** But **very much them at the family gatherings and all that sort of thing** (Respondent 6).

> So I think, when I thought of what does home mean to you, I guess I thought that **fundamentally it's the people** (Respondent 7).

Home is also a place of comfort, warmth and relaxation. These respondents consider their home to be a sanctuary and place of peace, a serene temple for living in. These are the qualities of the original temple-house which resonate with the human psyche (Marc 1977). They describe a connection between their psyche and the living psyche of the house, which provides insight in two ways. First, the house is, by definition, architecture (Boyd 1970); and second, the living psyche of the architecture is important for a house to become a home:

> It's a **very comfortable place**. It's a place I feel ... I don't go many places where I feel I've got something better than this. And I'm talking holiday places (Respondent 1).

> **You can continue to provide me with the tranquil, stimulating and uplifting environment which I need to continue my reading and my learning experiences** (Respondent 2).

> Then there's other people scattered around, but not heaps. I guess, we certainly have friends and visitors but **home is also a peaceful place where you're not surrounded by crowds of people** (Respondent 7).

> Um an artist friend stayed with us, and she wrote me the loveliest letter and she said um, well [partner] and I are not very religious at all. In fact we are atheists. And um, if you have to label anything - we don't bother with labels - but she's the wife of a Bishop, and Anglican Bishop, and she loves coming to stay, and ah she tells me that she **feels like she's in a cathedral when she's in our home. She loves our home. She really, really likes it, and loves coming to stay. And she feels like she's in a cathedral.** She says there's a serenity there ... which she **enjoys immensely** (Respondent 2).

The gathering of material possessions over time enables the home to become a site of identity expression (Noble 2004), and these respondents all describe this process. With great care and consideration, they collect things with which they identify. These artifacts personalise and distinguish their house as a home:

> But I guess they represent the, all the, **bright coloured artifacts that we gather around us**. That make our, they're **our collection of objects that make our place ours, and familiar** and. . . The things that we make and create, that aren't green and brown and natural colours or whatever. So it was sort of, but I also thought of them as pillows and comfortable (Respondent 7).

The following respondent explains in detail the items that she collects and displays in her home that convey something about herself:

> Well this is just got bits and pieces of things that are of significance to me at home. **My artwork is represented there. Books obviously. Artworks, paintings, orchids, music, flowers, plants. You know, just all of those things that I amass around me at home, which suit me and my lifestyle I guess** that's um, the um . . . So that's one aspect of just little bits and pieces just in that area where I relax and um, and just enjoy myself really, enjoy the benefits of living where I live (Respondent 2, see Figures 8 and 9).

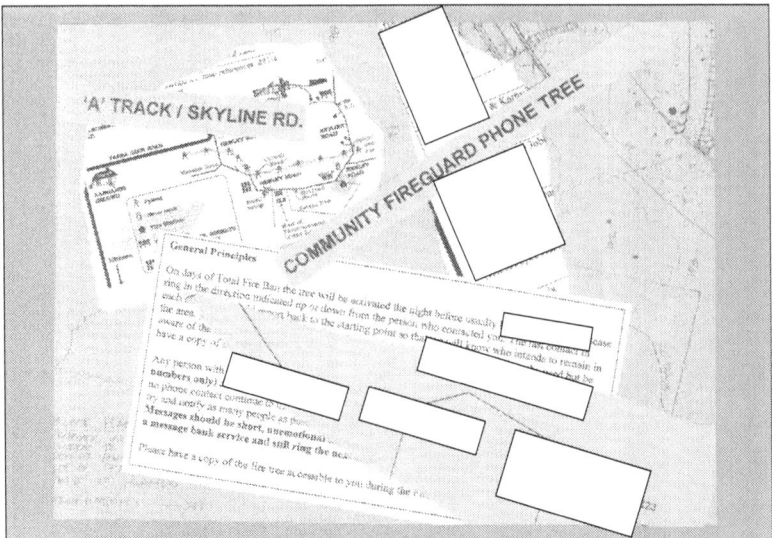

Figure 8: What Home Really Means . . . (Respondent 2)

- 109 -

Figure 9: What Home Really Means . . . (Respondent 2)

6.2.2 Theme 2: Memories of Home

Three of the four respondents in this category migrated to Australia at a young age. While the motivations for moving for each family were different, these respondents describe a shared sense of displacement as children. These feelings were exacerbated to some degree for two of these respondents by uncertain tenure and poor housing conditions on arrival, in contrast to what they considered to be comparatively good housing conditions they had experienced in Europe. Perhaps because of this, these three respondents indicate they have created an intense sense of rootedness and connectedness with Australia as home and place as adults. The following story from Respondent 1 describes this experience in detail:

> *My childhood is split into before Australia and Australia. There is a very precise split between the two, almost good and bad, happy and unhappy. After trying to come to terms with what to put here this separation helps me understand the **feeling I had of "not belonging".** I left a very pleasant easy going life where I fitted in and was well adjusted, to come to a country that had problems with new comers. I suddenly found myself surrounded by mostly unhappy people looking for a new start (mostly English migrants). **I was in opposition to anyone outside that community because of their rejection of us**. They were for the most part less well adjusted than my fellow countrymen. Most of them lived in and around the housing commission area of Heidelberg. **I never realised how much that tension of change has affected me.***
>
> ***For a long time I thought of myself as English not only because I was labelled "pom" but also because I didn't like the notion of being Australian.*** *In fact I probably took pride in not being Australian. I quickly adopted the Australian accent and apart from the people who really knew me . . . would pass as an Australian and yet I always felt the need at times to identify myself as British. **This probably would still be the case if I hadn't returned to England where I discovered that somehow; somewhere; in the space and time between I had become an Australian...***
>
> *When we came to Preston Hostel we often wound up throwing stones at the kids across the creek. Any trip was a trip into enemy territory, you were worried about who you might meet. On top of this **the hostel was a hostile environment**; the kids there were rough and tough compared to me. My parents came to Australia for us; most of the other migrants were there because they had been failing at making a life in Britain. So that was a tough place to be (we were there for 18 months).*
>
> ***To top everything off my parents lost their life savings in a failed house investment. They got nothing back and were very bitter about that.*** *My parents tried to create a family from the people who came with us; they became default*

*aunts and uncles. **It was never the same and while I now see the move to Australia as a positive experience for me as a child I had some deep seated regrets that I never really discussed with anybody. I have never properly looked at this issue before and it has been a bit of a personal awakening to finally sort some of this out**, thank you for this (Respondent 1, see Figure 10).*

This respondent's first years in Australia were distinguished by being an outsider, which was probably exacerbated by the identification of himself as British rather than Australian for a number of years. The process of identity-creation for this respondent was clearly challenging, and he indicates that he experienced a sense of exclusion shared by any "outsider" who does not conform to the prevailing social norms in terms of race, class, or sexuality (McDowell 1999; Gorman-Murray 2007). Furthermore, this respondent lived with his family in various government-provided forms of housing, from communal sheds to individual houses. Given that home is a home is a key site of identity-creation and stability (Blunt 2003), this uncertainty and mobility probably further complicated the process of identity-creation.

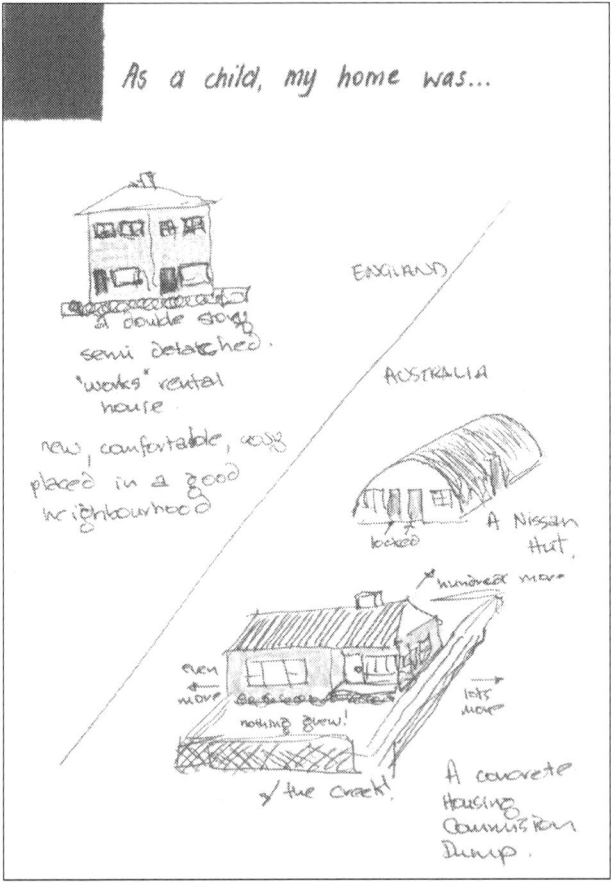

Figure 10: Childhood Homes (Respondent 1)

The following respondent, who also migrated to Australia with her family as a child, clearly experienced very challenging living conditions. On arrival she lived with her family in a migrant hostel. The long hut was shared by a number of families who demarcated space with hessian bags. This respondent describes a sense of having no control over her environment in terms of basic needs like privacy, but also in terms of personalising the space or facilitating creative expression. This experience clearly deeply impacted on the family:

> ***My childhood was just so different to anything I'm experiencing living in the bush, you know in the Australian bush. . . It was a long tin hut in the Broadmeadows migrant hostel.*** *It was situated in a former army barracks which were hurriedly and rather crudely converted to take the influx of displaced people - because we came from Europe after the war. . . We arrived in 1949. . .* ***Now, by***

today's standards I don't think that anyone would live anything like that quite frankly. You know, they were pretty dreadful. They were corrugated iron. They were unlined. Spiders, ants coming through, and everything else too. Anything. You know skinks... *And um, the ah, it took them a little while, but the residents you know actually, you know, did a fair bit of work to make the place liveable...*

When we first came to Australia it was, if you can imagine, it is not quite as big as, wide as this, **but there were you know long huts with three level bunks and everyone used to go into those. So if you were sick, too bad. If you were old and frail and you couldn't climb up there, well you were in trouble. And children and adults and everyone all together. And it was terrible. I think, you know.** That didn't last for very long. **The next step was hessian liners, and a family would have, a whole family would have, less than this room, and it would have some private bedding in there. So the hessian, you know pull-along curtains, that was the divider between families.** And then the next step was, you know, the army huts that were evacuated by the army, and um, three families would live in a hut...

It was, they were very crude, it was very crude. I mean as a child I didn't know any better. It was just you know, it was just the way it was. You just don't think about it, **but I know that my parents were quite anguished about it. In the um labour camp in Germany where they came from to Australia, the conditions weren't even that primitive** (Respondent 2, see Figure 11).

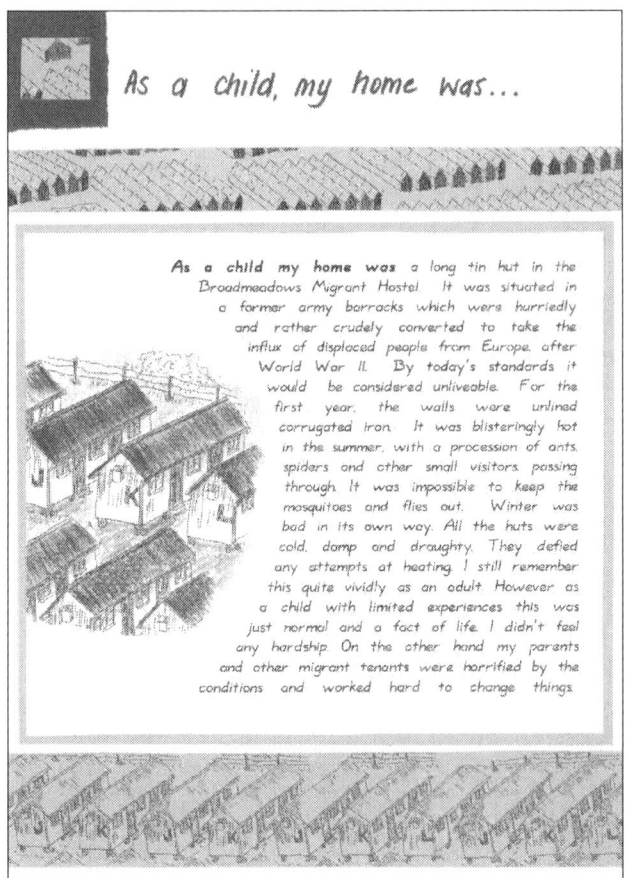

Figure 11: Childhood Homes (Respondent 2)

Conversely, Respondent 6 grew up in Melbourne surrounded by her extended family. She describes her childhood home as providing a profound sense of security, protection and stability, and has fond memories of her childhood. For this respondent, her childhood home was, in Bachelard's (1969) terms, her first universe that has framed later understandings about the world:

> *Oh yes, it was only sold a year ago this house. So it's been around forever.* ***So it's been like where all the family occasions have happened for . . . Not just my generation, first generation, but with kids to follow. So it's like home, it was like an anchor, a foundation where families are built around. . . So I guess, so the roots of home and house and things seemed to emanate from those times. Deep anchors and roots. Stability*** *(Respondent 6).*

6.2.3 Summary: Home as Symbiosis

Themes	Defining characteristics
Theme 1: Home Means Symbiosis	Home is the synthesis of house and place. Expansive sense of home. Entertaining family and friends. Symbolised by the kitchen, food and wine. Place of sanctuary, peace, comfort, warmth and relaxation. Gathered artifacts personalise and distinguish their home.
Theme 2: Memories of Home	Three respondents migrated to Australia as young children and experienced a profound sense of displacement and uncertain housing tenure and poor housing conditions in Australia. The fourth respondent grew up in Melbourne and experienced a secure sense of home.

6.3 Category of Description 2: Home as People

The respondents in this category associate the idea of home with the people they share their home with. Home is where their family and friends come together, especially to share food and conversation. For these respondents, the home provides emotional security and is seen as a foundation and anchor. It is a place to create and store memories. While these respondents had both positive and negative experiences of home as children, they all sought to create a secure and happy environment as adults.

6.3.1 Theme 1: Home Means Family

These respondents equate home with people, specifically immediate and extended family and friends. It is where people gather and communicate, and their understanding of home is as much about creating an environment that is conducive to this as it is about the people. Communal gathering spaces are the focus of their house, and for many this was the principal influence for the design. As such, the home is symbolised by a table, food, cooking, wine and conversation:

> *So home is essentially for me about the people. So without the people the home would sort of mean nothing really. So family is probably the core of the way our house is designed. Both for our immediate family, for [partner] and I and our children, as well as a place where our families are all the time coming for*

dinner. We've got this big table and all that. **It's a place where we can all, you know, sit down and share a meal and that type of thing** *(Respondent 8, see Figure 12).*

Figure 12: What Home Really Means . . . (Respondent 8)

And I guess the things that came to mind around that, talking about the **house as being a place where you can have fun, about interaction and mucking around,** *especially with [daughter] as she's growing up. A place for people to gather, talk, you know the communication element of people being in the one space (Respondent 9).*

We, I spend ninety percent of my day, and life, with the boys at the kitchen bench. When I'm cooking, they're on the other side drawing, when we're eating, I sit on one side, and they sit on the other side, and we eat and we cook together, talk together (Respondent 10, see Figure 13).

Figure 13: Home (Respondent 10)

The following respondent lives in a house with a number of families where the kitchen and dining area are communal spaces. This respondent identifies these places as the "heart" of the home, whereas the private areas are on the fringe of the communal spaces. While both private and public areas are important in a shared house, this respondent equates the public areas with the notion of home:

*I think we got to it before. **It's the place where the people are. So it's the kitchen, or it's the courtyard, it's the place where everybody gathers. And um then out on the edges of that are the places where you hide, the places where you do your own thing**, the places where you have adventures... But it's little things like that, that become um that are outside, but the core of it, **the heart of it, is where all the people are doing things**... Oh, maybe a kitchen table. Yeah maybe it's a* *sedentary thing. Maybe a bottle of wine, because I've often got a bottle of wine associated with it (Respondent 5).*

These respondents describe their homes as providing a profound sense of emotional nourishment and security. It is considered a foundation, a base, and an anchor that provides a safe and secure environment from which to participate in the world, all of which are normative meanings of home (Blunt 2003; Blunt & Dowling 2006; Mallet 2004):

From a personal point of view a house, **a home, it's constant that it's there for you. It's a base for you to operate from that's safe and warm** *(Respondent 8).*

Safety and sanctuary, *you know a place to come home to and shut out the hecticness of our job, or whatever else is going on,* **and just be able to relax and find some sanctuary**. . . *And that, I guess, is a bit of a contradiction to this, but it's sort of saying* **it's a constant and a foundation** *in that sense, but then you can get like a canvas and then you can change it (Respondent 9).*

These respondents describe their homes as welcoming, comfortable and relaxing. Their homes represent and emanate love and warmth. Many of these houses were designed to maximise natural sunlight and include working fireplaces, both of which contribute to this sense of warmth and comfort:

So words that describe that is that it's a **welcoming place** *and it's full*. . . **Light is obviously a big thing for us in that you can be in the space for the majority of the day and not have to have lights on. That it's restful** *(Respondent 8).*

Inviting, so it's welcoming for other people. A place to relax, *and I tried to draw reading books, magazines, having a drink, gardening - that's me digging with a spade, and playing - that's meant to be [daughter] and that's a ball*. . . *Fun, laughter, and* **the idea of relaxation, laughter, fun, somewhere where you can let your hair down** *(Respondent 9, see Figure 14).*

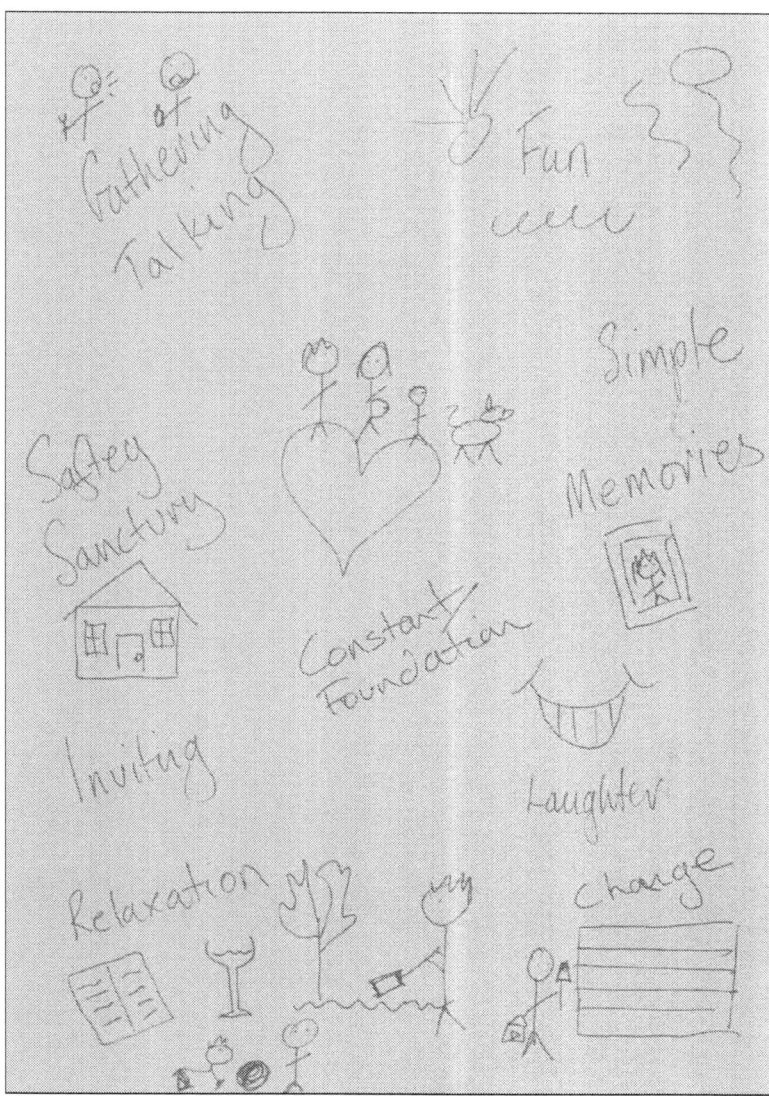

Figure 14: What Home Really Means . . . (Respondent 9)

Beautiful material. I started crying when I was doing this. . . **And then the red for the love and welcoming.** *And then um,* **this is the sun in the lounge room, and that kitchen bench area, because I love sitting in the light talking to the boys.** *. . . So that's my kitchen bench, and that light is this area here. Which, is* **so warm and nice, it's just lovely.** *. . . And that's* **the fireplace, which I suppose is a theme from my childhood, because we had a lovely fireplace at home.** *And, it really has* *a calming effect on the kids. And, um, like they,* **you light the fire and the house instantly calms down.** *Like they settle, and they sit in front of it, and we talk and things. Whereas* **without the fire, there's no sort of heart** *(Respondent 10, see Figure 15).*

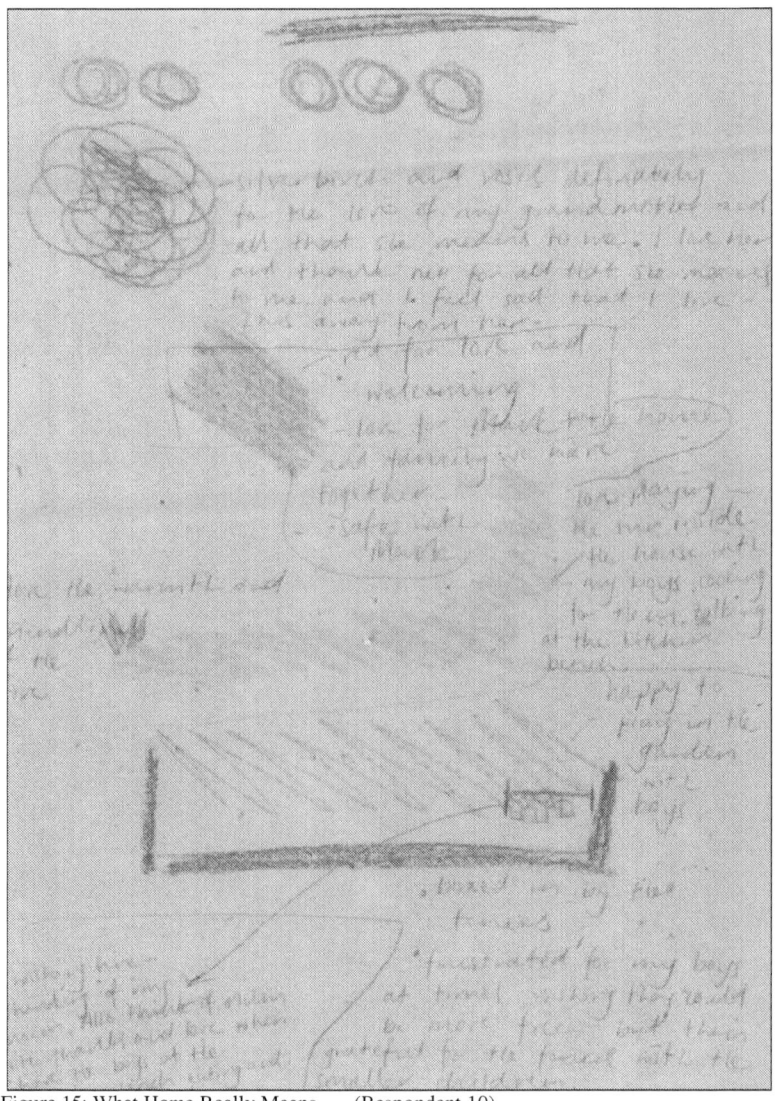

Figure 15: What Home Really Means . . . (Respondent 10)

*So, as you can see, it's very **important that a home is welcoming**, and I suppose too, it's something that I really value from my mum. . . **And I know what it feels like to be welcomed to a place, and I know that it feels good, and therefore that's something that I want to also be able to do in welcoming other people. That's what a home should be. It shouldn't just be a house, a thing, you know, that it should be a place where people feel comfortable, and conversation can happen,** and well, it's, many things are free to happen, people feel comfortable. You know, and **I think that welcome comes out of your heart, you know. It's something that comes from within.** It's not exterior type stuff (Respondent 13, see Figure 16).*

Figure 16: What Home Really Means . . . (Respondent 13)

For these respondents, their home is a place to create and store memories, especially of family and friends. Displaying these artifacts provides a sense of history, a connectedness to their extended family and network of friends, and also a sense of locatedness and rootedness in the world. For some of these respondents, this sense of history extends to their house, which they deliberately retained as part of the renovation:

*And **a place of memories where you can have photos on the wall as you walk down your hallway. Old furniture from different places and people, and a place*** *where you can store all that information as well. And display it in many ways (Respondent 9).*

*But it was **very important to us to keep the old part of the house because it has history and a place in this street. And we like the old part of the house so it's about bringing the two together** (Respondent 8).*

6.3.2   Theme 2: Memories of Home

These respondents describe a clear sense of how, as children, they wanted to feel in their home: safe, secure and happy. Some of these respondents describe experiencing this vividly and fondly, and have emulated it in their homes now with their own children:

*As a child your perceptions of the world are not as grand as they are as an adult. . . . And then as a child, well actually I drew the family holiday house which was at Phillip Island. . . **It's tiny but we would have twenty people staying there. So there would be loads of people in the bedrooms and there would be makeshift bedrooms and there would be people camping outside**. . . But it still provides the same function that it always did in that it provides **a place for people to go to and relax and it doesn't matter that it's so simple because it's so comfortable** (Respondent 8).*

*That's a good strong childhood image of a holiday house we had in Anglesea that Mum and Dad actually built. It was one of those log cabin ones. And that **big central fireplace was like, in a room like this it was at the end and it was just a really strong focus**. . . And it's those things that to some degree transferred into this arrangement, because I was trying to capture those sorts of things. It's funny how in my head somewhere there were visions of that (Respondent 9).*

*So as a child my home had a fireplace which was pretty pivotal to family life. . . **There were always lots of people in the house, and it was a nice family upbringing**. I was very lucky to have a lovely family. . . And memories of childhood was **mum at the washing line, and having dinner all together, and mum cooking at the bench. We have a bench similar to that, so I suppose I brought that to my own family, like hers**. . . So, and then, and then I, oh the clothesline, I love the clothesline. Like you can see it's in full view of the lounge room, it's just there. . . And I planned it deliberately so I could see the clothes on*

> the clothesline. It's just a nice thing for me, **because that's the way I remember Mum hanging clothes on the line all the time** (Respondent 10).

> Oh this is a place in my childhood. This is cool, I loved doing this too. So for me growing up, **my home always felt safe, happy, warm, friendly fun and active** (Respondent 12).

One of these respondents in particular did not feel she experienced this sense of safety, security and happiness in her childhood home. She has subsequently consciously reflected on the dynamics of her family as a child, and suggests that she did not feel this security and acceptance for two reasons. The first is growing up in a household that went through a divorce; and the second is that she feels her natural personality was modified as a child due to family expectations of how she should behave. For this respondent, the process of identity-creation in the home was curtailed. This respondent describes her experience below:

> As a home, **as a child my home was - as you can see, it's all in black** and I couldn't really put a lot of - I think I started drawing a picture, and then it just didn't, wasn't happening and I was really forcing it, and then **that's when I started to write, because it was in the writing was sort of letting out the most...**

> And I don't know if my mum took that consciously on or whether it was just the type of kid I was, **but it just seemed any adventure I got up to, I ended up getting into trouble.** So **I really felt that my personality, the type of kid that I was, was really squashed**, and I think it took me a bit of time to rediscover it. **So I probably think that that's why I was a bit confused and anxious**. Because it didn't seem - whatever I did, I got into trouble for it, to the point where **I became very, very quiet, insecure, anxious child and teenager. Plus the things that were happening within the house, which impacted the way that I felt, you know. Things were happening, not very nice family things, to make me not particularly secure.**

> And I like the Italians next door, when they made [tomato sauce] - even though it smelt disgusting - there was a scent - I used to just like looking over because there was this hive of activity. There was the extended family, you know. It was a whole day of work. **You could see that lots of things were going on, and they**

were just happy and cheerful, obviously getting into the wine and there was lots of laughter, and I think I just enjoyed it (Respondent 13, see Figure 17).

As an adult, this respondent has intentionally sought to create a sense of welcoming, warmth, acceptance, security and happiness in her home now.

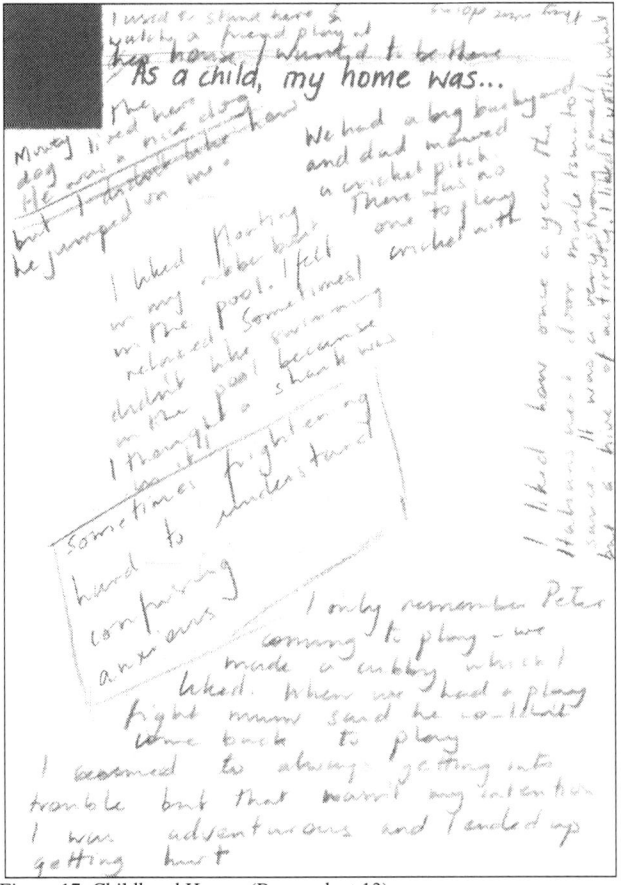

Figure 17: Childhood Homes (Respondent 13)

6.3.3 Summary: Home as People

Themes	Defining characteristics
Theme 1: Home Means Family	Home is people. Where people gather and converse, symbolised by a table, cooking, food, wine. Provides emotional security; it is a foundation, a base and an anchor. Welcoming, comfortable and relaxing. Emanates love and warmth, sunlight and fire. Place to create and store memories.
Theme 2: Memories of Home	From a child's perspective, a home should feel safe, secure and happy. Respondents who experienced this as children recreated it in their homes as adults. Respondents who did not experience this as children consciously chose to create this feeling in their home as an adult.

6.4 Category of Description 3: Homelessness

The respondents in the third category of description imply a sense of homelessness. They have difficulty articulating what home means to them, especially in terms of what home is and where it is experienced. These respondents express a sense of transience and displacement as children and adults.

6.4.1 Theme 1: Home Means Nothing

These respondents tend to be quite vague and elusive about what home means to them. For some, there is a clear hesitation to identify a single home, which includes two levels of confusion. Firstly, uncertainty about what home actually means; and secondly, indecision about where home is, which further compounds their doubt. These reservations are reflected in their inability to complete this activity in the cultural probe:

> *I thought I had finished it all. And I looked at it and I thought . . .* **Because I didn't know where 'home' was suppose to be for you**, *I didn't get any . . . And I*

> *was actually sitting down at Barwon Heads and I was thinking . . .* **No, it's still not doing anything.** *. . So that was why . . . . So I can do something but I couldn't get actually get anything out of it. . . But it's not really, I mean if you see what I've written, its been about Barwon Heads, and it really is because of . . . I don't feel anything for Barwon Heads because it is going. . . No, I mean, the problem was that I was trying to do it at Barwon, and it was when I couldn't, you know, I thought this is crazy. . .* **Now. Yeah I can do, I actually find, I think my difficulty with all this was it was directed to one home.** *And, I have more than one home, um, and so,* **home doesn't necessarily mean anything in particular to me**, *because you, yeah . . .* **I mean, this is, this assumes that you have an affinity with the idea of home** *(Respondent 11).*

For one of the respondents in this category, confusion about what home means is partly the result of not having any positive experiences of, or associations with, the houses he has lived in. He suggests that the unhappiness in these houses was intimately entwined with the negative emotional experiences within them; in this respect, the house is a depository for feelings of pain and anxiety (Sibley 1995). This respondent doesn't actually use the term home, preferring instead to use house, an indication that the issue is not about physical shelter, but an absence of the complex psychological and social phenomena associated with having a home (Zaborowski 2005). Perhaps because of this, he did not complete this (or any other) activity in the cultural probe:

> ***I don't have very many, um, positive connotations about this house, or any other houses.*** *Um, I mean* ***this house is probably a bit of a refuge for me, but it's also a house that I built with my ex partner, and has a lot of memories about that, which aren't always necessarily good.*** *Um, and, so probably* ***the image that comes to mind is probably a bit of a cave type image, not an open sort of image.*** *And um, the only other house that comes to mind was a house that belonged to my auntie and uncle when I was a youngster. And that was in Yalourn, that was a very traditional house, but that was probably, um,* ***I used to spend holidays there and my aunty and uncle had a completely different family from my family, or they were a completely different family from my family.*** *. . So yeah, so that was probably something I remember, not because of the house per say or whatever,* ***but more about the dynamics of the family that lived in the house, yeah*** *(Respondent 3).*

A strong sense of displacement comes through in these responses, which seems to contribute to their inability to identify what home means. These respondents describe varying degrees of transience which, they suggest, has contributed to their incapacity to create a sense of home:

> *No it's, I mean, only that I, as I've said, **I did feel that, it was, you know you really had to have one place. . . You had to be living an area, rather than two or three, in order for it to be more meaningful.** You know, I realised that as I was doing it, that um, you can't really write about somewhere where you're not very often. Even though I plan to be there often in the future. **But even then it will never be my only home** (Respondent 11).*

> *Part of like my background, I guess, what home means to me is being a traveller. **So, and I've had, I've generally had my home on my back. So the snail, and I'm just moving around slowly, and travelling around, and in a comby around the country**, so that's sort of been the way that I've lived from about, when was it? The late 90s. . . (Respondent 4, see Figure 18).*

Figure 18: What Home Really Means . . . (Respondent 4)

> *So I've been very transient. Um, and home is pretty, been where I hung my hat really. . . Yeah. And one thing I really disliked about living in the city is um renting – I've only ever stayed in places for like one year at a time, and had to um - basically the houses I've chosen have been ones that are about to be demolished*

or something, just basically to have a roof over my head and pay as little as possible, and so they get knocked down and I'm out again, and I only have a year there. ***And so I've never been able to make my mark. Like plant trees, or paint things, or connect with the place*** *(Respondent 4, see Figure 19).*

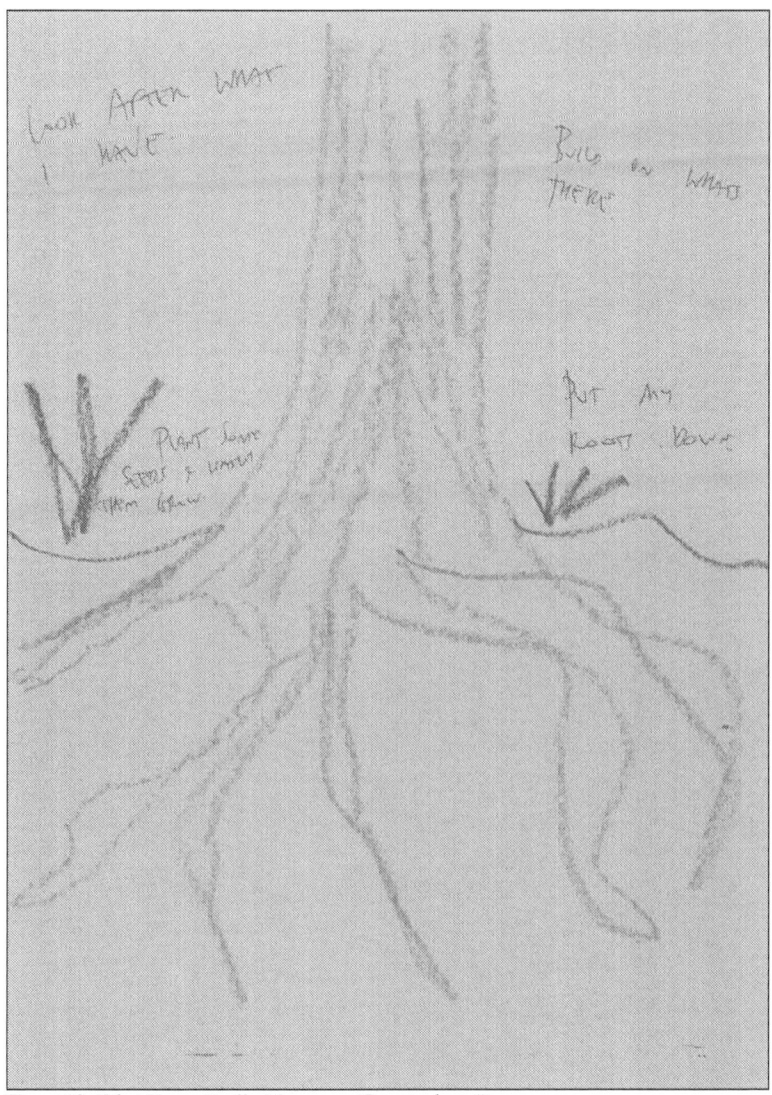

Figure 19: What Home Really Means . . . (Respondent 4)

This respondent's commitment to sustainability has informed his choice of where to live, which is in an alternative community (a cooperatively managed bush property) in rural Victoria. While he considers his home to be essentially on the fringe of society - metaphorically and physically - he describes a desire to connect into the mainstream to share ideas about sustainable living. He explains this through his drawing of What Home Really Means (Figure 20):

> ***It's about connecting. Doing things differently, but still connecting with mainstream. Because I want to share the things I've learned.*** *So this is sort of like, in some ways it's like the internet, like . . . this sort of branching out, and things to say and do,* ***a view from the outside looking in.*** *So it's about, I guess,* ***taking a step back from the mainstream and looking at it from a big picture perspective.*** *. . .* ***Observe and have input, but also be able to take a step back from it.*** *. . . I sort of feel that the changes that need to happen in the city um, are, sort of more attitude. . . I guess it's a way of thinking. And going to that you need to sort of take a step away from it because you feel bombarded with all the things that are happening. But I still want to sort of, ah, be a part of it. . . . This is like the planet, I suppose. And this is . . . Oh, like, almost like a, yeah something,* ***like a kite, or like a, like the um umbilical cord or something, you know? Connected, but somewhere else*** *(Respondent 4, see Figure 20).*

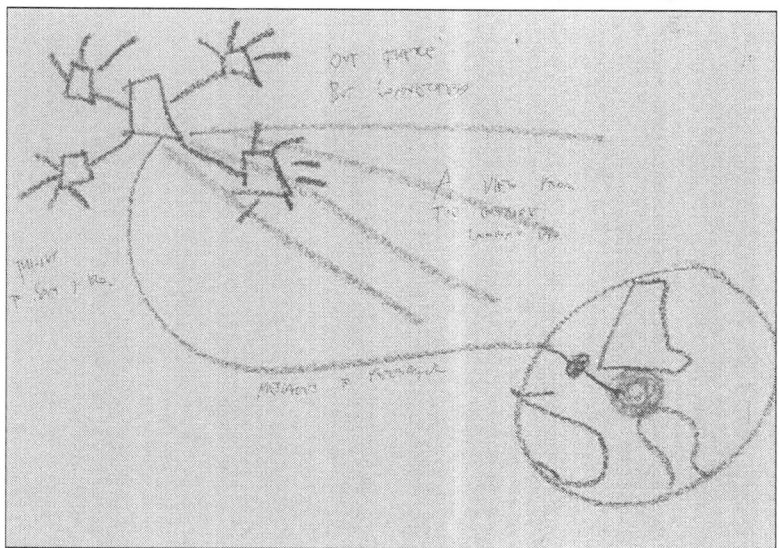

Figure 20: What Home Really Means . . . (Respondent 4)

6.4.2 Theme 2: Memories of Home

While these respondents experienced childhood homes differently, the result of these experiences seems to be that, as adults, they share a sense of homelessness. The first respondent was quite distressed discussing experiences of home as either an adult or child, and describes memories of an unhappy childhood home characterised by family conflict. In contrast to this were positive experiences of a relative's home, which highlighted, and possibly heightened, this unhappy experience of their own home:

> *Oh look as a child my, I think my childhood homes went through probably three stages. And the first one I barely remember at all. I mean I don't have, I don't have very many memories of my first home.* ***And then the home that I spent probably right through my teenage years into my adult years, or my early adult years, was um, not a black hole, a grey hole. It was a pretty depressing place, with a fair bit of conflict taking place in it.*** *And I was, at that stage I had one sister who is um about 11 years older than me I think, so that period of time I was the only one at home.* ***So yeah, so I don't have good memories of it, no. So my auntie's house stood out as an alternative to that*** *(Respondent 3).*

The following respondent also has negative memories of his childhood home. He clearly did not identify with the suburban environment the house was located in, which probably impacted on his sense of home:

> *As a child my home was... I was just thinking about the little, like I grew up in the suburbs,* ***and actually I mean I despised it, growing up, in some ways.*** *Just the, sort of the outer suburbs (Respondent 4).*

This respondent encountered difficulty in responding to this exercise for the same reason she did not complete the 'What Home Really Means to You. . . ' drawing: she lived in many houses as a child, and therefore no single house clearly represented home for her, however after some reflection she was able to identify one with which she felt most connected:

> ***Ok, childhood was an interesting thing, because I lived in lots of homes as a child****, so I had to think which one I had the most connection with I suppose. And it was a place I lived for most of my Primary school years. . .* ***So that's my childhood. Yeah, so that was um, what I thought of in terms of my childhood. So nothing like what I live in now*** *(Respondent 11).*

6.4.3 Summary: Homelessness

Themes	Defining characteristics
Theme 1: Home Means Nothing	Vague and elusive about what home means. Confusion about what home is and where it is. Sense of transience and displacement. Sense of home is entwined with emotional experiences of house.
Theme 2: Memories of Home	Two distinct experiences of home as a child. The first included negative memories and experiences of home as a child. The second included living in many houses as a child, therefore no single house was clearly considered a home.

6.5 Structural Aspect: Home

The internal and external horizons of the categories of description together form the structural aspect of the experience of the phenomenon, which is the way in which the respondents describe their understanding and experience of home. As previously noted, the internal horizon of the categories of description includes the aspects that make up the experience of the phenomenon. Within the context of home, these aspects include the way in which the respondents describe their understanding and experience of what home really means to them, and their childhood memories of their experience of home.

The external horizon for home is represented by the categories of description, and therefore includes three ways of viewing home in its context. The first is that home as a harmonious synthesis of house and place; within the second perspective home is inextricably linked to family and friends; and the third viewpoint described a sense of homelessness. These internal and external horizons make up the structural aspect of the respondents' understanding and experience of home in this study.

7 Place

And I think, I mean I've sort of done the little houses, but I've identified the houses which are of the people we are close to. I mean we sort of know everyone, but then there's people we're close to. And I've put our place in red. And then there's the beaches, and the wetland, and I guess some of the little things . . . Little, like there's this little path through the forest that we just call the Fairy Forest. And all the neighbours call it the Fairy Forest, but I don't really know who else calls it the Fairy Forest (Respondent 7).

7.1 Introduction

This chapter explores the qualitatively different ways the respondents described their understanding and experience of place. Four conceptual categories of description emerged from the data. In the first, the respondents described place as the area for which they held deep feelings of care and respect. The interviewees in the second described place in terms of the services and amenities they used in their local neighbourhood. The respondents in the third category described an increasing sense of alienation from place; and in the fourth they felt an immediate affinity with place. Within the four categories, one theme was explored: the multitude of connections with place for each of the respondents, which then defined its boundaries. As noted previously, the four categories of description of place directly correspond to the four qualitatively different ways the respondents described their understanding and experience of their house.

This chapter contributes to answering the first of the following three research questions:

1. *How do people describe their understanding and experience of house, home, and place?*

2. *How do people describe their understanding and experience of the relationship between house, home, place and sustainability?*

3. *How do people describe the relationship between childhood memories and their understanding and experience of home?*

There is significant overlap between the themes that have determined the four categories of description. For example, all of the respondents describe place as somewhere with which they identify to a greater or lesser extent. Therefore, the categories bear the title of the respondents' strongest overall descriptions of their understanding and experience of place. The four categories of description outlined in this chapter contribute to the overall outcome space within this study.

7.2 Category of Description 1: Place as Dwelling

The respondents in the first category of description suggest a sense of place as Dwelling, in the Heideggerian sense of sparing and preserving. They describe profound feelings of care and respect for their environment and community, and are frequently involved with community projects to nurture and protect the area. They describe their community and neighbourhood in terms of a field of care, and feel intimately connected them.

7.2.1 Theme: Expansive Place Boundaries and Connections

These respondents all consider place to be the areas with which they identify, which includes the neighbourhood. Two of them live in a conservation cooperative on the fringe of Melbourne, the third lives in a small coastal town that is dominated by coastal sand dunes and vegetation, and the fourth lives in an urban eco village. The identification with their neighbourhoods is developed and nurtured through physically traversing their surrounding environment for either pleasure or community projects, such as weeding and vegetation maintenance programs. They describe deep feelings of care and respect for their environment, and are routinely involved in community projects to ensure the ongoing survival of these natural areas:

> ***Yes we contribute substantially to the fire brigade in the area, and so we have things like Cinema Pompadour.*** *That's once every two months. . . They have what they call, and you'll probably see the ads going out, they have Café Benders on Saturday where they,* ***you go along and buy a cup of coffee and have a cake and sit and have a chat with the neighbours, and again, it's a fundraiser*** *(Respondent 1).*

> ***Oh, on foot really, mostly.*** *But, I mean the kids ride bikes.* ***There's a few walks that you do repeatedly.*** *So from our place we might go all the way down to the point and then actually come back along the wetland.* ***When the kids are going down to some of the neighbours, they use this little path through the trees and then go down here.*** *So, and sometimes, particularly probably before I had kids, and* ***we used to do quite a lot of community weeding, and that's still an issue, but I haven't been as involved in it.*** *. . But, so I know the dunes quite well from those community weeding projects. . . And I mean I go in there in the guise of weeding, which you know, we've done heaps of over time. But it is quite fun just*

wandering through the dunes, all along really, getting lost for a while (Respondent 7).

There is a sense of intimacy and delight for their place that is conveyed in the interviews with these respondents. Their detailed knowledge of these areas has been gained over many years, and while these areas are open to the public, they have been personalised. The respondent below describes how the community named parts of the sand dunes:

And then there's the beaches, and the wetland, and I guess some of the little things . . . **Little, like there's this little path through the forest that we just call the Fairy Forest. And all the neighbours call it the Fairy Forest, but I don't really know who else calls it the Fairy Forest.** *. . . We'd walk up the back and there's little sandy glades that are surrounded by ti-trees and* **we'd have Sandy Patch and Mossy Patch. And they'd be the little, I guess, place names** *(Respondent 7, see Figure 21).*

These emotional connections are visually depicted in the map of the neighbourhood drawn by Respondent 7 (see Figure 21).

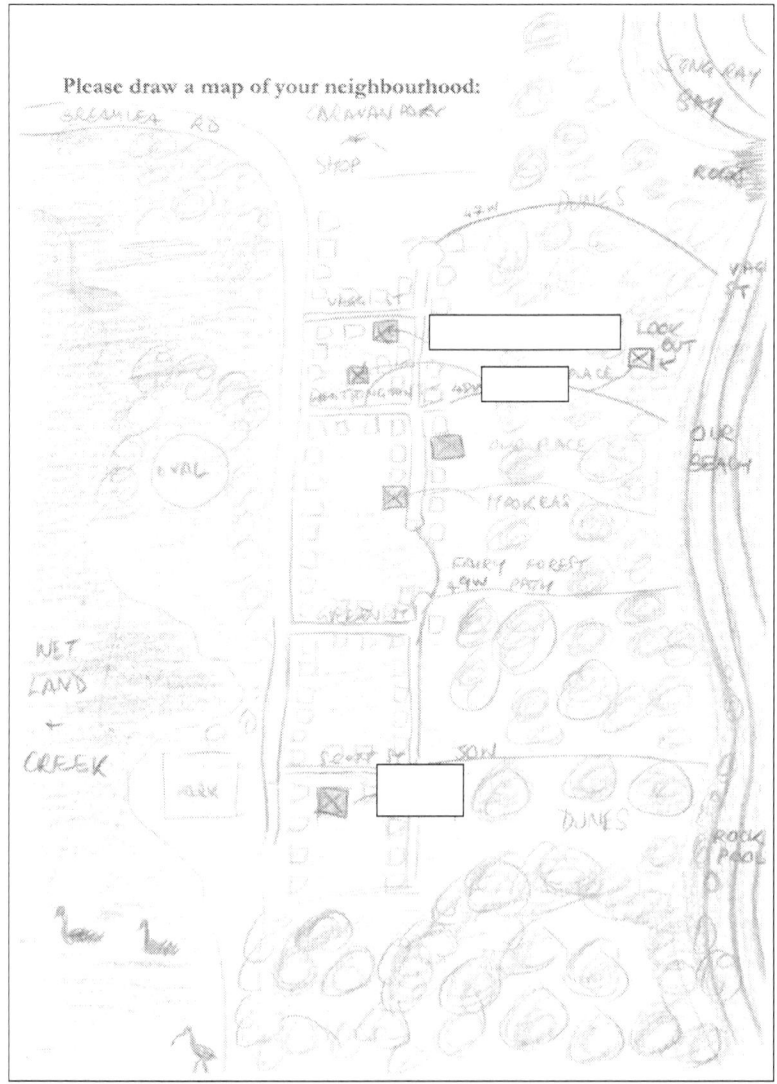

Figure 21: Map of Neighbourhood (Respondent 7)

The respondent below defines environmental features of significance – two creeks and large park – as providing three clear boundaries of her sense of place. These are within walking and cycling distance, and include within them services and amenities such as shops and recreation failities:

> *Um, it made me think I was pretty privileged in um what's around, what's nearby. So rough boundaries to my immediate neighbourhood: Merri Creek to the East, Moonee Ponds Creek to the West, Royal Park to the South, and then **I didn't give***

a boundary up here because it just wanders off into the bigger suburbia. . . Um, and it just made me think of all the amazing facilities that exist within a stone's throw. Um, a few local shops nearby, sadly a bank went which made it almost an entire little shopping centre, but there's still a newsagent, a butcher, a chemist and a few other things. Um, and then tennis courts nearby, parks nearby. . . Um, this is all parkland with the Brickworks housing estate in the middle of it. *But all interesting places to walk on a daily basis. Um, a few friends nearby, mostly they're beyond the immediate neighbourhood, but there's a scattering towards the periphery of this little map.* . . And um, so these are the sort of, the physical things. . . All these places I walk to (Respondent 6, see Figure 22).

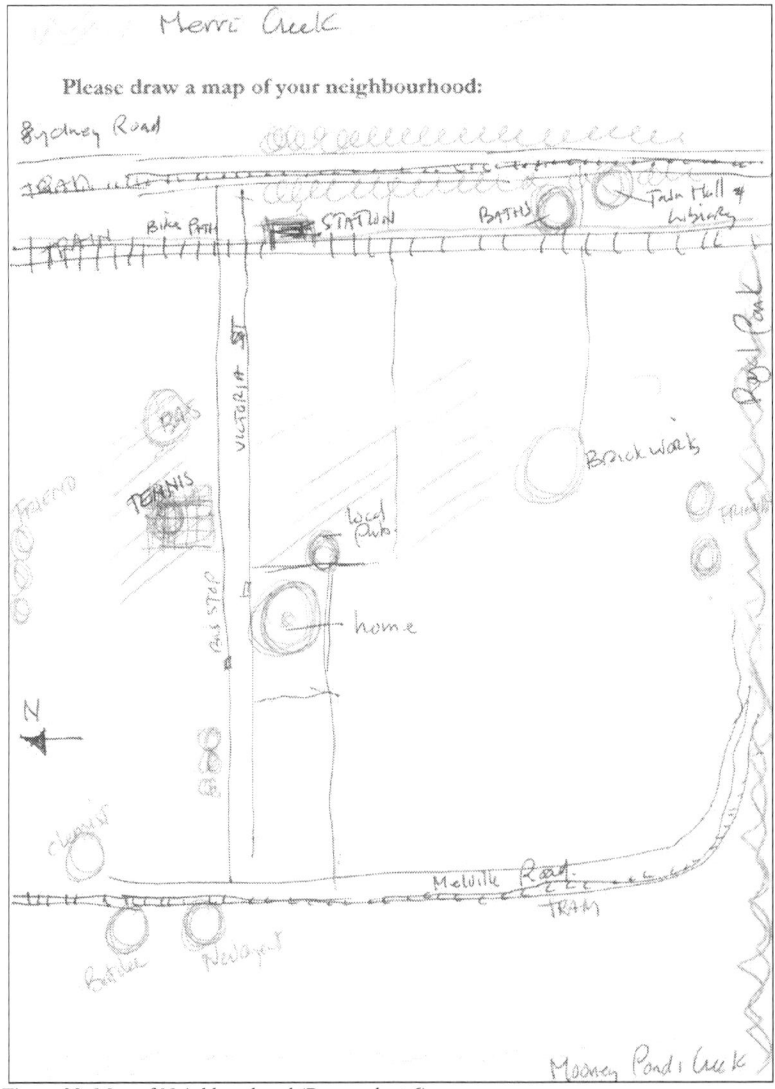

Figure 22: Map of Neighbourhood (Respondent 6)

Place for these respondents is intimately associated with a strong sense of community, which was developed over time through participation in community activities, including social gatherings and working days. They describe a profound sense of rootedness, belonging and identification with their community and place (Relph 1976):

> *Ah, it's, over time we've won quite a lot of them over. Particularly, because the, ah, especially the [neighbours] who you met, are so keen on community. Um,*

> *quite a few of those people, the male has died so it's left a little old lady who is in desperate need of support,* **and the community has moved in behind them and helped them.** *Over time they've said 'Well we can help you with those agapanthus' . . .* **So we have a work party, and people move in, and while were there we'll chop her some wood and stuff like that. . . And there's a lot of community support,** *like we've got a bus that comes up and drives our old people to um the shops once a week and that sort of stuff. . .* **But um, you know the locals really get into it, they're very good here** *(Respondent 1).*

> **So there is a sense of community of a different sort within its new metamorphis. There's definitely an awful lot of community stuff happens here, there's many meetings, and people feel fairly free to come and knock on the door at all sorts of times.** *Um, there is a community forming here, of a more, slightly more - not such a broad school community, but a different community.* **Um, so that feeling of it's communal, community, semi-owned by others, that's important.** *. . Um, it was a natural place for people to come to because we could host bigger gatherings (Respondent 6).*

> *Um we liked the notion of, um the cooperative notion, we're both a bit left wing, oh probably very left wing,* **and liked the notion of common property and common responsibility** *and um we even went to the trouble of doing that for our daughter and her education. You know* **the notion of learning how to use a facility without causing any sort of deterioration, in fact adding something to it. So we just liked it, and the people that we met we also liked** *(Respondent 1).*

These respondents describe a strong sense of commitment and loyalty to the community as a whole, and have formed close friendships with some residents. These feelings for other people are inextricably linked with their deep care and respect for place. For these people, house, home and place are a field of care (Relph 1976), and provide for the needs of the soul (Weil 1952). They are existential insiders and demonstrate a complete and unselfconscious commitment to their community and place (Relph 1976):

> *It is very much like that. It's not that that happens right through everybody.* **What we found is that you get groups of four or five friends that are like that. Much closer than family in many ways.** *All of us maintain our, I mean we've got strong family links, probably stronger than any of the others, um, but they've still got*

those family links, and yet we see even more of each other than we do of those people (Respondent 1).

And I think, ***I mean I've sort of done the little houses, but I've identified the houses which are of the people we are close to****. I mean we sort of know everyone, but then there's people we're close to (Respondent 7).*

7.2.2 Summary: Place as Dwelling

Theme	Defining characteristics
Theme: Expansive Place Boundaries and Connections	Consider place to be the areas with which they identify. Describe a deep level of care and respect for their environment and community. Routinely involved in community projects. Sense of intimacy and delight for their place. Knowledge of these areas has been gained over many years. Places have been personalised through naming.

7.3 Category of Description 2: Place as Amenities

The respondents in the second category of description think of place in terms of the services and amenities in their neighbourhood that they routinely use. They place a high value on the accessibility of these services and amenities, especially those that facilitate social interaction with the community such as the local park and oval. Furthermore, the services and amenities they place the highest value on are within walking distance of their houses, creating further opportunities for interaction and fostering a sense community.

7.3.1 Theme: Contained Place Boundaries and Connections

The respondents in this category described place as the area in their neighbourhood with which they identify, which tend to be the amenities, facilities and services they use frequently. While the respondents in the first and second categories converge in defining the boundaries of place as the area of their neighbourhood they identify with, the activities that fostered this identification are quite different for these groups of people. Where the first group (Place as Dwelling) cultivated their connection and identification with place through community-oriented activities and projects, those in the second category developed this through regular informal contact with local residents, rather than participation in community projects. The sites for these informal meetings are local facilities and amenities, including the park and the shopping centre, and the routes they walk in order to reach these destinations. In this sense, places are backgrounds for activities, which Relph (1976) defines as incidental insideness:

> *And then there's neighbourhood again in **Baker's oval and the role it plays, it's good for people walking their dog, playing footy, it's just a meeting place. Access to reasonable shops is fantastic, really good butcher, friendly old milk bar guy,** down Sparrow Park and the trees that set in and the playground down there. And then obviously the **good connection through to Pakington Street and all the activity that goes on there**. Trying to show tables and chairs and people moving around there and all that sort of thing (Respondent 9).*

> ***So the thing that I most connect with in the neighbourhood is that there is an oval for the dog and we actually meet up with, 4 o'clock in the afternoons, all these people around our neighbourhoods who have got dogs who gather and all run around with little kids. . . Dogs obviously connect all these people together and it's a public facility that's easy to use. Some of the other main things we like about our neighbourhood is that we've got a butcher and a milk bar within one hundred metres of us. So having that access to shops is really convenient. There's also schools nearby*** *and I just wanted to show that we're walking all the time. There's a big children's park about two to three hundred metres away which is a great place to go. There's always other children there, and that's important. Here I've just shown Pakington St with different services that are available.* ***And that's the main community area. I guess that's why we love living where we are because we can access it all within walking distance*** *(Respondent 8, see Figure 23).*

Figure 23: Map of Neighbourhood (Respondent 8)

While easy access to services and amenities is important for the following respondent, he has emphasised the location of his friends' houses in the neighbourhood. His connection to the people in the community and neighbourhood is an integral part of his identification of this area as place, and is clearly shown on his drawing of the neighbourhood (Figure 24):

> *So, what are the things that sort of stand out for me? Well, there's Brian. And there's us in the centre of things. . .* ***But um, so you can see most of our sort of***

linkages are over this side. And I suppose it's not surprising because we live in the front there. *So we see Janine and John and Brian and um, ah David's place. . .* **And then there's Marty's pub and I've done that in red because that's linked to us. So the places I did in red are Marty's um pub, the manse, even though the people in the manse are no longer our mates.** *But our mates Al and Claire, Al who's the moderator of the Uniting Church lived there, and they've moved around here now.* **And um, ah Brian's place, um, so they're the ones we're most closely connected to.** *. . So it's sort of you know, our neighbourhood is pretty much out here and like that. It's not really um, because we live here we don't have so much to do with the people over there (Respondent 5, see Figure 24).*

Figure 24: Map of Neighbourhood (Respondent 5)

These respondents demonstrate a significant sense of rootedness and attachment to place which is founded on their familiarity with their neighbourhood and interaction with local residents. They describe a sense of knowing and being known (Relph 1976):

> *The map of my neighbourhood consists basically of Geelong West, because I think Geelong West has a really good village feel. . .* **And even though it's inner city, it's really like living in a country town. Because you go down the street and say**

hi to people that you know all the time, the shopkeepers know you, women in prams stop and have chats even though they don't know each other. It's really, really friendly (Respondent 10, see Figure 25).

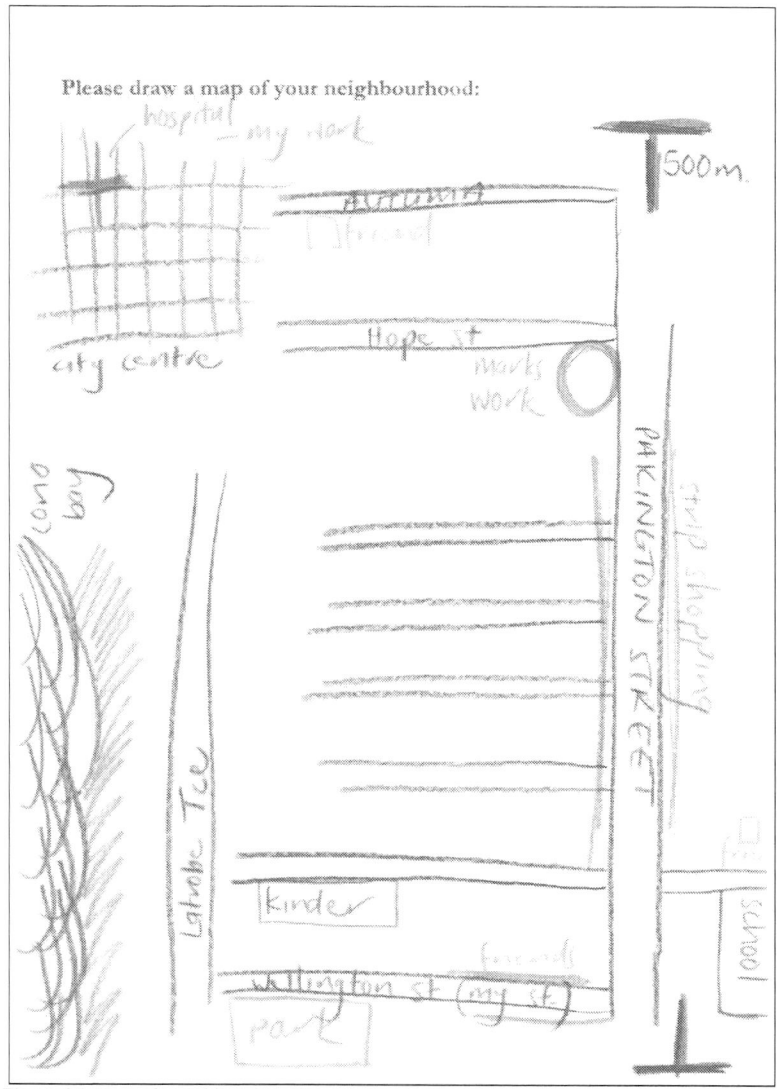

Figure 25: Map of Neighbourhood (Respondent 10)

These respondents suggest they have an inclusive sense of community, and articulate their appreciation for diversity in the neighbourhood:

*This was just to show that the **neighbourhood has evolved over time** so there are some anomalies like 1960's two storey boxes amongst the older housing stock. **So I think that also contributed to the character of the neighbourhood... Whereas our neighbourhood has a history to it and it's evolved over time... But I think I don't dislike those things in the neighbourhood because they are representations of time past. So, I like the fact that there is a mix. It says something about the community, that there is a mix in the community** (Respondent 8).*

*I think the other thing that makes our neighbourhood interesting and good to live in is that it's not, so **I tried to draw different types of people but I gave up in the end**... There's all those sort of people here and I walk down into the street with [dog] and there's a bloke a few doors down, he's always out on the verandah and smoking and having his beer every night. And he's a big old rough looking bloke, but he's just really friendly and he pats [dog] and he's got a couple of little girls who are always running around. And then a couple of doors down, there's another bloke who, yeah, rocks up in his brand new merc and fully painted house and all fitted out and everything like that. **So there's such a diversity of people around it makes for an interesting – plus nationalities – as emphasised in Pakington Street. That diversity creates a really dynamic place** (Respondent 9, see Figure 26).*

Figure 26: Map of Neighbourhood (Respondent 9)

The provision of public transport routes, and especially the ability to walk to a local shopping centre, are important elements in developing this sense of community and connection to place for these respondents. They describe a level of intimacy that developed over time from walking, rather than driving, through their local neighbourhood. Their various walking routes provided the opportunity for incidental contact with neighbours, the ability to stop and talk, and for noticing details that make the neighbourhood unique.

I got the bus route in, and the tram route in, and the bike, so that's you know, that's our mobility out of here. And then there are parks we go to here, a park I just squeezed that one in there, and the Moonee Ponds Creek is down the bottom (Respondent 5).

I guess that's why we love living where we are because we can access it all within walking distance. We can get out and about without having to rely on the car. . . I mean, that's what I think makes our neighbourhood and that's why I like it. . . when you're walking you have more freedom. You can take a different route, look at different things. . . Oh yeah, you can see what's happening, what's changing. You can see if people are renovating their house. Or you see something in someone's garden that you like, an idea. It makes you more intimately contacted with your neighbourhood. . . You connect with other mothers with young children so you would stay in the immediate locality. . . They're just symbolic, just to show that there's always people walking around, that there's life in the streets because you see people all the time (Respondent 8).

And realised how good it was to walk to work, walk to the shops, walk to school, walk to kinder. And the community network that we became part of was really nice. So I thought that's too good to turn your back on. So then we decided to stay here, so after a couple of months of living here we bought this house, then renovated it for about nine months and then moved in... Looking at the map of the neighbourhood, it's really important to us that our neighbours are our friends. And that we can walk to school, walk to kinder, walk to the park. . . So really, I don't ever really need to leave Geelong West practically. It's great. . . Like this morning, I've walked to school, out to [partner's] work, to the bank, done my fruit and veggie shopping and come home (Respondent 10).

Respondents 8 and 9 both indicate that forming friendships with their neighbours is important, and contributes to their sense of belonging in the neighbourhood. This is a phenomenon that Pratt (1999) discusses in terms of women balancing their identities and responsibilities as mothers and paid employees. Pratt (1999, p. 151) argues that middle-class working mothers use their networks to 'create safe spaces within their neighbourhoods for their children', thus extending the safety of their home into the neighbourhood. While these two respondents are not working at this time, they are actively and intentionally creating relationships and networks within their neighbourhood that extend the boundaries of home.

7.3.2 Summary: Place as Amenities

Theme	Defining characteristics
Theme: Contained Place Boundaries and Connections	Place is the area in their neighbourhood that they identify with. Developed a connection to place through the use of local facilities and amenities, including the park and the shopping centre. A strong sense of community is fostered through regular, informal meetings and use of local facilities. There is an appreciation for diversity. Walking is a key element in developing this sense of community and connection to place.

7.4 Category of Description 3: Alienation from Place

The respondents in this category live in vastly different types of neighbourhoods: one of them lives in an alternative community of protected bushland (a cooperatively managed bush property) on the fringe of metropolitan Melbourne, and the other two live in a master planned residential development in Melbourne's outer west. While their physical neighbourhoods are clearly different, they share the experience of alienation from the community, neighbourhood, and therefore place.

7.4.1 Theme: Fragmented Place Boundaries and Connections

These respondents define the boundaries of place as the areas they identify with in terms of connections with people and the amenities they use, in the same way that the respondents in the category of Place as Amenities. While the respondents in the previous category described a cohesive sense of place, the respondents in this category describe a highly fragmented sense of place which is partly due to the physical structure of the neighbourhood, and partly due to their scattered emotional connections with the community, neighbourhood, and place:

> *I probably would think of my neighbourhood as being all of [community], and probably the narrow strip of road down to Healesville... So yeah, I think I'd probably include Healesville as part of my neighbourhood, yeah in that sense...*

> *Yeah, I think, sort of like an onion, it's just that getting past [community], it becomes much more fragmented, you know I have a few friends in Healesville, not . . . But yeah, in terms of layers, yes I'd say it's the cluster, and **I've often thought about the cluster here, and members of the cluster here as my extended family, and then the co-op, and then the broader community I guess**, yeah (Respondent 3).*

Respondents 12 and 13 indicate that their sense of place is limited to the areas of the estate where they feel intimately connected, which is defined by two aspects. The first is familiarity with discrete parts of the neighbourhood, and this connection is fostered by routinely using the same paths into, and around, the estate. The second aspect is a sense of acceptance and friendship with specific people in the local community. While these respondents described an intense feeling of alienation from the community in general (see Chapter 5), they have formed close friendships with the neighbours in their street. However, over time these neighbours have moved out, and the sense of security and acceptance that came with these friendships is diminishing. Overall, their sense of place is highly disjointed. It includes their street, the path to the two local parks where they walk their dog, and the route they take driving in and out of the estate. These connections are depicted in the map of the neighbourhood drawn by Respondent 12 (see Figure 27).

> ***So I've just drawn the way I drive home, to my little house. Love this park. Walk [dog] around that park. This big lake is beautiful, and [partner] walks [dog] around there.*** *This is our little home, and this is our little street.* ***So for me neighbourhood is, when we all moved in, we had street Christmas parties, and we'd all go to each other's house, and we were all out the front doing the garden, so we all got to know each other.*** *. . So Rob and Jody they're my good mates, lots have moved like Mark and Julie across the road they're Kiwis, they've gone home to New Zealand. Rob and Jody, hang out with them, you know, if I'm away they'll collect my mail all that kind of stuff.* ***Felt secure with them, and Mark and Julie. . . Yes, that's where I drive. . . That's my route in and out*** *. . . Yes, that would be my neighbourhood (Respondent 12, see Figure 27).*

Figure 27: Map of Neighbourhood (Respondent 12)

*So I've really, you know, there's been, I like Jodie and Rob across the road, they're really terrific. And just some other people in the street have just been really friendly, not overly friendly, but fine... **And I suppose my neighbourhood sort of is the streets, a few streets around here and around here. Because there's this really good little lake around here and I like to take [dog] around here...** It's a really nice place, and I like going there because I can take [dog] off the* *lead, and she likes running around there. And I've met some interesting people there, like some people who will say hello as you go along, but there's a little park here with some equipment and a couple of times I've come across this . . . It doesn't matter where you are, if you can stop and talk to people and you get to know familiar faces, and people say hello, and there's other dogs. . . So, having some conversations. So I suppose that's what neighbourhood is, you know, talking to people* (Respondent 13).

For these respondents, a sense of connection with place is entwined with their feelings of connection and acceptance within the community, which they feel has diminished over time. They suggest that the most significant factor in this is that they do not, and are not, going to have children, which they feel excludes them from participating in local clubs and schools, and therefore connecting with the other residents to a greater extent. Furthermore, they choose not to attend the local church as they assume the church will not accept them, though there has been no explicit communication about this. These respondents do not feel any sense of belonging to the community, instead they describe a profound sense of alienation from their community and place, and as such they are existential outsiders. In this sense, they also display an inauthentic attitude to place, which is characterised by 'no sense of place' (Relph 1976, p. 82):

I didn't draw that because I reckon I don't feel connected to that bigger neighbourhood like I did when I was growing up in Mildura, because I don't have kids, I'm not involved in any sporting clubs. I go to, I'll go to mass sometimes, but you know once again, going to church, unless you're a family, no one really talks to you. Do you know what I mean? . . . Yeah, like [partner] and I don't even go to the shopping centre together, we go by ourselves in case someone sees us. . . And I guess it's my choice I haven't got involved with the community as well. You know, it's a choice I've made. But . . . I've loved it, and I'll miss it, but I'll love Kensington way more. . . And it's funny because I moved from Flemington out there, and now I'm moving back to Kensington. So, that's where I always wanted to be, I just couldn't afford it, even now. That was the means to an end (Respondent 12).

Respondent 12 describes a general dissatisfaction with the neighbourhood amenities in terms of the lifestyle they facilitate, which is heavily family-oriented. She also expresses a sense of both social isolation and decreasing safety in public areas. This couple no longer identify with their surroundings, nor feel that their environment nurtures them (Marcus 1995). Furthermore, the affection Respondent 12 feels for her house as home does not compensate for the sense of alienation from the community:

> Also, all these people now have had young babies who are now growing up and are now teenagers. **There's lots of teenagers walking around, bored, nothing to do. A big problem for these outer suburbs I reckon, that are being developed.** I think a huge problem... **They hang around the park and just graffiti, and it's like I walk [dog] around there and it's almost like I'm intimidated to walk round my own park**, within seven years...
>
> **But you can't walk, you can't, like there's no good restaurants, there's, you can't walk anywhere, like to go for a drink or anything, or ... There's just nothing there, just houses...** It's very much suburbia, kind of, and that's why I'm moving closer to the city, because it doesn't suit my lifestyle any more. It did, **but it's very family orientated... I think I've done everything I can there. I've realised being out there I'm not near my friends and stuff... You can't be spontaneous. You can't just ring up a mate say meet you in the bar in 10 minutes** (Respondent 12).

For Respondent 3, the desire to live in an alternative community was explicitly connected with his desire to develop and nurture interpersonal relationships with the community, which he thought would be more successful in this environment:

> One aspect was the notion that **I would be able to live and participate with a group of people who were maybe doing some reasonably significant things about changing the world.** Um, I think another one was the notion that **I would have an opportunity maybe to learn more about myself**, and learn how to err, **interact with people in better ways, more easily...** And maybe another part was the notion that um I could, that it would be easier for me to, to develop some **close, good, relationships with people up here than to try to do it under my own steam in normal nuclear suburbia** (Respondent 3).

However, this resident now feels a growing sense of alienation from this community, which is intimately connected with the breakdown of his marriage and his own conflicted feelings towards his house. Furthermore, he suggests there is tension between himself and the community for two reasons. First, he believes they should have, or at least could have, intervened in his relationship with his wife; and secondly he suspects they would have preferred his wife, rather than him, to stay when the marriage ended. This respondent's growing sense of alienation from the community is due to this dissonance between his feelings towards house, home and place (Marcus 1995). Respondent 3 describes this experience:

> *And also I think that um, being in the cluster, and I've never discussed this with anybody else, so I don't know,* ***being in the cluster um, might have made it easier for [partner] and I to co-habit together even though things weren't good. So we were probably getting an enormous amount of energy, um, from the fact that we were mutually interacting with this group of people***. . . *That meant that we didn't make much effort, I guess, to try and resolve anything that was happening between the two of us. . .*
>
> *And then I think the other thing that I have, sort of, struggled with for the last few years, since we split up, and this is very much about me, but it's about the cluster as well I guess, is that um* . . . ***I feel quite angry with the people on the cluster****, because um - probably misplaced anger, but -* ***because I feel as if um, they failed. They failed me in some way****. This is very personal stuff, but um, in the sense that* ***I assumed that they probably all sensed that there was trouble in our relationship, and none of them ever bothered to say anything, or do anything about it, at least to me***. *And I feel that's a much broader issue now, I feel as if that's some aspect of friendship that just doesn't seem to work out. . .*
>
> *And then the other thing is that I still sometimes feel as if . . . [Partner] is the one who, when we decided to split up, [partner] is the one who moved down to the city, or she already had a place down there.* ***So she's the one who's now off the mountain. Um. But I still sometimes have the feeling that she's the one that they would all rather have here***. ... *But that's me, that's really got nothing to do with the house or whatever,* ***but it's an interesting aspect of, of being here, that um, and about me I guess, that I have those feelings****. But I don't know if that was anything about this.* ***So to a certain extent, the sense that the house is a bit of a cave and a refuge is sometimes from the rest of the cluster as well*** *(Respondent 3).*

7.4.2 Summary: Alienation from Place

Theme	Defining characteristics
Theme: Fragmented Place Boundaries and Connections	Place is defined by connections with people and the amenities they use in their neighbourhood. Connection with place is directly related to feelings of connection and acceptance within the community. Now feel a growing sense of alienation from their community, the neighbourhood, and therefore place.

7.5 Category of Description 4: Affinity with Place

The two respondents in this category now live in quite different neighbourhoods and community structures; however they both describe an affinity with their respective places that was immediate. Their connection to place is stronger than their connection with house or home, and this rapport is with place in general rather than specific locations.

7.5.1 Theme 1: Amorphous Place Boundaries and Connections

The two respondents in this category describe a connection with place that was not built up over time through familiarity and friendships within community, but was an immediate feeling or knowing. As one of the respondents suggests, this may be due to her history of transience, and as a result she knows if she feels comfortable somewhere immediately:

> *So um, something I identify with. Well, I took that, something that I really identified with because I really like the bridge and the river, and you know like I was actually looking through the bridge there. . . Yeah, I guess possibly because I've moved all my life, I do, if I like something I like it, but you know . . . So, but I have a real sense of connection when I go down through the forest and out to the beach and to the bridge and all that sort of thing. And we were involved in, sort of, the fight to keep the bridge as it was,* so . . . *(Respondent 11, see Figure 28).*

Figure 28: Forest with Bridge in Distance (Respondent 11)

The connection and affinity these respondents feel is with place in general, and therefore tends to be amorphous. Unlike the respondents in the other three categories, these people do not describe a deep attachment to it, nor a sense of familiarity, belonging, and rootedness (Weil 1952). While this does not diminish the depth of their connection, it simply means that these respondents found it more difficult to define the boundaries of place or describe it in detail:

> *That's the church, that's right. Yeah, that's the church, so that's Hitchcock, that's the church up on the corner of Ozone where, and so, yeah that's Hitchcock, **so we're down here somewhere... Yeah. I'm down there, and then ... Yeah then I'm down here, and then I walk, this is the path ... The reason I drew it this way is, this is actually the part that I walk around the most**, and I go down, so that's the river, and the Jetty's at the end of it.*
>
> *[... And so are these, sort of like building outlines?]*
>
> **Oh yeah, or blocks of buildings. That's just to really show that that's built up** *(Respondent 11, see Figure 29).*

This lack of familiarity is conveyed in this respondent's drawing of her neighbourhood, which shows a generic outline of streets, buildings, and the river, but provides no further detail about these landmarks (see Figure 29):

Figure 29: Map of Neighbourhood (Respondent 11)

A history of transience not only means the following respondent immediately knows whether he feels comfortable in a place, it has perhaps contributed to his current desire to deeply connect with a place and make it his home:

> ***Um, so ever since coming here it's really been about getting off wheels.*** *Like, because I stayed in a caravan before, when I first moved here, for about a year and it was like **really important to me to just put my roots down**. And have a like*

a roof over my head and that's why I sort of did up the hut, was to feel like I could really connect with the place and make it my own.

[So, symbolically, and physically?]

Yeah. Yeah. . . ***And so I've never been able to make my mark. Like plant trees, or paint things, or connect with the place.*** *So here I've been able to do that. So I've done it pretty loudly and really made a mark (Respondent 4).*

Bound up in this respondent's feelings for place is his sense of connection with the other people living in this alternative community:

But here, the people I connect with here are much more like minded (Respondent 4).

This respondent is clearly suggesting a long term investment in this community, and discusses visions for the future development of his immediate neighbourhood (cluster of huts) within the larger community and collection of facilities. He demonstrates a level of commitment and involvement in both the community and the infrastructure that was not possible in his previous transient living situations:

So this is my little neighbourhood. *Which, really, I probably spend, I spend more time in this building than here. But this is my physical neighbourhood. So like the hut and the octagon and the buildings that are around it. . . And since this building has been built,* ***this has been sort of left, and the huts have sort of falling apart a bit, so I came in and um added a bit of life to them, and what I'm hoping to see happen is that this becomes another living space****. And that younger people perhaps who ah want their own space, but who aren't as needy like we will be soon, can sort of have their independence and little spaces,* ***and this will become a little community****. . . And I sort of see the, this space as offering different things for different needs. So, as a young family our needs would probably be more in this building. As a single person, probably here's good, you've got a bit of space (Respondent 4, see Figure 30).*

Figure 30: Map of Neighbourhood (Respondent 4)

7.5.2 Summary: Affinity with Place

Theme	Defining characteristics
Theme: Amorphous Place Boundaries and Connections	Affinity with their respective places was immediate. Feel a connection with place in general rather than specific locations in their neighbourhoods. Boundaries of place amorphous and difficult to define. For one of the respondents, connection with place is entwined with a connection with people.

7.6 Structural Aspect: Place

The structural aspect of the respondents' understanding and experience of place is created from the internal and external horizons of the categories of description. The internal horizon of the categories of description includes the aspects that make up the experience of the phenomenon. Within the context of place, this aspect is the way in which the respondents describe their understanding and experience of the multitude of connections with place, which then defined its boundaries.

The external horizon is defined by the delimitation of the phenomenon from the context, and the relation of the phenomenon to the context. Within the context of place, these boundaries are represented by the categories of description, and therefore include four ways of viewing place in its context. The first is as the area for which they held deep feelings of care and respect; within the second perspective, place is defined by the services and amenities the respondents frequently used; the third viewpoint describes an increasing sense of alienation from place; and in the fourth they felt an immediate affinity with place. These internal and external horizons make up the structural aspect of the respondents' understanding and experience of place in this study.

8 Sustainability

It's like that, the starfish. You know when you're walking along the beach, and this person's throwing all the starfish back in to the sea, and a man comes along and says 'What are you doing?' And he says 'I'm making a difference'. And he goes 'No you're not, there's thousands of starfish in the sea'. And he said 'I've made a difference to this one.' And that's what it is. We've got to act. So, sustainability. Yep. I want my life to be more sustainable (Respondent 12).

8.1 Introduction

This chapter explores the relationship between the qualitatively different ways the respondents described their understanding and experience of their house, place and sustainability. Two conceptual categories of description emerged from the data. In the first, the respondents described sustainability as Being, as a holistic approach to the world and a mode of thinking and behaving that permeates their whole lives. The interviewees in the second described sustainability as doing, as a moral obligation to the greater good, and viewed conservation as something "out there". Within these categories, three themes are explored with respect to sustainability. The first theme examines the respondents' definition of sustainability; the second considers the relationship between sustainability and house; and the third is the relationship between sustainability and place.

The relationship between home and sustainability will be explored in Chapter 9 for three reasons. The first is that it is more subtle and complex, involving emotions and memories to a greater extent than house and place in this context. The second is that the four categories of house and place directly correspond (Self/Dwelling, Agora/Amenities, Refuge/Alienation, Shelter/Affinity), whereas there are only three categories of home. The third is that respondents articulated more clearly the relationship between sustainability, house and place, probably because house and place are tangible, physical things.

This chapter contributes to answering the second of the following three research questions:

1. *How do people describe their understanding and experience of house, home, and place?*
2. *How do people describe their understanding and experience of the relationship between house, home, place and sustainability?*
3. *How do people describe the relationship between childhood memories and their understanding and experience of home?*

There is some overlap between the categories for each of the themes and these nuances will be considered in further detail in Chapter 9. The two categories of description outlined in this chapter contribute to the overall outcome space for the respondents' understanding and experience of the relationship between house, place and sustainability within this study.

8.2 Category of Description 1: Sustainability as Being

The respondents in this category described a holistic and inclusive understanding of sustainability. They are conscious of the balance between human and non-human activities and needs, and view sustainable practices as those that are infinitely renewable. The house for these respondents is a physical manifestation of their inclusive and holistic definition of sustainability, and it is considered to be a centre for learning and teaching in this respect. These respondents believe that the presence of their house should enhance, rather than disturb, the environment in which it is located.

8.2.1 Theme 1: Holistic Definition of Sustainability

These respondents describe a definition of sustainable development that is holistic and inclusive of human and non-human life, and that aims to achieve harmony and balance between the human-made and natural environments. It extends beyond the immediate environment of themselves and their house to their community, neighbourhood and place:

> *For me 'sustainable' means the provision of the best outcomes for both human and natural environments* for the present and for the future (Respondent 2).

> I always had the view, and not really I suppose my parents, but their concern *about looking after where you live*, and they were fairly much ahead of their time I think in that sort of way, *but for me it means just not making the place any less as a result of being there* (Respondent 1).

> So for me sustainable means: to last forever, to keep using things, and to throw out very little (Respondent 7).

The following respondent defines sustainability in terms of the preservation of natural resources and understanding the processes of ecosystems, and suggests that human activities should be respectful of these:

> Yes, sustainability, it's probably, as I say I would have liked to have gone on much more than that... *It's an underlying pattern that needs to be respected...* So I think I was thinking about, it's really about something that's, well I started off *infinitely renewable so that it can keep coming and coming, and not be threatened...* So to me that *renewability is about being respectful*, and um, *of where you are, and hoping that you'll do something that will not be detrimental but that others will enjoy being there in the future*, and that you'll have helped

that to happen. . . So, all those sort of things. But yeah, but very much the ***interdependence of each thing and species, and um the bigger picture, the um underlying cycles of the earth and all that*** *(Respondent 6, see Figure 31).*

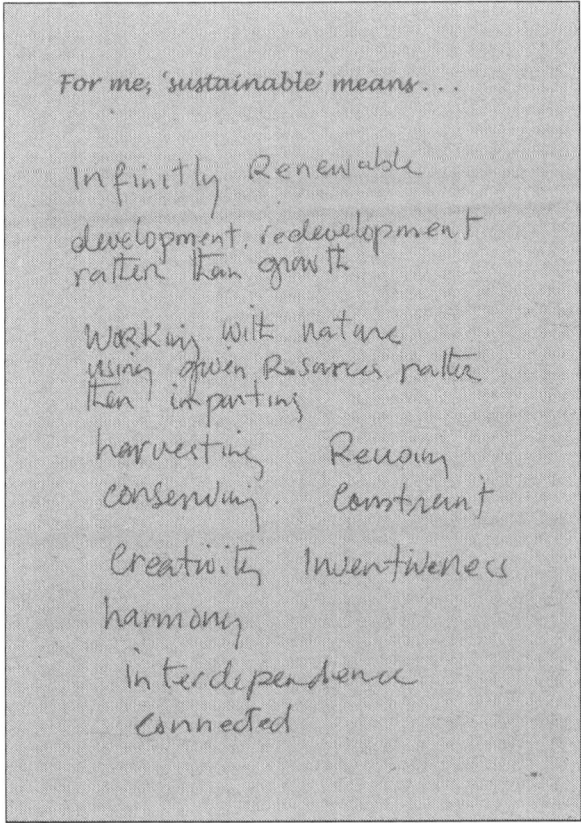

Figure 31: The Meaning of 'Sustainability' (Respondent 6)

These respondents' definitions of sustainability demonstrate an understanding and acknowledgement that the world exists in and of itself, with its own inherent value. There is a respect for the natural environment, an understanding that it was indeed there before they were. They imply that the "in-the-World" aspect of our existence is not merely a coincidence, but, as Heidegger (1951) suggested, an essential component of it.

8.2.2 Theme 2: House is an Example of Sustainable Living

These respondents believe their house is an integral element of living sustainability. Two of the interviewees describe the presence of the house as having a positive overall impact; they believe the house and its inhabitants contribute to the balance, stability, and ongoing survival of the local ecosystem. Respondent 1 describes below how the house makes a minimal impact on the landscape, and provides shelter for these respondents who nurture and care for their surrounding environment:

> *House I built you because . . .* **We wanted a place that would fit into the bush, a place in harmony with its surroundings. We built you using resources that surround you.** *We wanted a place that made the best use of space and resources. And so you catch our water on your tin roof, you are squat and compact and require little heating. You are a giant solar collector storing heat in the day and slowly releasing it at night. In summer you use the earth to cool you.* **Your presence has been an important factor in making the survival of this environment possible. You have allowed people with a commitment to preserving something very special and quite rare to make a stand, to make a statement.** *Now at night you glow orange, warm and inviting.* **You are a home.**
>
> *We chose to build you because of the community as well as the natural features of the land. You share a property with many others similar to yourself built by people with a shared vision of conservation and sustainability. . .* **We've tried to build you so you have a minimum impact on the place you occupy. You have a small footprint.** *You contain your waste, filtering it through the septic system and then through a transpiration bed. There is no observable run off of excess nutriments - this is usually easy to detect around similar sized homes. You catch the water we drink and use.* **Very rarely do we ever need more than what you provide.**
>
> *This cooperative is sustainable in a very special way.* **It sustains a disappearing part of Australia, a part that rarely gets incorporated into community living at all.** *Australia itself! Even the garden that manages to provide fresh food supplements for our lifestyle, is managed and screened to protect it from marauders but also to protect the surrounding environment from potential invasions and population distortions.* **You, house, are now an integral part of this environment, you allow resource hungry and demanding invaders from another era to sit on the edge of wilderness, care for it, love it, and most importantly, let it survive by minimising the impact** *(Respondent 1, see Figure 32).*

Figure 32: Sustainable Home (Respondent 1)

Respondent 2 shares this house with Respondent 1, and expresses similar views about their role in the ongoing preservation of the environment surrounding their house:

> *Now, as a resident of the [planning scheme zone] in the [community]* ***sustainable living means the meeting of personal needs for a harmonious existence, in a natural environment, without compromising the biodiversity and the natural ecosystems of the area****. It means planning and achieving the ability to maintain these ideals into the indefinite future. I live in the [Conservation Co-operative] in the [planning scheme zone] which is comprised of 326 acres of dry sclerophyll forest, about 50km north of Melbourne GPO. The land has been divided into 32 shares or house sites in an effort to minimise the ecological footprint of the inhabitants in the area.*
>
> ***The co-op has been set up to act as a guardian of the environment. It has got strict rules for building and site management for all inhabitants. It shows good governance and respect for the ecosystem and for the people residing within it. The result is the achievement of joint human and ecosystem well-being, which to my mind is a very positive slant on the concept of sustainability. . . There's just a limit to how much you can keep giving long term if it's very one sided, its got to sort of fit for both I think. . . Our efforts to achieve sustainability within the area have been to erect a house which has been designed specifically to blend into the bushland and to commit ourselves to fitting in and preserving the***

natural environment... We weed our site regularly to exclude non-indigenous plants. Any disturbed areas have been mulched and replanted and the areas around the house regularly maintained (Respondent 2).

For these respondents, the house is considered to be an example of how people may live in a more sustainable manner. The house is described as a centre of learning, and is intended to impart a message to the community about sustainable living:

*So the house asks: what is it that you can give me? You can stay strong, **maintain your beliefs and spread the message. It would not occur to many that there are real benefits to themselves and the broader community to live in sustainable, environmentally friendly, housing in a bush setting**. Houses are built and they can be abandoned or demolished. We only continue to be homes while people appreciate what we have to offer, and keep wanting to live in us. We must appear to be useful and functional or appeal to people's aesthetics or ideology (Respondent 2).*

But it was a place of learning and it seemed important it continues that sense of learning and experience. *Um, and so we still have many tours and public days and I feel again that sense to be **sharing all that experience with as wide a public as possible** (Respondent 6).*

These people view their house as a physical manifestation of their understanding of sustainable living, and as such they carefully chose the architects who designed their houses. The respondents describe trust and a shared vision of what sustainable means for domestic architecture as an essential component of the decision making process. These houses, therefore, are a physical manifestation of what Boyd (1970) describes as the architect's vision – the combination of the architect's personality, the site, the place and the clients:

I remember listening to a radio program in the 1970s and hearing about a group of conservationally-mided architects who were working in the School of Architecture at RMIT. **When I met them, I heard about their ideas on energy budgeting and sustainability, and I felt as soon as I met them I felt sure that um, they were the right people and they would suit our needs**, *um ah in, you know, designing, or working on a design of a house (Respondent 2).*

I think I liked working with [architect] because I knew he was more particular than me. And I wouldn't have to do all the research. So if I was working with an architect who wasn't at all green, I would have had to say, 'Oh now we want', like say for example 'We want water tanks', and they said 'Oh no, that won't quite fit in with my grand design.' *Whereas with [architect], you knew he would just design them in to the design, because they were important to him*. . . *But he, I knew he was more informed than I was, and that, I guess that expertise was really good. And to know he wouldn't do something damaging to the environment* (Respondent 7).

8.2.3 Theme 3: Sustainability Extends to Place

All the respondents in this category suggest that their understanding of, and approach to, sustainability extends beyond their house to the community, neighbourhood and place. Their attitudes to Australia as place in general, and their place in particular, are characteristic of people who consider themselves as "Being-in-the-World" (Heidegger 1951). Three of the four respondents have chosen to live in areas dominated by the natural environment, and experience these environments as beautiful, living, dynamic systems. They demonstrate a profound respect for all life, human and non human, and a genuine desire for minimising their impact on the ability of all life to continue undisturbed. This behaviour is characteristic of what Heidegger (1951) describes as sparing; it is a positive action that preserves the essence of something. One interviewee describes in detail his understanding that the presence of his house and himself in any environment should have a positive impact rather than a negative one:

*I always had the view, and not really I suppose my parents, but their concern **about looking after where you live**, and they were fairly much ahead of their time I think in that sort of way, **but for me it means just not making the place any less as a result of being there**. . . **We, our imprint on this place, and we're in amongst a whole lot of others, is just tiny**. . .*

*For me, I mean one of the things that was interesting in Mitchener's comments in, ah Hawaii, where he says the people that are living there - and he names them, the Chinese woman, the American - **they're the golden people because their interests are in Hawaii, they're not interested in being missionaries or making money, they're just interested in Hawaii being their home. I kind of feel - even though I'm a new Australian - that we still haven't come to terms with this*** *country. Wherever we build, we seem to build another little part of Europe. We get rid of the vegetation, we get rid of the animals...*

And ah, I mean that I don't understand why we can't be a bit more sensitive about what it is we've got, you know, because this sort of forest is a classic example. It's going; there isn't much of it left. One of the natives in this area, the tuans, you know, they're almost extinct... **Um, we like the pretty birds, and we're happy enough to put a bit of seed out for them, but they've got no idea what the rest of the birds are like, and that sometimes by doing that you can actually drive out some of the bird populations.**

The native animals that we see here and are a part of our environment, most kids don't even know about it, some of them haven't even seem them before. I think that's very, very sad, **and I think it's a bit of a comment about the way we use land as a resource...** *I just think that we should,* **you need to teach people how to share resources...** *And that way you get better resources, they last longer if you care for them, but we just don't do that.* **We actually teach selfishness,** *I believe. I think it's a big issue for me (Respondent 1).*

Respondent 1 has raised an issue that, while not the focus of this study, is worth briefly addressing. Australia's recent cultural history has focused to a significant extent on the tension between the European aspect of Australia's cultural and intellectual heritage, and the physical realities of the Australian landscape (Cameron 2003). In the quote above, this respondent makes it clear that he is aware of this conflict. His ability to reconcile these tensions was probably assisted by this recognition and understanding of his own cultural background juxtaposed with the Australian landscape, and his conscious endeavour to come to a peaceful accommodation with these.

8.2.4 Summary: Sustainability as Being

Themes	Defining characteristics
Theme 1: Holistic Definition of Sustainability	Inclusive and holistic understanding of sustainability. Maintaining a balance between human and non-human needs. Infinitely renewable.
Theme 2: House is an Example of Sustainable Living	House as a physical manifestation of their inclusive and holistic definition of sustainability; this is an intimate and complex relationship. House is considered to be a centre of learning and a message about sustainability. Selection of the architect for their house was critical to their understanding of sustainable living coming to fruition. Key factor within the client-architect dynamic was a shared vision for sustainable living.
Theme 3: Sustainability Extends to Place	Presence of the house and its inhabitants does not disturb the natural environment. The house and its inhabitants enhance the ongoing balance and survival of the ecosystem within which the house sits.

8.3 Category of Description 2: Sustainability as Doing

The respondents in the category of sustainability as doing describe an anthropocentric understanding of sustainability. They suggest a utilitarian approach to the natural environment, and are primarily concerned with the preservation of resources for future generations. Their behaviour associated with sustainability is contained to the boundary of their house, and they do not identify a relationship between sustainability and their community, neighbourhood or place.

8.3.1 Theme 1: Anthropocentric Definition of Sustainability

These respondents describe an anthropocentric understanding of sustainability. Their definition focuses on the preservation of resources for future generations, especially from the perspective of their children:

> *So, sustainability. I guess is just about **continuation, and not destroying what's here today for future generations**. That you know there's always opportunity for …um…**the opportunities that are available today should be available for tomorrow** and that every person makes an individual contribution to sustainability (Respondent 8, see Figure 33).*

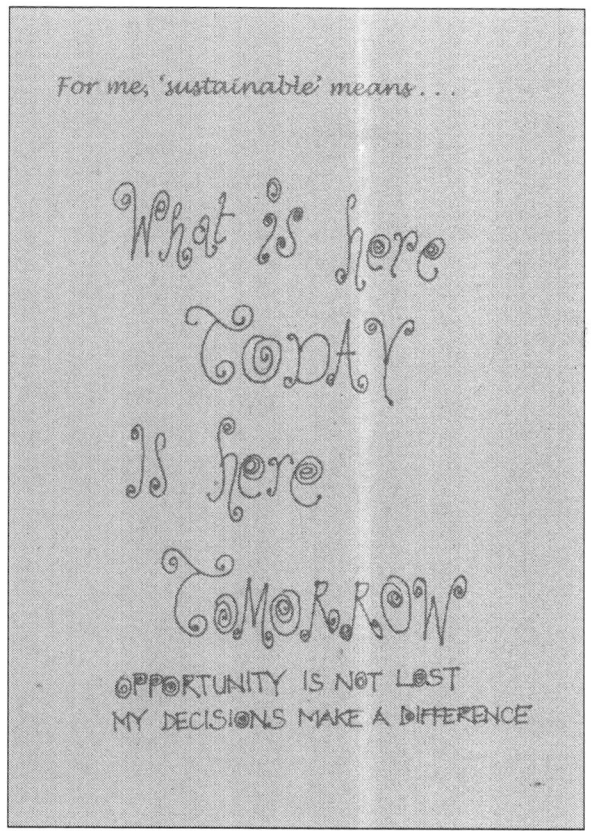

Figure 33: The Meaning of 'Sustainability' (Respondent 8)

> *In terms of what sustainable means to me this isn't the most creative set of words, but **using what we have now wisely so that future generations can use them too.***

That's probably, it's maybe a bit broader than that, but what I did try to draw was pictures of things that I, both professionally and privately, have some relevance to that. **So the idea of water, and we've got the tanks on the house, all that sort of thing. Energy in terms of double-glazing, the solar efficiencies...** *This idea of movement and being close to recreation areas but also promoting people to walk and move to things rather than jump in the car and go and do it that way. Agriculturally, the idea of producing some of your own food...* **And then just capturing some of all that in terms of housing, how you might design it with slabs and solar efficiency and tanks and having some sort of garden connection too** *(Respondent 9, see Figure 34).*

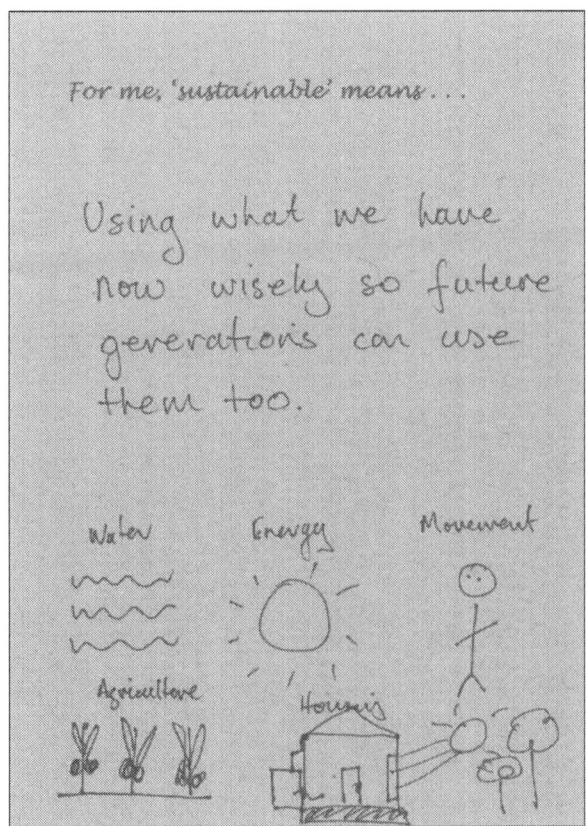

Figure 34: The Meaning of 'Sustainability' (Respondent 9)

So I wrote here for sustainable it **means being ecologically sound...** *So I said that* **there is minimal damage done to the environment, or that it is not using**

> *resources that are exhaustible or damaging. And it means adding rather than taking (Respondent 10).*

> *Well I think **sustainable really means that um [daughter] going to be able to live here, [partner's] kids are going to be able to live here, um and their kids are going to potentially be able to live here**. That um, that you know, it's a sense of community that others can come and join, and that it's not um, **it's not casting a heavy footprint on the earth. It treads lightly** (Respondent 5).*

The following respondent understands sustainability in terms of stable social and political systems which are mutually dependent on maintaining secure access to (natural) resources. The goal of this form of social and political sustainability is to maintain a high quality of life:

> *Yeah, ok, well I certainly think of it in a broader sense. . . . **I'll put it in a human perspective, but um, I think of it as being about having human communities that have a high quality of life - whatever that means – um, but in the context of, they, having the processes, and the values, so that the communities can continue to function into the future. And that their impact on their surrounding environments enables those to continue into the foreseeable future.***

> *Um, and I guess what I mean by the part about communities is that the processes and so on that **the communities use enable them to maintain their quality of life into the future**. . . Well, yeah, **I guess for me sustainability implies coming up with the right sort of social and political structures that enable the environmental impact side of it to happen as well** (Respondent 3).*

The same respondent also demonstrates a selective approach to sustainability, which probably derives from his dualistic understanding of the relationship between humans and the natural environment. He has established clear boundaries between species of trees in his immediate environment, a phenomenon that Head and Muir (2006) identified within a study of people who live at the edges of bushland. Respondent 3 has identified one species that he believes belongs there (gum tree), and one that does not (silver wattle), despite both being indigenous to the area in which he lives. He also suggests that he accepts the gum trees within his domestic space, but that the silver wattles should be contained to the adjacent bush reserve.

He describes the gum trees in anthropomorphic terms, bestowing qualities on them that perhaps also justify his distinction between the two species. There is a sense of a shared history with the trees, as he designed his house around them. Furthermore, there is an underlying implication that they also reflect how he feels about himself and his standing within the community, especially given his growing sense of alienation from the people in his immediate neighbourhood:

> *No I think of it more about their stature and their, um, oh I think they've got sort of, they're like, they're like the dignitaries of the cluster*, *or the . . . And, so, you know,* **I think their existence should be honoured**, *whereas I must admit now when there are wattle trees around, we had these big tall silver wattles, and* **I don't have any qualms about cutting them down.** *So it's a bit of that.* **Because I should really get these [gum trees] cut down, because they potentially could fall down on the house, but you know I sort of feel that's a risk I'm prepared to take and so on... Yeah they're very much something about um, about the house, and my life here. They were there when, um, started building the house and, in a sense designed the house with them there** *and so on, and the same, there's a couple out here which you walked past here.*
>
> *Um, so it's just that like, they're um, I don't know* **they're probably fifty or sixty years old now, so I think they should be honoured in that sense** *and not defaced, or killed. . . And I think it's because the wattles, ah, they're not weeds, but they are a bit like a weed in the sense, that they . . . grow like weeds. They live for about seven years, and then they fall over anyway, so you know* **in that sense I feel that cutting the wattle down is not as significant as cutting one of these [gum trees] down that takes decades to grow. So that's why I think of them as a bit more um, deserving of our respect or whatever** *(Respondent 3).*

This anthropocentric approach to sustainability also tends to include a dualistic, and utilitarian, approach to the natural environment. For example, the following respondent feels that trees that impinge on human activities in streets should be removed, but more trees should be planted in public spaces where people would derive more benefit from them. She suggests that nature is something that 'should be contained, preserved and valued "out there"' (Head & Muir 2005, p. 85), where it is more appropriate and may be fully appreciated:

> **It makes me feel very uncomfortable. I need to write to the council about it. . . The fact that the function of the footpath is compromised. To maintain some trees that don't offer any shade and** *. . . I know you should retain as many trees as possible* **but to maintain or retain half a dozen street trees that look crap anyway now, at the expense of a footpath, seems silly to me. I would rather see a**

whole lot of trees planted around the outskirts of the oval or in a public space where they really could provide some usefulness (Respondent 8, see Figure 35).

Figure 35: Footpath (Respondent 8)

The following respondent outlines a reasonably detailed knowledge of what sustainable means to her, especially in terms of natural resource use and her own ecological footprint. She describes a sense of urgency about the current state of the world, and clearly articulates the changes she believes are necessary in order to achieve a sustainable outcome within her house and lifestyle. While Respondent 12 has not yet implemented these ideas in her current house, she intends to do so in the house she is moving to:

> *And we're teaching it, and* **I'm thinking how can I do that in my life?** *Like sustainable, you know, you talk about being sustainable. . .* **And I guess being sustainable means that you leave the world in a better environmental place than when you first entered it.** *. . . So, and it's about reducing, reusing, and recycling, which I don't think we, you know we're such a, western society is so consumer based. . . So we're, [partner] and I, are trying to be more aware, making decisions about what we're buying. . .*
>
> **And I used to really just talk about it and it wasn't really true, but now, it's like, you know, we can't screw up any more. . . And we've got to act now. . . It's vital. Every minute counts. The clock's ticking.** *. . . So many people are just so selfish, and just want to make money at the expense of the environment. You can't buy it*

back. Once you've screwed it, you can't buy it back, it's gone. **You know like I remember when I was a kid learning about resources and what's the word, finite and infinite. Didn't really get it. But now I bloody get it. We're running out***.*

Well that, you know, everyone's got to make. . . It's like that, the starfish. You know when you're walking along the beach, and this person's throwing all the starfish back in to the sea, and a man comes along and says 'What are you doing?' And he says 'I'm making a difference'. And he goes 'No you're not, there's thousands of starfish in the sea'. And he said 'I've made a difference to this one.' And that's what it is. **We've got to act. So, sustainability. Yep. I want my life to be more sustainable** *(Respondent 12).*

In the following description, Respondent 13 indicates that she understands the broad concepts of sustainability, but articulates a sense of confusion about how best to implement any of these principles. She emphasises the effort required to significantly changer her lifestyle, and indicates that this is the barrier to her implementing these changes. This may be due to a number of factors. The first is likely to be the current location of her house in a housing estate where opportunities for significant change are limited, and the dominant form of transport for almost everything (other than walking the dog) is driving. The second may be due to her previous experience of 'going against the flow' of society, which she notes can be quite difficult. She conveys a sense of being overwhelmed by the perceived enormity of the task ahead, and suggests that she has largely chosen to 'opt out':

Oh well this is just a . . . I feel like a bit of a mishmash here. **So I suppose, because there's so much stuff on it, I feel that I don't really have it clear in my own mind.** *Therefore that's why I've written down all these things.* **Trying to maintain balance by respecting and considering the natural environment**. *Thinking about needs and not so much about wants.* **Yeah, I really think that we live a materialistic lifestyle, and it's very difficult not to get caught up in it, and you have to be really conscious not to do that, and it's really going against the flow. And as a human being to go against the flow is, can be quite difficult**, *because of all the things that go with it. And so that's really, yes. Yes, that's a bit of a struggle. . .* **Sometimes I just opt out, and go the easy way, because it always demands more work to go the hard way**. *Absolutely.*

So, to recycle and reuse, and I was just using those typical things and I couldn't even think of the third one, that's how non-thinking I am about it. . . Reduce. There you go. **Gaining and maintaining knowledge about your environmental footprint. So it's not about the knowledge, it's what you also do with the knowledge. Sometimes I feel I have the knowledge and I don't follow it through.** *Many a time. Yeah. Because that takes effort (Respondent 13, see Figure 36).*

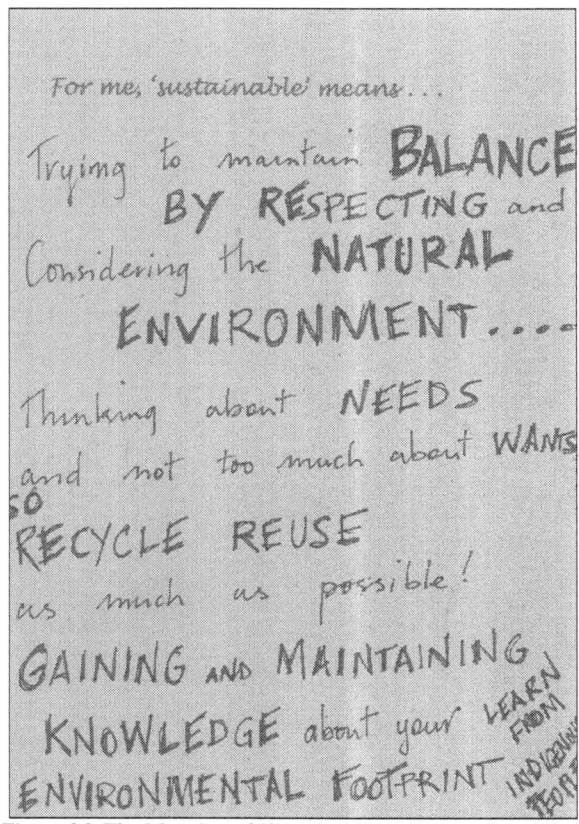

Figure 36: The Meaning of 'Sustainability' (Respondent 13)

The following respondent defined sustainability in terms of his life and achieving a balance between work and leisure. He suggests that sustainability is not so much about where he lives (his hut) but how he lives. For this respondent, work is a means to an end that enables him to pursue his interests:

> *So for me sustainability means . . .* ***To keep going. For me it's about finding ways that I can sustain what it is that I want to do.*** *It's a process that changes according to my knowledge, my abilities, and my priorities at the time.* ***It's not always important to sustain what I'm doing. Sometimes it's a means to an end, and that's OK. What's important to me is that I'm conscious of what I want to sustain, and what I don't. . . If I want to keep something in my life, I want to find a way to make it sustainable.*** *So, I guess it's not, it's malleable, it changes. . . . I guess it's general.* ***It's not really about the hut.*** *It's um, it's probably a bit more about my attitude to work and what I'm doing. . .* ***But I'm finding, in order to sustain what I'm doing, I need to work to earn money. So in some ways that's a part of being sustainable, is actually working there…*** *Um, I don't want to work too much to earn money. Just enough to do what I want to do at the time (Respondent 4, see Figure 37).*

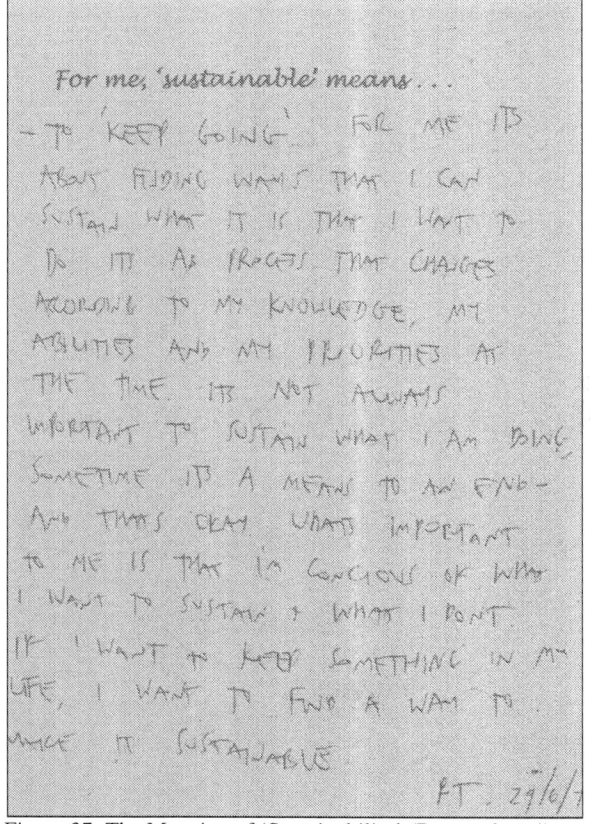

Figure 37: The Meaning of 'Sustainability' (Respondent 4)

8.3.2 Theme 2: Sustainability Contained to the House

These respondents generally describe a strong commitment to sustainability, and indicate that the relationship between sustainability and their house is manifested through their desire for simplicity in the design of their house:

> **Strong, simple, close to activity and open space** *and had this good locational setting.* **I like that design philosophy of the bungalow and that sort of earthy, grounded, sort of thing and the lines that went with that.** *I like that design philosophy of that era and that time, and so that was sort of a thing that captured me initially. . . Lots of potential, that's one of the reasons for the house, north facing, all that sort of stuff and then able to be close to stuff (Respondent 9).*

Similar to the respondents in the first category of Self/Dwelling, these people describe their house as a centre of learning, and consider it to be an example of how people may live in a more sustainable manner:

> *[Responding from the house's perspective] I've been in the heart of this community and I've watched it change. I've been part of its changes. And just when I thought my time was up I was resurrected and cast into a different centre of activity, a centre of community.* **I'm proud to impart a new message of learning. So it's always been about, it's always been about learning, this house, it's always been about ah, ah, growth and that sense of change** *(Respondent 5).*

This respondent suggests that the achievement of environmental sustainability is linked to a sense of spiritual and intellectual satisfaction within people, which may be provided by their house and home:

> **Sustainable also though needs to be something about the, for people associated with their home, it needs to be about their spirits, and it needs to be about their intellect, and it needs to be about their psyche. So we need to feel all of those things are being satisfied if we're going to have a sustainable environment.** *So everything needs to be in balance, needs to endure, and needs to be um, and mustn't be rapacious, mustn't draw too much from the earth.* **But it needs to give, it needs to give to the community around it, and give to those who live in it** *(Respondent 5).*

Respondents 12 and 13 live in a master planned community in a house that was purchased off the plan. However, they have recently purchased a house in an inner city suburb. Respondent 12 suggests that her desire to live more sustainably has been thwarted to a degree by a perceived lack of opportunities in her current house and neighbourhood. However, she indicates that moving into an inner city suburb may provide greater scope to implement a more comprehensive approach to sustainable living, including reducing her car use, and possibly renovating their house according to ESD principles:

> **But you know like we do things in the garden, like we've got a compost bin, and we haven't put in a um, what do you call it, a water tank, but I'm going to put one in our new property.** *. . .* **One of the reasons too, for moving closer, is we're hoping to get rid of one of our cars.** *We just want to have, and we'd like to get rid of both our cars, you know, like just really making a difference. Reducing car*

*emissions... **Even in our new house, even the plants I'll plant in the garden, I'm so much wiser now than seven years ago... So thinking about my actions and how they impact on the environment** (Respondent 12).*

These respondents view their house as a physical manifestation of their understanding of, and commitment to, sustainable living. They describe a commitment to simplicity as an important factor in being sustainable, and their houses reflect this:

***I always wanted a hut in the bush, a small simple**... and away from the buzz of activity, a place to escape and invite friends to visit. Close to rain water, in the winter I can hear the creek flowing, it soothes me (Respondent 4).*

The following respondent describes a significant commitment to sustainability, which motivated her to engage an architect to design a new house for her based on sustainability principles. The selection of architect was foundational to her vision being realised, and necessitated the architect sharing her basic understanding of sustainability, while providing the technical expertise required to translate this into domestic architecture. This respondent indicates immense trust and respect for the architect she selected:

*Because I had, **I knew I wanted to get something that was sort of environmentally sound, and I had been to another Architect and he had come down and I just didn't feel good about it. I met [architect], and [architect] had, there was a real gelling of ideas**, and um so he came up with some conceptual stuff, and we've found all the way through because we talk a lot about it, about what we want, and **he's interpreted our ideas almost spot on**. So we've made very few changes. **As it's developed, we've really not made many changes because he's interpreted our ideas exactly how we want them** (Respondent 11).*

8.3.3 Theme 3: No Connection Between Sustainability and Place

For Respondents 5, 8, 9 and 10, the "in-the-World" aspect of Being-in-the-World is intimately associated with the people they connect with in their immediate surroundings. Given these respondents all live in inner urban areas, their focus tends to be on the human-made rather than the natural environment. While these respondents do not directly comment on the relationship between sustainability and their neighbourhood, community, and place, they are committed to minimizing the use of their cars. They have deliberately chosen to live in an inner city area where there are many services and amenities within walking distance. The following two respondents have young families, and they are proud of the fact that their proximity to the kindergarten, schools, shops, the park and work ensures that they rarely use their cars during the week:

> *Looking at the map of the neighbourhood,* ***it's really important to us that . . .we can walk to school, walk to kinder, walk to the park. . . And walk to work****. And then my work, because I work at the hospital, is just in the city, and I actually bike ride around the bay. . . So I bike ride to work which is really nice to me. . .* ***So really, I don't ever really need to leave Geelong West practically. It's great. . . Like this morning, I've walked to school, out to [partner's] work, to the bank, done my fruit and veggie shopping and come home. So it's great, the car doesn't have to leave the driveway except for one day a week. Monday to Friday it doesn't, so it's good*** *(Respondent 10).*

> *Some of the other main things we like about our neighbourhood is that we've got a butcher and a milk bar within one hundred metres of us.* ***So having that access to shops is really convenient. There's also schools nearby and I just wanted to show that we're walking all the time****. . . I guess that's why we love living where we are because we can access it all within walking distance.* ***We can get out and about without having to rely on the car****. . . I mean, that's what I think makes our neighbourhood and that's why I like it (Respondent 8).*

The two respondents who live in a master planned community do not discuss a relationship between sustainability and their community, neighbourhood or place. Their understanding of sustainability is individualistic in the sense that they feel the actions that need to be taken are by individuals (for example, recycling), but collective in that they believe everyone should be undertaking them. While they do not convey any desire for participating in caring for their community, neighbourhood or place, this may be due to the lack of opportunities rather than an ideological stance against it. In fact, one of these respondents believes as a society we could, and should, be learning from indigenous practices and ways of relating to place:

> ***And I think from my experience with Aboriginal people, I've learnt from indigenous people, you know of their whole, I think they've got a good perspective****. And I think that we're, you know, it's such a pity we can learn so much from the indigenous people, but we disregard them. And you know like, it's such a great opportunity to, for them, well in so many ways for them to be empowered, you know.* ***For us to develop a relationship, a respectful relationship, but in the context of looking after ourselves as people, and the***

> land that we live in. *And it's just slipping by. It's just so unfortunate. Yes (Respondent 13).*

The following respondent lives in an alternative community which, as one of its founding principles, has environmental conservation. However, he explicitly states that this was not the primary reason he chose to live in this community. He does not believe the only method for conserving the natural environment is to separate it from human activity. Respondent 3 suggests instead that he supports an approach of managed conservation, including selective logging and sustainable harvesting of 'bush tucker' (food native to Australia):

> *Yeah look I don't um,* ***I don't think of the notion that it was protecting an area of land was by itself a significant part. Like I think that it was a mixture of the social structure, and maybe the idealism implied in that, combined with the fact that [community] did have, you know, a whole range of things about environmental issues that were forward looking.*** *And so the protection of the forest was one of those, but I wasn't, I wasn't particularly attracted to [community] because of that aspect of the sort of environmental stuff...* ***I thought that was a good thing, but that probably wasn't a super significant one, and I probably still have some issues with that anyway...***
>
> ***Because I'm probably not a, I'm not a um, I'm not a person who sort of thinks that the only way that you can look after land is not to touch it at all, so I sort of, I sort of envisage that we could probably have some practical productive uses of the, of that land that um, that are different from leaving it untouched.*** *But um, I'm in a very small minority there so . . .* ***Oh look I'd even go as far as saying really selective logging. . . But also I think maybe harvesting of um, harvesting of bush tucker, and harvesting some foliage that might be useful. . . I guess I would fall into the line of people who think that it is possible for humans to use these areas of land without destroying them*** *(Respondent 3).*

Similarly, the following respondent does not overtly discuss sustainability in terms of his community, neighbourhood or place. However, he made an indirect reference to a greater focus on subsistence living through growing his own food and maintaining a worm farm to contribute to this:

> *This is somewhere I enjoy being, something I identify with.* ***Growing my own food I like to sort of get into the garden from time to time. And this is kind of where I want to focus more of my energy now, growing food...*** *Um, that's my little worm*

farm. . . I guess in some ways that is nature as well. Like this is about speeding up the process of breaking things down. I guess in some ways, it's using nature, it's accelerating it. **Um, it's, I don't know, it's a great way to recycle and feed the garden.** *And, this is the garden it feeds (Respondent 4).*

8.3.4 Summary: Sustainability as Doing

Themes	Defining characteristics
Theme 1: Anthropocentric Definition of sustainability	Anthropocentric. Primarily concerned with resource conservation for future generations, and to maintain stable political and social systems. Utilitarian approach to the natural environment. Selective approach to conservation.
Theme 2: Sustainability Contained to the House	Ideas about sustainability are contained to the house. Relationship between sustainability and their house is manifested through a commitment to design simplicity. Perceived lack of opportunities for sustainable behaviour in current house/ neighbourhood for two respondents.
Theme 3: No Connection Between Sustainability and Place	Do not overtly mention the link between sustainability and place. Demonstrate a commitment to a simple lifestyle. Focus in minimising car use and dependence. These respondents do not discuss a relationship between sustainability and their community, neighbourhood or place.

8.4 Structural Aspect: Sustainability

The internal and external horizons of the categories of description together form the structural aspect of the experience of the phenomenon. In this case it is the way in which the respondents describe their understanding and experience of sustainability, and the relationship between this and their understanding and experience of house and place. The internal horizon of the categories of description for sustainability includes three aspects that make up the experience of the phenomenon. Within the context of sustainability, the first aspect includes the respondents' definitions of sustainability; the second considers the relationship between sustainability and house; and the third aspect is the relationship between sustainability and place.

The external horizon is the delimitation of the phenomenon from the context, and the relation of the phenomenon to the context. Within the context of sustainability, these boundaries are represented by the categories of description, and therefore include two ways of viewing sustainability in its context. The first is sustainability as Being, and the second perspective is sustainability as doing. These internal and external horizons make up the structural aspect of the respondents' understanding and experience of sustainability in this study.

9 Outcome Space: Sustainable Dwelling

House I built you because . . . We wanted a place that would fit into the bush, a place in harmony with its surroundings. We built you using resources that surround you. . . Your presence has been an important factor in making the survival of this environment possible. You have allowed people with a commitment to preserving something very special and quite rare to make a stand, to make a statement. Now at night you glow orange, warm and inviting. You are a **home**. *. . We chose to build you because of the community as well as the natural features of the land. You share a property with many others similar to yourself built by people which a shared vision of conservation and* **sustainability**. *You have much in common with these other buildings and yet you are unique, you are ours. We've tried to build you so you have a minimum impact on the* **place** *you occupy. You have a small footprint. . . Very rarely do we ever need more than what you provide. . . You, house, are now an integral part of this environment, you allow resource hungry and demanding invaders from another era to sit on the edge of wilderness, care for it, love it and most importantly let it survive by minimising the impact (Respondent 1).*

9.1 Introduction

This chapter presents the outcome space for this study. The connections between the qualitatively different ways the respondents described their understanding and experience of house, home, place and sustainability are discussed. These are related to the theoretical framework established in Chapter 3. The outcome space is also represented visually in order to highlight the relationships between the phenomena of house, home, place and sustainability, and the categories of description within each. This chapter is divided into two sections according to the two qualitatively different ways the respondents described their understanding and experience of sustainability.

The first section includes the respondents who view Sustainability as Being, and describe sustainability from a holistic perspective. This category includes the respondents in the Self/Dwelling combination. The second section includes the respondents who view Sustainability as Doing. The respondents in this category all define sustainability from an anthropocentric perspective. This category includes the respondents in the house/place combinations of Agora/Amenities, Refuge/Alienation, and Shelter/Affinity. Within each section, the research questions provide the structure for synthesising the results and the theory, and are organised into three themes. The first is the experience of house, home and place. The second is the relationship between house, home, place and sustainability. The third theme is childhood memories and the experience of home.

This chapter contributes to answering all the research questions:

1. How do people describe their understanding and experience of house, home, and place?
2. How do people describe their understanding and experience of the relationship between house, home, place and sustainability?
3. How do people describe the relationship between childhood memories and their understanding and experience of home?

The outcome space is visually represented in the following diagram:

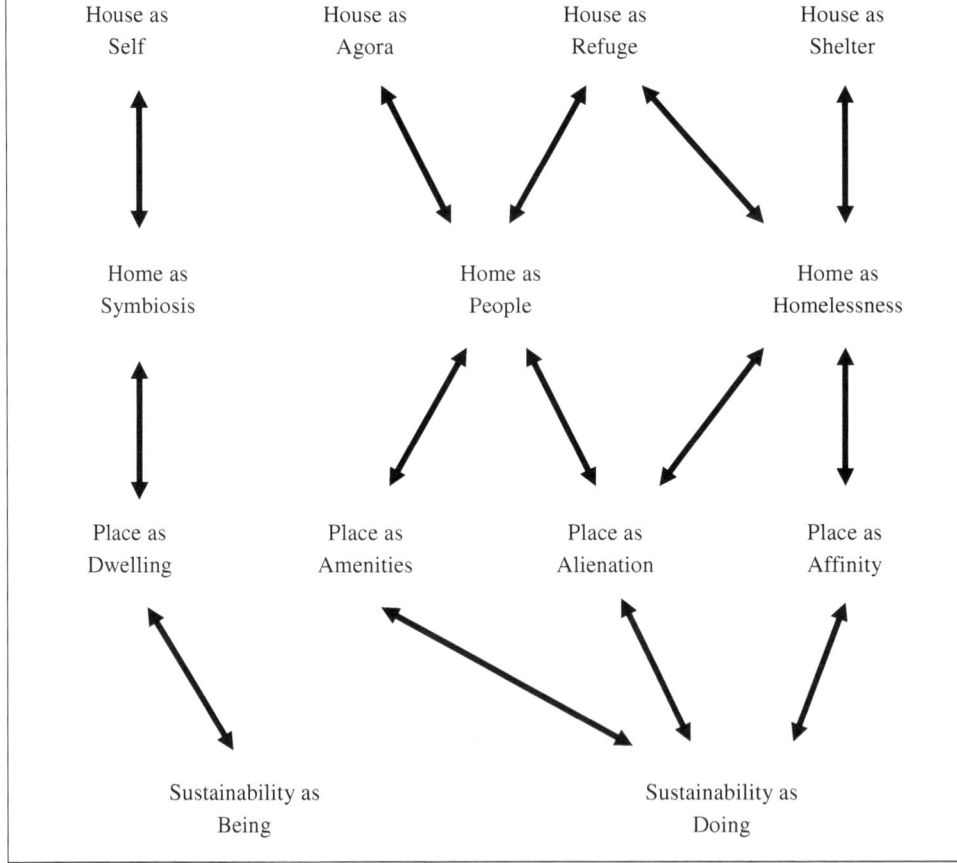

Figure 38: Outcome Space

9.2 Sustainability as Being

9.2.1 House, Home and Place

The respondents who view sustainability as Being describe a holistic perspective of their understanding and experience of house, home and place, and as such the distinction between these phenomena is blurred to the extent that they are inseparable. These respondents use the terms house, home and place interchangeably. As each of these phenomena clearly informed their experience and understanding of the others, they have a profound connection to all three. The boundaries of home are expansive and extend beyond the walls of their house and the title of their property to their neighbourhood (place) and the earth as a whole. The care and nurturing they create within their house as home extends beyond the threshold of their house to the earth as home.

These respondents describe a profound sense of rootedness in their community, which they view as place. They actively participate in the life of the community in various ways, which include perfunctory activities such as weeding and maintenance, and also social and supportive activities such as fundraising events and celebrations for community members. Moreover, Respondent 1 described an additional level of care and concern for members of the community in who were in need of support, and in these instances the community 'moved in behind them and helped them' (Chapter 7). These respondents describe a strong sense of commitment and loyalty to the community, and they have formed close friendships with some residents. These feelings for other members of the community are inextricably linked to their deep care and respect for place.

For these people, house, home and place provide for the needs of the soul. Collectively, they are a field of care, and 'call forth an entire complex of affections and responses' (Relph 1976, p. 38). This is especially true in times of illness and need. The house, as a home, has provided 'a cocoon' that has sheltered Respondent 1 through his hours of pain and sickness, and contributed to making his 'last few years more bearable' (Chapter 5). In this sense, house as home and place provides a sense of safety and enclosure, and a secure place from which to engage with the world.

The respondents in this category describe a sense of belonging to, and identifying with, their community and place. They are existential insiders, and demonstrate a complete and unselfconscious commitment to their community and place. They describe a sense of intimacy and delight for their place, and have personalised areas by naming them. For example, Respondent 7 has named parts of the surrounding sand dunes the 'Fairy Forest' (Chapter 7). They all have detailed knowledge of these areas which has been gained over many years, and there is a sense of being both surrounded by, and an integral element of, their place. The identification with place is incredibly strong for these respondents, and as such it provides a sense of knowing who they are. Respondents 1, 2, 6 and 7 impart a clear sense of where they feel inside, which is essential to Dwelling (Norberg-Schulz 1971).

An authentic attitude to place is a direct and genuine experience of place. It is associated with the experience of rootedness and belonging, and is generally expressed by an existential insider. Respondents 1, 2, 6 and 7 all describe an attitude to home and place that is authentic. They display a 'deep and multi-faceted attachment to a single, clearly defined home area' (Relph 1976, p. 83). For Respondents 1 and 2, the area they feel attached to is the Conservation Co-operative in terms of both the residents and the geographic area (326 acres of dry sclerophyll forest) it is responsible for.

Respondent 7 defines this area as the geographic area the community inhabits, which is reasonably clearly defined for this coastal town.

9.2.2 House, Home, Place and Sustainability

These respondents demonstrate an understanding and acknowledgement that the world exists in and of itself, with its own inherent value. There is a respect for the natural environment, an understanding that it was indeed there before they were. Like Heidegger, they imply that the 'in-the-World' aspect of our existence is not merely a coincidence, an added extra, but an 'essential and irreducible feature of it' (Glendinning 1998, p. 46). Their attitudes to Australia as place in general, and their place in particular, are characteristic of people who consider themselves as Being-in-the-World. They demonstrate a profound respect for all life, human and non human, and a genuine desire for minimising their impact on the ability of all life to continue undisturbed. Being-in-the-World is the basic state of Dasein, and as such, these respondents are living in a state of Dasein (Heidegger 1962).

Three of the four respondents have chosen to live in areas dominated by the natural environment, and experience these environments as beautiful, living, dynamic systems. Respondent 1 describes the pleasure he derives from looking out the windows of his house, which evokes a feeling of being 'instantly transfixed by the raw beauty... Each time I do this I tune again in to the ongoing story of a world in balance, a world that sustains itself' (Chapter 5). While these respondents derive pleasure from these environments, they acknowledge that this choice also implies a responsibility to neutralise their impact on the local ecosystems. For Respondent 2, sustainable living means 'the meeting of personal needs for a harmonious existence, in a natural environment, without compromising the biodiversity and the natural ecosystems of the area' (Chapter 8). Similarly, Respondent 1 feels that his house enables him to 'sit on the edge of the wilderness, care for it, love it, and most importantly, let it survive by minimising the impact' (Chapter 8).

As an existential foothold, the primary function of building as architecture is to enable Dwelling, which is the basic state of Being. Building, therefore, enables and facilitates Being. In this respect, the importance of how, where, and why people build houses should not be underestimated. This also suggests that there is a powerful dynamic relationship between the designer-builder and occupier. As Respondent 7 notes, the architect's 'expertise was really good' and she trusted that the architect 'wouldn't do something damaging to the environment' (Chapter 8). The experience of Respondents 1, 2, 6 and 7 demonstrate that the outcome, the house as an existential foothold, is most successful when the intended inhabitants are included in the design and construction process.

These respondents all demonstrate an awareness of, and respect for, what Heidegger (1962) defines as the fourfold – the earth, sky, divinities and mortals. The fourfold provide a constant reference point to orient ourselves. All of the respondents in this category demonstrate this sense of orientation; they all have chosen to live in an area with significant native bushland, rather than a primarily human-made environment. Because these respondents are all aware and respectful of the fourfold, this respect and mindfulness simultaneously consciously informed the design and construction process, and unconsciously concretised this understanding and respect within the house. Respondents 1, 2, 6 and 7 have, through their house as an existential foothold, achieved a 'peaceful accommodation' between themselves and the world (Sharr 2007, p. 37). In this peaceful accommodation Dwelling occurs, and a profound sense of home is experienced.

Dwelling in the Heideggerian sense also means sparing, which is something positive that 'safeguards a thing in its essence' (Heidegger 1951, p. 351). Dwelling in this sense was the intent for Respondent 2, who states that efforts to achieve sustainability within her home has included building a house which was 'designed specifically to blend into the bushland and to commit ourselves to fitting in and preserving the natural environment' (Chapter 8). Similarly, Respondent 1 states that concern and care for where he lives means 'not making the place any less as a result of being there' (Chapter 8). Through Dwelling, these respondents feel at home.

These respondents describe an intimate connection with the physical structure of their house, especially Respondent 1 who feels that the house is an extension of himself (Chapter 5). The house, therefore, is an external manifestation of these respondents, and importantly, it is a manifestation of them in place. It is an expression of these respondents, and their sense of care and responsibility for themselves is extended to the house. Furthermore, place is created when a building gathers the fourfold around it, and it is experienced as gathering.

For respondents 1 and 2, the house was formed out of the earth on which it stands; in this sense the house is both an extension of themselves, and a part of the earth, of place. Drawing on Norberg-Schultz's concept of *genius loci* as the concretisation of spirit of place through architecture, these respondents have concretised *their* spirit *in* place through the architecture of their house. In this sense, their house provides an existential foothold which enables Dwelling. For all of the respondents in this category, their houses enable them to orientate themselves within, and identify themselves with, their environment and their place, and as such they experience their environment as profoundly meaningful.

9.2.3 Childhood Memories and Experience of Home

Three of the four respondents in this category migrated to Australia as children, and experienced a profound sense of displacement. Moreover, for two of the respondents in this category, the living conditions in Australia were perceived to be significantly worse than those they had experienced in Europe. Despite these beginnings in Australia, these three respondents have consciously chosen to embrace Australia and its flora and fauna, to really know the place they live in, and to become part of the Australian landscape. Respondent 1 describes a sense of disappointment and frustration that 'we still haven't come to terms with this country', and that 'wherever we build, we seem to build another little part of Europe' (Chapter 8). He laments the fact that the once vast expanses of dry sclerophyll forest he lives within are fast disappearing. Moreover, the native fauna that depend on this forest are also nearing extinction. Respondent 1 suggests that this is due in significant part to the reality that many Australian fauna are still referred to by their Latin names and children aren't educated about them, which is 'a comment about the way we use land as a resource' (Chapter 8).

9.2.4 Summary: Sustainability as Being

The respondents who view sustainability as Being impart a sense of belonging to a connected, interdependent global community. While they do not suggest they are taking on all of the world's environmental issues, there is an understanding that their actions within their home and place have an impact at a global scale. As such, sustainability permeates their life and way of being in the world. For these respondents, house is an external manifestation of themselves, an existential foothold, and is experienced as home and place. In this sense, these respondents experience the Earth as their home, which is essential to Dwelling. Furthermore, place is a way of seeing, knowing and understanding the world.

The important factor in determining the way these respondents think about house, home, place and sustainability, and the relationship between these, is their understanding and boundaries of home. They all have an expansive understanding of home, and home as place extends well beyond the threshold of their house. For these respondents, home is the Earth. As such, the respect, responsibility and care they demonstrate for their house as home is extended to the Earth as home. This behaviour is described by Heidegger (1951) as sparing.

9.3 Sustainability as Doing

9.3.1 House, Home and Place

The primary difference between the respondents who think of sustainability as Being and those who think of sustainability as doing is the boundary of home. For both of these groups, sustainable activities are undertaken in the home as a centre of meaning and field of care. As such, the respondents in the latter category indicate that their ideas about sustainability are generally contained to the house as home. These ideas do not extend to home as place in the broader sense. For the respondents in the former category, house, home and place fuse to become a whole experience, and as such their ideas about sustainability extend to the Earth as home and place. The experiences of house, home and place can be generalised into the house/place categories of Agora/Amenities, Refuge/Alienation and Shelter/Affinity, defined in the results chapters.

The respondents in the Agora/Amenities combination consider their house as a meeting place and gathering place, an agora. The focus is on bringing people together, especially family and friends. The neighbourhood has meaning through their connections with people, services and amenities. They have an anthropocentric understanding and experience of both house and place, and all of these respondents live in an inner urban area. House, home and place are defined by the human connections between them, and these respondents describe a very strong connection to all three.

The respondents in the Agora/Amenities combination demonstrate a significant sense of rootedness and attachment to place which is founded on their familiarity with their neighbourhood and their interaction with local residents. They describe a sense of knowing and being known (Relph 1976). Respondent 8 explains that the local oval is an important site in the neighbourhood for her because she meets up with other residents to walk their dogs and allow the children to play (Chapter 7). For Respondent 10, it is the 'village feel' of the area she lives in, 'Because you go down the street and say Hi to people that you know all the time, the shopkeepers know you' (Chapter 7). These respondents also describe a profound sense of belonging to place.

Respondents 5, 8, 9, and 10 define their neighbourhood as place in terms of services, facilities and amenities that provide opportunities for connecting with other people. In this sense, places are backgrounds for other activities, which Relph (1976) describes as incidental insideness. While these respondents describe a significant connection with place, and a sense of insideness and belonging, it is not to the same extent or depth as the respondents in the category of Sustainability as Being. However, they could be described as having an authentic attitude to place, as the defining factor for Relph (1976) is that this sense of insideness and belonging is 'unreflected and unselfconscious', which it appears to be for Respondents 8, 9, and 10.

The respondents who comprise the Refuge/Alienation combination describe their house as a refuge. For these respondents, there is an intense sense of alienation from the community and neighbourhood, and therefore place. The house is viewed as a safe haven from this perceived threat of the community and neighbourhood, and the house and home compensate for the acceptance that is lacking from the neighbourhood by being welcoming, warm and safe. The emphasis for these respondents is on their house as home rather than place.

These respondents do not feel any sense of belonging to the community; in fact they feel the opposite. Respondent 3 perceives animosity from the community because, after the breakdown of his marriage, his wife moved away and he remained, whereas he believes that the community would have preferred that his wife had stayed and he left. Similarly, Respondents 12 and 13 do not feel connected to 'that bigger neighbourhood' and they feel intimidated by the groups of teenagers hanging around the nearby park (Chapter 7). They do not participate in the community, though this is due to some extent to the fact that they do not have children. While Respondent 12 feels sad about moving and leaving her house, she makes it clear that it's not the house that she is leaving, 'it's the location' (Chapter 5).

These respondents describe a profound sense of alienation from their community and place, and as such they are existential outsiders. In this sense, they also display an inauthentic attitude to place, which is characterised by 'no sense of place' (Relph 1976, p. 82). Despite this, Respondent 13 hints at a deeper understanding of the potential for a more meaningful role for place in her life: 'for us to develop a relationship, a respectful relationship, but in the context of looking after ourselves as people, and the land that we live in' (Chapter 8). These respondents demonstrate an understanding and experience of place that Relph (1976) defines as placelessness.

The respondents in the combination of Shelter/Affinity regard their house as utilitarian shelter. For these respondents, the distinction between house and home is very clear, and these people are aware of having a house with the aim of creating a home in the future. Moreover, they purchased or moved into the house with the intention of either significantly changing it or building a new one in order to make a home. They feel a strong connection and affinity with place rather than the house, and especially the spirit of place. For both of these respondents, the feeling of comfort and affinity with place was immediate. As Respondent 11 suggests, this may be due to a history of transience: 'I guess possibly because I have moved all my life, if I like something, I like it' (Chapter 7).

While these respondents feel some level of connection to place, they do not demonstrate a deep attachment to it, nor a strong sense of familiarity and belonging, and as a result place is not experienced as a centre of meaning and field of care. As such, this relationship would not be characterised as embodying a 'significant spiritual and psychological attachment to somewhere in particular' (Relph 1976, p. 38). However, given the nature of the connection that these respondents described – an immediate resonance with place - this suggests that the connection was at a deeper level. In this situation, a distinction may be drawn between the experience of a resonance between the spirit of place and the human psyche, and the experience of place as a meaningful entity which nourishes the human psyche. The former may be experienced immediately, whereas the latter is generally the product of a long-term investment in a community and place.

For Respondents 4 and 11, places are treated as concepts and locations, and as such they demonstrate objective outsideness. Yet they also demonstrate a direct and genuine experience of place. The former is characteristic of an inauthentic attitude to place, however the latter is characteristic of an authentic attitude to place. This inconsistency may be the outcome of the length of time these respondents have lived in their neighbourhoods (less than a year), and suggests that over a longer period of time they would develop a sense of rootedness, insideness and belonging.

9.3.2 House, Home, Place and Sustainability

Respondents 5, 8, 9 and 10, who comprise the Agora/Amenities combination, do not overtly describe a wonder about life in the Heideggerian sense, but they certainly have a positive perspective and an understanding of themselves in a 'bigger picture, in a time span much longer than a life' (Sharr 2007, p. 8). For these respondents, the "in-the-World" aspect of Being-in-the-World is intimately associated with the people they connect with in their immediate surroundings. Given these respondents all live in inner urban areas, their focus tends to be on the human-made rather than the natural environment.

Dwelling, as the basic state of Being, is achieved when individuals reflect on the fourfold and reach a peaceful accommodation with their surroundings. Given the anthropocentric perspective of the world described by the respondents, they give primacy to humans rather than non-humans. As such, they prioritise mortals above the other aspects of the fourfold – the earth, sky and divinities. This is reflected in their house, which, in gathering the fourfold around it for reflection, prioritises people. For example, Respondent 8 states 'the main thing I really wanted in the house was a big space that people could gather in' (Chapter 5). In this sense, they have not reached a peaceful accommodation with the fourfold and therefore, by definition, they do not Dwell.

The act of building a house does not necessarily ensure that it will gather the fourfold and thereby enable Dwelling, particularly as these respondents only partially gathered the fourfold in the construction of their houses. Furthermore, these respondents do not view the house as an extension of themselves. Rather, the house is a meeting place, it serves a utilitarian purpose. They do not feel a connection with the spirit of place, the *genius loci*, but rather with the people who live in this place. In this sense, their houses are not a concretisation of themselves in place, nor the place itself.

The respondents in the Refuge/Alienation combination do not overtly acknowledge that the world exists for its own inherent value. While they suggest an understanding of themselves in a broader context, it is from an anthropocentric perspective. They do not discuss a sense of Being-in-the-World, which is probably due to their experience as existential outsiders. Rather, they feel their immediate community does not accept them, and as such their interaction with the community is to a large extent avoided. Respondents 3, 12 and 13 have sought shelter from this perceived threat within their house, which has become the focus of their physical environment.

Given that Dwelling is the basic state of Being, and may only be achieved when individuals reach a peaceful accommodation with the fourfold, these respondents do not suggest a sense of experiencing either of these states. This is reflected in their houses, and the way in which they relate to their houses. Rather than their house being an external expression of themselves in the world, it provides a place within which to hide from the world, somewhere the world cannot judge them, harm them or hurt them, somewhere Respondent 3 describes as 'a bit of a cave' (Chapter 6). This is a profoundly different way of viewing house. Furthermore, these respondents describe intense feelings of alienation from the community, neighbourhood and place. As such, they have not connected with place, nor have they concretised the *genius loci* of place in their house.

The respondents in the Shelter/Affinity combination suggest an awareness, like Heidegger, of the 'remarkable but often overlooked fact that human life exists' (Sharr 2007, p. 28). These respondents indicate that are aware of themselves in a 'bigger picture' and a 'time span much longer than a life' (Sharr 2007, p. 8). For these respondents, the "in-the-World" aspect of Being-in-the-World is intimately associated with the deep connection to place that they feel. These respondents live in rural and coastal environments, and as such their focus tends to be on the natural rather than the human made environment.

While Dwelling is the basic state of Being, and these respondents suggest they are at least partly aware of Being, they do not achieve a sense of Dwelling for two reasons. The first is that their focus is primarily on one element of the fourfold – the earth. The second is that they share a history of housing transience, and until recently houses have not been an external manifestation of themselves in the world, instead they have been utilitarian shelter. However Respondent 4 has made a conscious decision to put down some roots and 'really connect with the place' and make it his own (Chapter 7). The hut he has renovated reflects his 'choice for a simple life' and his 'desire to connect with nature' (Chapter 5). It gathers the earth around itself for reflection, and to some extent concretises both the *genius loci* of place, and himself, in place.

Conversely, Respondent 11 has plans to demolish her existing house in a coastal town. She purchased it with this intention, hence from her perspective the house only provides basic protection from the elements. She is building a new architect-designed sustainable house which is a closer reflection of her values and how she chooses to be in the world, and communicates her 'thoughts about protecting the environment' (Chapter 5). The new house will possibly concretise the *genius loci* of place, and to some extent, her affinity with place. However, this house will not necessarily guarantee that Dwelling, and therefore sparing, will occur because Respondent 11 notes that while she will stay there more often when it is complete, it will never be her 'only home' (Chapter 6).

9.3.3 Childhood Memories and Experience of Home

Respondents 5, 8, 9, 10, 12 and 13 view home from the perspective of people. These respondents describe a clear sense of how, as children, they wanted to feel in their home: safe, secure and happy. Some of these respondents describe experiencing this vividly and fondly, and have emulated it in their homes now with their own children. For these people, their childhood homes were a place of protected intimacy which framed the way they went on to view the world. Respondent 10 vividly recalls aspects of her childhood home – her mother at the washing line, the kitchen bench, and the family gathering around the fireplace - which she has re-created in her current house with her family (Chapter 6). Similarly, Respondent 9 recalls his experiences in the family holiday house which he has transferred into his current house. He notes: 'It's funny how in my head somewhere there were visions of that' (Chapter 6). In contrast to these very positive childhood experiences of home, Respondent 13 describes a more troubled and confusing experience, and as a result she has intentionally sought to create a sense of welcoming, warmth, acceptance, security and happiness in her home now.

Respondents 3, 4 and 11 do not describe any specific sense what home means to them. While these respondents experienced childhood homes differently, the result of these experiences seems to be that as adults they share a sense of homelessness. Two of the three respondents in this category did not complete the drawing exercise 'What does home really mean to you' which suggests they found it difficult to articulate a sense of home. Respondent 3 describes an unhappy childhood home characterised by family conflict, and distressing experiences of home as an adult. In contrast to this were positive experiences of a relative's home as a child. Respondent 11 encountered difficulty in discussing childhood experiences of home as she lived in many houses as a child, none of which clearly represented home to her. These respondents do not view the world as their home in the Heideggerian sense, which is probably due to their childhood experiences of home.

9.3.4 Summary: Sustainability as Doing

The respondents in the Agora/Amenities combination suggest that sustainability is a moral duty to other people, especially to future generations. While they are deeply committed to what they define as sustainability, it is easily compartmentalised as one aspect of their lives, rather than permeating their entire way of Being-in-the-World. Their ideas about sustainability are generally contained within their house as home. The respondents in the Refuge/Alienation combination also describe sustainability in anthropocentric terms. While they demonstrate a reasonably detailed knowledge of what sustainability entails, they have not yet introduced this into their lifestyles. Their ideas about sustainability suggest they associate it with an approach of environmental conservation which is "out there", rather than inside their homes. Respondents who comprise the Shelter/Affinity combination describe sustainability from the perspective of future generations and themselves. They describe a deep connection with place, especially the natural rather than the human made environment, which they view as home more than their house. This connection with place is currently being incorporated into their houses through sustainability measures which are a closer representation of themselves and their values.

The respondents who describe home as people define sustainability in terms of preserving resources for future generations, especially their children. The focus of their house as home is the family and friends with whom they share it. While these respondents indicate they have strong ties to place, they are through other residents and the social connections they have developed. As such, they do not view place as home, nor do they extend their understanding of sustainability beyond their house as home. The respondents who describe a sense of homelessness articulate an anthropocentric understanding of sustainability, which for Respondents 3 and 4 is focused on themselves and social and political structures.

9.4 Conclusion

For the respondents who view sustainability as Being, sustainable behaviour is directly linked to the way in which they understand and experience home. They have expansive boundaries and understanding and experience of home. For these respondents, home is the Earth. Their behaviour is characteristic of Being-in-the-World. They have reached a peaceful accommodation with themselves and the fourfold, and as such they Dwell. In so doing, they 'spare' in the sense that they safeguard their place in its essence. They experience existential insideness, and describe a profound sense of rootedness and an authentic attitude to place. Rather than the *genius loci*, they have concretised their spirit in place through the architecture of their houses, which provide an existential foothold. While three of the four respondents shared a sense of displacement as children new to Australia, all of the respondents have consciously chosen to make Australia their home, and to learn about and protect the indigenous flora and fauna. For these respondents, sustainability is fully integrated into their lives. It is unreflected and unselfconscious, and because of this it is an integral element of who they are and how they choose to be in the world.

The respondents who view sustainability as doing indicate they are deeply committed to what they define as sustainability. The primary difference is that the definitions of sustainability diverge. Home is very clearly compartmentalised – for some respondents, it is the house; for others, it is place; and the remainder impart a sense of homelessness. Their behaviour is only partially characteristic of Being-in-the-World, and again it is compartmentalised. Some of them find a peaceful accommodation with parts of the fourfold, but none of these respondents describe this for all of the fourfold, and as such none of them could be defined as Dwelling, nor sparing. Respondents 5, 8, 9 and 10 experience incidental insideness and an authentic attitude to place. While these respondents describe a significant connection with place, and a sense of insideness and belonging, it is not to the same extent or depth as the respondents in the category of Sustainability as Being. Respondents 3, 12 and 13 describe a profound sense of alienation from their community and place, and as such they are existential outsiders who display an inauthentic attitude to place which is characterised by no sense of place. For Respondents 4 and 11, places are treated as concepts and locations, and as such they demonstrate objective outsideness. Furthermore, given that none of these respondents Dwell, they have not concretised the *genius loci* in their houses.

These respondents' childhood experiences of home vary from positive to negative. The respondents who described positive childhood experiences of home have emulated these in their own homes as adults, however those who did not experience a sense of safety and protection in their homes as children now describe a sense of homelessness.

Overall, these respondents indicate that sustainability is compartmentalised into one aspect of their lives. They consciously reflect on what it means for them and how they may incorporate it into their lives, and while they are deeply committed to sustainability, it does not completely permeate who they are and how they choose to live in the world.

10 Conclusion

Every spirit builds itself a house; and beyond its house a world; and beyond its world, a heaven. Know then, that the world exists for you. . . Build, therefore, your own world (Emerson 1836, p. 224).

10.1 Introduction

The purpose of this study was to gain a rich understanding of the experience of house, home, place and sustainability, and the relationships between these, for people who have built houses based on sustainability principles. The study explored the respondents' complex, multidimensional lived experiences within a framework based on theories of place. This was situated within the broader context of suburban sustainability. This chapter summarises the findings of the study, and provides comments regarding the implications of these. The chapter is organised into two sections. The first section provides a synthesis of the results with the theory to answer the three research questions:

1. How do people describe their understanding and experience of house, home, and place?

2. How do people describe their understanding and experience of the relationship between house, home, place and sustainability?

3. How do people describe the relationship between childhood memories and their understanding and experience of home?

The second section discusses the implications of the study, especially for housing sustainability policies and trends.

10.2 Research Questions

10.2.1 Research Question 1

Research question one explores the qualitatively different ways people describe their understanding and experience of house, home, and place. Within this study, four categories of description emerged for house, three for home, and four for place. The place theory relevant to answering this question is Relph's concepts of place and placelessness, which include notions of rootedness, insideness and authenticity.

Respondents 1, 2, 6 and 7 view their house as an extension of themselves, home as the symbiosis of house and place, and place as the area they identify with and within which they Dwell. Furthermore, they describe an expansive sense of home, which extends to the Earth as a whole. They indicate they have a holistic perspective of house, home and place, and that these collectively provide for the needs of the soul. These respondents describe a profound sense of rootedness and a strong commitment and loyalty to the community. The identification with place is incredibly strong for these respondents, and as such it provides a sense of knowing who they are. They are existential insiders, and demonstrate a complete and unselfconscious commitment to their community and place. As such they also express an authentic attitude to place that is a direct and genuine experience of place.

Respondents 5, 8, 9, and 10 view their house as an agora with a focus on bringing people together, and home from the perspective of the people with whom they share it. For these respondents, place has meaning through their connections with people, services and amenities. As such, house, home and place are defined by the human connections between them, and these respondents describe a strong connection to all three. These respondents demonstrate a significant sense of rootedness and attachment to place which is founded on their familiarity with their neighbourhood and their interaction with local residents. These respondents also describe a profound sense of belonging to place. Respondents 5, 8, 9, and 10 define their neighbourhood as place in terms of services, facilities and amenities that provide opportunities for connecting with other people. As such, places are backgrounds for other activities, which is characteristic of a sense of incidental insideness. These respondents, therefore, feel a significant connection with place and a sense of insideness and belonging, and could be described as having an authentic attitude to place.

Respondents 3, 12 and 13 view their house as a refuge and feel an intense sense of alienation from the community and neighbourhood, and therefore place. The respondents in the Refuge/Alienation combination of categories are divided between two of the three categories of home – home as people and home as homelessness. The emphasis for these respondents is on their house as home, which is viewed as a safe haven, rather than place. These respondents do not feel any sense of belonging to the community, and as such they are existential outsiders. In this sense, they also display an inauthentic attitude to place, which is characterised by no sense of place. These respondents demonstrate an understanding and experience of place that is characteristic of a sense of placelessness.

Respondents 4 and 11 describe their house as utilitarian shelter and also describe a sense of homelessness. For these respondents there is a clear distinction between house and home, and they purchased or moved into the house with the intention of either significantly changing it or building a new one in order to make a home. They feel a strong connection and affinity with place rather than the house, and especially the spirit of place. Despite this connection to place, they do not demonstrate a deep attachment to it, nor a strong sense of familiarity and belonging, and as a result place is not experienced as a centre of meaning and field of care. Instead, places are treated as concepts and locations, and as such they demonstrate objective outsideness.

10.2.2 Research Question 2

Research question two explores the qualitatively different ways people describe their understanding and experience of house, home, place and sustainability, and the relationships between these. The theories of place relevant to answering this question include Heidegger's approach to place as Being-in-the-World and place as Dwelling. Implicit in the concept of Dwelling is the notion of sparing - safeguarding a thing in its essence - which is critically important to sustainable behaviour. Dwelling is also the point of departure for the third place theory relevant to this question, *genius loci*.

The respondents who describe their house as an extension of Self, home as the symbiosis of house and place, and place as Dwelling, also describe sustainability as Being. These respondents indicate that the world, and especially the natural environment, exists in and of itself with its own inherent value. Their attitudes to place are characteristic of people who understand it as Being-in-the-World, and that the "in-the-World" aspect of our existence is not merely a coincidence but an essential feature of human existence. Beyond this, these respondents reveal a gratitude for life in general, suggesting it is a privilege rather than a right. They demonstrate a profound respect for all life. The basic state of Dasein is Being-in-the-World, and as such these respondents behave in a way that is characteristic of both.

Three of the four respondents in this category have chosen to live in areas dominated by the natural environment, and experience these environments as beautiful, living, dynamic systems. All these respondents are aware of the fourfold, and this informed the design of their houses, which provide an existential foothold. These respondents have concretised their spirit in place through the architecture of their houses. Furthermore, the houses gather the fourfold around them for reflection, and provide a constant reference point for the respondents to orient themselves within and identify themselves with their environment and their place. As such, the inhabitants experience their environment as profoundly meaningful, which enables them to find a peaceful accommodation in the world. In this peaceful accommodation Dwelling occurs, and a profound sense of home is experienced. Dwelling in the Heideggerian sense also means sparing, which these respondents demonstrate.

The respondents who describe their house as an agora, home as people, and place as amenities, describe sustainability as doing. For these respondents, the "in-the-World" aspect of Being-in-the-World is intimately associated with the people they connect with in their immediate surroundings. All these respondents live in inner-urban areas. They describe an anthropocentric perspective of the world, and this permeates their understanding of the fourfold, within which people are given primacy. This understanding informed the design of their houses, which are essentially gathering places for people, and as such, their houses do not gather the fourfold around them for reflection. These respondents do not feel a connection with the spirit of place, the *genius loci*; instead they feel a connection with the people who live in this place. Therefore, their houses are not a concretisation of themselves in place, or of the place itself. In this sense, they have not reached a peaceful accommodation with the fourfold and therefore, by definition, they do not Dwell.

The respondents who describe their house as a refuge, home as either people or homelessness, and place as alienation, define sustainability as doing. They do not discuss a sense of Being-in-the-World, which is probably due to their experience as existential outsiders. Rather, they feel their immediate community does not accept them, and as such their interaction with the community is to a large extent avoided. These respondents have sought shelter from the community within their house which is the focus of their physical environment, and has taken on a heightened status to compensate for their perceived alienation. These respondents have not reached a peaceful accommodation with the fourfold, and as such they do not indicate they experience either Being or Dwelling. This is reflected in their houses and the way in which they relate to their houses. Rather than their house being an external expression of themselves in the world, it provides a place within which to hide from the world.

The respondents who describe their house as shelter, home as homelessness, and place as affinity also describe sustainability as doing. The "in-the-World" aspect of Being-in-the-World is intimately associated with a strong connection to place for these respondents. They live in areas dominated by the natural environment, and this tends to be their focus. While these respondents feel a strong connection to place, they do not feel any connection to their house, or a significant connection to home, and as such they do not Dwell. While Dwelling is the basic state of Being, and these respondents suggest they are at least partly aware of Being, they do not achieve a sense of Dwelling due to their focus on one element of the fourfold, and their housing transience. Until recently houses have not provided an existential foothold or concretised the spirit of place; however these respondents indicate that they are consciously seeking this now.

10.2.3 Research Question 3

Research question three explores the qualitatively different ways people describe the relationship between childhood memories of home and their current understanding and experience of home. The place theory relevant to answering this question is Bachelard's approach to memories of home, especially childhood memories of home, and the way in which these frame the way people go on to experience the world. The relationship between these understandings of home and sustainability are also explored.

Respondents 1, 2, 6 and 7 view home as symbiosis. Three of the four respondents migrated to Australia as children, and experienced a significant sense of displacement. Perhaps because of this, these respondents consciously chose to embrace Australia as a place and to make Australia their home. The fourth respondent in this category was born in Australia, and has always felt a profound connection to Australia as her home. Their responses suggest that this profound connection with Australia as place and home inspired them to embrace native, and especially indigenous, species of flora and fauna. As such, they all made the decision to learn about the flora and fauna in their local areas, and to participate in activities that minimise their intrusion into these ecosystems.

These respondents discuss an understanding of the interdependence of human and non-human systems, and that people have a responsibility to support these larger processes. Furthermore, they describe a sense of disappointment about the prominence of introduced species of flora, and consciously chose to view native flora as beautiful. These respondents identify with the natural environment as their home, and they all displayed native flora in their homes. These respondents all describe an expansive understanding of home, and define sustainability from a holistic perspective.

Respondents 5, 8, 9, 10, 12 and 13 view home from the perspective of people. These respondents clearly articulate that they wanted to feel safe, secure and happy in their childhood homes. Some of these respondents describe experiencing this vividly and fondly, and have emulated it in their homes now with their own children. Their childhood homes were a place of protected intimacy within which the family was the most important aspect. Home in this sense was intimately associated with family, and as such extended as far as the house. This experience has framed the way these respondents have gone on to view the world, which is from the perspective of people, especially family and friends. In contrast to these positive experiences of childhood homes, one of the respondents describes a more troubled and confusing experience, and as a result she has intentionally sought to create a sense of welcoming, warmth, acceptance, security and happiness in her home now. However she also views the world primarily from the perspective of people. These respondents all defined sustainability from an anthropocentric perspective, and their responsibility for sustainable activities extends to their house as home.

Respondents 3, 4 and 11 do not describe any specific sense of what home means to them. These respondents describe a range of experiences of their childhood homes; however the outcome of these experiences is that as adults they share a sense of homelessness. Two of these respondents had difficulty discussing and articulating what home means to them as adults, and all these respondents lived in a number of houses as either children or adults (for one respondent, both). Their responses suggest that the outcome of this housing transience is that they have not experienced a profound sense of home in any of these houses. Similarly, their connection to place is characteristic of objective outsideness, and as such place does not provide a sense of home for them either. They all define sustainability from an anthropocentric perspective, and two of the three respondents understand sustainability to be directly related to them and their involvement in social systems rather than the natural environment.

10.3 Implications

This study provides insight into the connections between house, home, place, and sustainability. The implications of this study are presented in four categories. The first category highlights the relationship between house, home, place and the human psyche, and the implications of this. The second includes implications for the relationship between home and sustainability revealed in this study. The third category includes an overview of the implications of these findings for housing policy and trends, and the fourth outlines the potential development and application of the methods used in this study. Overall, the results suggest that there is a critical link between domestic architecture and sustainable Dwelling.

10.3.1 House, Home, Place and the Human Psyche

While a sense of home may be experienced anywhere, in its purest sense, the home is created from the temple-house. As one of the most profound and important examples of architecture, the house is a primal, yet universal, expression of the human psyche. It is a microcosm intimately connected to the macrocosm; as domestic architecture it represents the opportunity for, and necessity of, creative expression. The house provides physical protection, and an anchor and base from which to engage with the world. More importantly, it provides a foundation from which consciousness is formed and the Self defined. As our first cosmos, the house as home frames our understanding and experience of the world. While the architectural expression of the house may be unique to a region, climate, and culture, the purpose and meaning of the house to the human psyche transcends all of these.

The house, as domestic architecture (in Heideggerian terms, "building"), is critically important to facilitating Dwelling, which is the basic character of Being. Houses, therefore, have a direct effect on the human psyche and our relationship with the world. Furthermore, this study reveals that there is a dynamic relationship between the designer/builder and occupier in the creation of domestic architecture. This architecture, as house, provides an existential foothold in the world for the occupier, which in turn facilitates their Being, especially Being-in-the-World. This suggests there are profound implications for all of the architecture we surround ourselves with on a daily basis, especially the most intimate place we define as home.

A sense of home is essential for the human psyche. The emotional attachment to home, and place as home, is as important as meaningful relationships with other human beings. This bond with home and place calls forth a complex range of affections, including a sense of deep care, respect, responsibility, and commitment to that place, which may be realised as sparing. Simultaneously, home and place are understood to be a field of care. When home and place are experienced as a centre of meaning and a field of care, the human psyche is fulfilled.

When the human psyche is nourished through significant connections to home and place, it experiences life as meaningful, all of which are necessary for Dwelling. These are also critical experiences to avoid the conditions of either an existential vacuum (Frankl 1984), or status anxiety (De Botton 2004). People who describe a sense of feeling satisfied with life, and deeply connected to home and place, experience their house as an existential foothold that facilitates Dwelling, rather than viewing their house as a status symbol. Furthermore, people who Dwell are also more likely to engage with sustainable behaviour in the home and all aspects of their life.

10.3.2 Home and Sustainability

The house, as domestic architecture, is the mechanism through which we orientate ourselves in our world, find a peaceful accommodation within our world, and come to know it as home. All of these are necessary pre-conditions in order to Dwell. Furthermore, when home and place are experienced as a field of care, the associated deep sense of respect, responsibility, and commitment generally inspire behaviour towards that place that Heidegger refers to as sparing. This behaviour preserves the essence of "the thing", and is characteristic of those who Dwell.

Sparing in this sense is akin to acting as a custodian of the environment, rather than as an owner or conqueror. Thus sparing essentially rejects the western notions of property rights and ownership. This perspective is intimately linked to a world-view that acknowledges the "in-the-World" aspect of our existence is an essential feature of being human. Within this context, the natural environment is understood to have value in and of itself, not simply that which humans accord to it. The respondents who behave in this manner understand that environmental "issues" are in fact environmental symptoms of a human problem, and are actively seeking to address them from this perspective.

The results of this study strongly suggest that sustainable behaviour extends to an individual's understanding of the boundary of their home. For some, this may be the Earth; for others, the boundary is the threshold of their house. Those who view the Earth as their home also describe sustainability as Being; those who have a more limited understanding of home describe sustainability as doing. This has profound implications for sustainable housing policy and behaviour change programs, and indicates that technology and education are unlikely to develop holistic approaches to sustainable behaviour. A "deep" approach to sustainability – sustainable Dwelling - is a way of Being, rather than simply a way of doing. It is intuitive and comes from the human psyche, rather than something that is learned or taught, and it is intimately connected to an individual's sense of home, place, and belonging.

10.3.3 Implications for Housing Sustainability Policy and Trends

Given the results of this study, what are the implications for housing sustainability policy and trends in Victoria? While the Victorian Government has been elusive regarding strengthening the existing residential building standards, current initiatives in this area are being led by the private sector. For example, a joint venture between the CSIRO, Delfin Lend Lease, and Henley Property Group has developed a 'ground breaking eco-home', the Zero Emission House (Green 2008). This house includes a minimum 8 Star thermal efficiency rating, passive-solar design, solar panels (and possibly mini-wind turbines) for electricity production, and the most efficient fittings and appliances available. Delfin Lend Lease has supported this project on the basis that their research indicates that the 'marketplace wants a more sustainable housing option. But their preparedness to pay for it is another matter' (Green 2008).

While the Zero Emission House will become more affordable over time, the anticipated price is higher than a house of equivalent size that meets the current residential sustainability regulations. This is a concern for peak bodies such as the Housing Industry Association (Lamont 2008) and Master Builders Association of Victoria (Welch 2007), who argue that any escalation in house prices will have a significant impact on housing affordability. This is becoming an increasing issue as the full impacts of the global economic crisis reach Australia.

There are two considerations within the affordability debate. The first is that the ongoing running costs will be significantly lower for the Zero Emission House, due to both lower energy requirements, and the capacity to produce as much energy as is uses. This is a significant financial advantage given the estimated price increases in energy due to the proposed Carbon Pollution Reduction Scheme. The second consideration is that Australians have been purchasing increasingly larger houses which require more energy to operate. The increased costs of including sustainability measures could be offset by decreasing house size.

Initiatives such as the Zero Emission House are critical to transforming the residential housing market from both a supply and demand perspective, and contributing to a paradigm shift within both of these spheres. From a supply perspective, potential for improvements are generally contained to design, technology and construction techniques. However, a significant, and relatively unknown, limitation to the success of initiatives such as the Zero Emission House is the complex relationship and interaction between the occupant(s) and the house.

This study has demonstrated that an individual's desire to live in a sustainable house does not necessarily guarantee sustainable behaviour in a broader sense. In fact, according to research undertaken in England, sustainable behaviour alters according to the context. For example, people who 'regularly recycle rubbish and save energy at home are the most likely to take frequent long-haul flights' (Adam 2008). As such, if sustainability practices and initiatives do not relate to what people value, then education and technology are unlikely to make a significant difference. If people value environmental sustainability then both of these should encourage more sustainable attitudes and behaviour. However, in terms of this study, this sustainable behaviour would be classified as sustainability as doing, rather than sustainability as Being.

While initiatives like the Zero Emission House are important for transforming the housing market, ultimately they are still mass-produced housing designed to be constructed on a generic block of land (though probably with restrictions on the potential orientation of the house). While they are a step towards sustainability, they are unlikely to instigate and inspire sustainable Dwelling from their inhabitants. Conversely, domestic architecture is a physical manifestation of the architect's spirit combined with the unique qualities of the client's brief and the site to create an existential foothold. The respondents who describe sustainability as Being all live in unique, architect-designed houses that respond to, and gather, the environment they are located in. The results of this study suggest there is a critical link between domestic architecture and sustainable Dwelling, one that is unlikely to be realised through mass-produced housing.

10.3.4 Development and Application of Methods

There was no precedent found for the unique combination of data collection techniques and research approach. As a data collection technique, a cultural probe is useful for eliciting rich descriptions of memories, feelings, and experiences. They are especially useful as an interview tool when researching potentially sensitive issues, as they enable the respondent to reflect on these issues prior to discussing them with the researcher, thereby minimising the potential for the respondent to feel uncomfortable during the interview. The creative exercises simultaneously create intimacy, and distance, between the interviewer and interviewee, both of which are useful when discussing sensitive topics. This also enables the interviewee to move on to another exercise if they are feeling uncomfortable.

As a research approach, phenomenography has remained largely within the field of education research. It is a particularly useful approach, however, for exploring conceptions of the world relating to social issues, especially where there is likely to be a diversity of experiences. Within this study, the second-order approach adopted by phenomenography requested that respondents consciously reflect on the meaning of the phenomena being studied, thereby enabling the respondents to take ownership of their conceptions and understanding of house, home, place, and especially sustainability. This approach was successful in highlighting that environmental problems are an environmental symptom of a human problem, and reframing environmental issues from this perspective.

However, a limitation of this study is that it stopped at this point. The next step in this process is to go beyond the reframing of environmental issues to using this understanding as a teaching and learning tool. As noted earlier, a "pure" phenomenographic approach was used in this study, with the intention of describing conceptions of the everyday world. In contrast, developmental phenomenography provides a framework for understanding how people experience an aspect of the world (as does "pure" phenomenography), but with the intention of enabling them to intervene in the way their world operates (Bowden 2000).

Within developmental phenomenography, the research findings are not the aim of the study, it is the application of these findings to enable the research participants to gain a more 'powerful understanding of the phenomenon', and thus change their views and behaviour (Bowden 2000, p. 4). This process is particularly suited to enabling people to come to a deeper understanding of contested concepts like sustainability, home and place, and decide what it means for them as an individual. The aim of this process is to enable the participants to change the way the world operates, or more importantly, change the way they operate in the world. The future development of this research could include a sub-group of respondents who go through this process based on the outcome of this study.

10.4 Conclusion

To return to the story of WALL-E: after 700 years aboard the spaceship Axiom, the humans have lost all sense of what it is to be human, and aimlessly move about the spaceship while being bombarded by holographic screens instructing them what to do. They have grown morbidly obese, and for the most part lost the ability to walk. Most importantly, they appear to have lost both the desire and the ability to think for themselves, which Descartes (among others) argued defines humans as rational beings separate from the non-human world. They have become de-humanised and robot-like.

Meanwhile, the robot that was left behind on Earth has developed what are considered uniquely human traits: a personality, curiosity, and a desire to create a home and develop meaningful connections with other living beings. The sub-text running through this story suggests that a physical connection with the Earth is an integral part of being human. As Heidegger suggested, Being-in-the-World is not a fortunate accident, but an essential and irreducible aspect of being human.

Moreover, the results of this study strongly suggest that this connection with the Earth as home is fundamental to sustainable Dwelling, and is characteristic of those who view sustainability as Being. The house, as domestic architecture, provides an existential foothold and is critical to facilitating this experience. It provides a constant reference point for the inhabitants to orient themselves within and identify themselves with their environment and place. As such, the inhabitants experience their environment as profoundly meaningful, which enables them to find a peaceful accommodation in the world. In this peaceful accommodation sustainable Dwelling occurs, and a profound sense of home, especially the Earth as home and place, is experienced.

11 References

2007, *Household and Family Projections*, ABS, vol. 3236.0 Australian Bureau of Statistics.

2008, *Average Floor Area of New Residential Dwellings*, ----, vol. 8731.0 Australian Bureau of Statistics.

Adam, D 2008, 'Green-aware people 'key drivers of global warming", *Guardian*, September 25, 2008.

Agnew, J 1987a, *Place and Politics: The Geographical Mediation of State and Society*, Allen & Unwin, London.

---- 1987b, *The United States in the World Economy*, Cambridge University Press, Cambridge.

Anderson, K 1991, *Vancouver's Chinatown: Racial Discourse in Canada, 1875-1980*, McGill-Queen's University Press, Montreal.

Ashworth, P & Lucas, U 2000, 'Achieving Empathy and Engagement: A Practical Approach to the Design, Conduct and Reporting of Phenomenographic Research', *Studies in Higher Education*, vol. 25, no. 3, pp. 295-308.

Auge, M 1995, *Non-Places: Introduction to an Anthropology of Supermodernity*, Verso, London, New York.

Australian Government: Department of the Environment, W, Heritage and the Arts 2007, 'Ecologically Sustainable Development', viewed December 19, 2007, <http://www.environment.gov.au/esd/index.html>.

Bachelard, G 1969, 'Poetics of Space', in N Leach (ed.), *Rethinking Architecture: A Reader in Cultural Theory*, Routledge, Oxon, UK, pp. 85 - 97.

---- 1994, *The Poetics of Space*, Beacon Press, Boston.

Banks, M 2001, *Visual Methods in Social Research*, SAGE Publications Ltd, London.

Beatley, T 1994, 'Land Development and Endangered Species: Emerging Conflicts', in S Wheeler & T Beatley (eds), *The Sustainable Urban Development Reader*, Routledge, London., pp. 116-9.

Beer, A 2008, 'Housing: Mirror and Mould for Australian Society?' *Census Series 3*.

Blunt, A 2003, 'Home and identity: life stories in text and in person', in A Blunt, P Gruffudd, J May, M Ogborn & D Pinder (eds), *Cultural Geography in Practice*, Arnold, London.

---- 2005, 'Cultural Geography: Cultural Geographies of Home', *Progress in Human Geography*, vol. 29, no. 4, p. 505.

Blunt, A & Dowling, R 2006, *Home*, Key Ideas in Geography, Routledge, London.

Bourdieu, P 1990, 'Structures, Habitus, Practices', in A Elliott (ed.), *Contemporary Social Theory*, Blackwell Publishers Ltd, USA.

Bowden, JA 2000, 'The nature of phenomenographic research', in JA Bowden & E Walsh (eds), *Phenomenography*, RMIT University Press, Melbourne, pp. 1-18.

Boyd, R 1968, *Australia's Home*, Penguin Books Australia Ltd, Ringwood, Victoria.

---- 1970, *Living in Australia*, Pergamon Press (Australia) Pty Ltd, Rushcutters Bay, NSW.

---- 1972, *The Great Australian Dream*, Pergamon Press (Australia) Pty Ltd, Rushcutters Bay, NSW.

---- 1979, *The Australian Ugliness*, Second edn, Penguin Books, Ringwood, Victoria??

Boyden, S 2004, *The Biology of Civilisation*, UNSW Press Ltd, Sydney.

Bryman, A 2004, *Social Research Methods*, 2nd edn, Oxford University Press, Oxford.

Busch, A 1999, *Geography of Home: Writings on Where We Live*, Princeton Architectural Press, New York.

Buttimer, A 1976, 'Grasping the Dynamism of the Lifeworld', *Annals of the Association of American Geographers*, vol. 66, no. 2, pp. 277-92.

Calthorpe, P 1993, 'The Next American Metropolis', in S Wheeler & T Beatley (eds), *The Sustainable Urban Development Reader*, Routledge, London, pp. 73-80.

Cameron, J 2003, 'Introduction: Articulating Australian Senses of Place', in J Cameron (ed.), *Changing Places: Re-Imagining Australia*, Longueville Books, Double Bay, NSW.

Carnevale, E, Cohn, DV, Kent, M, Maki, S, Malsawrna, Z, Skolnik, R & Yin, S 2007, 'World Population Highlights', *Population Bulletin*, vol. 62, no. 3, September 2007.

Carroll, J 1998, *Ego and Soul: The Modern West in Search of Meaning*, HarperCollins Publishers, Sydney.

Casey, ES 1993, *Getting Back Into Place: Toward a Renewed Understanding of the Place-World*, Studies in Continental Thought, Indiana University Press, Bloomington, Indianapolis.

---- 1997, *The Fate of Place*, University of California Press, Berkeley and Los Angeles, CA.

Clayton, DW 2000, *Islands of Truth: The Imperial Fashioning of Vancouver Island*, UBC Press, Vancouver.

Cresswell, T 1996, *In Place/Out of Place: Geography, Ideology and Transgression*, University of Minnesota Press, Minneapolis.

---- 2004, *Place: A Short Introduction*, Short Introductions to Geography, Blackwell Publishing Ltd, Oxford.

Daniel, G 2003, *The First Civilisations: The Archaeology of their Origins*, Phoenix Press, London and New York.

Davison, G 1997, 'The Great Australian Sprawl', *Historic Environment*, vol. XIII, no. 1.

De Botton, A 2004, *Status Anxiety*, Penguin Books, Australia.

de Certeau, M 1984, *The Practice of Everyday Life*, University of California Press, Berkeley, CA.

DOI 2002, *Melbourne 2030. Planning for Sustainable Growth*, Department of Infrastructure, Melbourne.

Dovey, K 1999, *Framing Places: Mediating Power in Built Form*, Routledge, London.

Dowling, R & Mee, K 2007, 'Home and Homemaking in Contemporary Australia', *Housing, Theory and Society*, vol. 24, no. 3, pp. 161 - 5.

Dresner, S 2002, *The Principles of Sustainability*, Earthscan Publications Ltd, London, Sterling VA.

Drew, P 1985, *Leaves of Iron: Glen Murcutt Pioneer of Australian Architectural Form*, The Law Book Company Limited, Melbourne.

Easthope, H 2004, 'A Place Called Home', *Housing, Theory and Society*, vol. 21, no. 3, pp. 128-38.

Edinger, E 1972, *Ego and Archetype*, Penguin Books, New York.

Eisler, R 1990, *The Chalice and the Blade: Our History, Our Future*, Mandala Unwin Paperbacks, London, boston, Sydney, Wellington.

Eliade, M 1963, *Patterns in Comparative Religion*, Cleveland and New York.

Emerson, RW 2003, 'Nature', in WH Gilman & C Johnson (eds), *Selected Writings of Ralph Waldo Emerson*, Published by Signet Classic, pp. 181-224.

Escobar, A 2001, 'Culture Sits in Places: Reflections on Globalism and Subaltern Strategies of Localization', *Political Geography*, vol. 20, no. 2, pp. 139-74.

Feldman, RM 1990, 'Settlement-Identity Psychological Bonds with Home Places in a Mobile Society', *Environment and Behaviour*, vol. 22, no. 2, pp. 183-229.

Fell, JP 1979, *Heidegger and Sartre: An Essay on Place and Being*, Columbia University, New York.

Fletcher, B 1987, *A Hisotry of Architecture*, 19th edn, Butterworth Group, Sydney.

Frankl, V 1984, *Man's Search for Meaning*, Washington Square Press, Boston.

Frede, D 2006, 'The question of Being: Heidegger's project', in C Guignon (ed.), *The Cambridge Companion to Heidegger*, 2nd edn, Cambridge University Press, New York.

Friedan, B 1963, *The Feminine Mystique*, Penguin, Harmondsworth, England.

Gardiner, S 2002, *The House: Its Origins and Evolution*, Second edn, Constable & Robinson Ltd, London.

Gaver, WW, Boucher, A, Fennington, S & Walker, B 2004, 'Cultural Probes and the Value of Uncertainty', *Interactions*, pp. 53-6.

Gaver, WW, Dunne, T & Pacenti, E 1999, 'Cultural Probes', *Interactions*, pp. 21-9.

Girardet, H 1999, 'The Metabolism of Cities', in S Wheeler & T Beatley (eds), *The Sustainable Urban Development Reader*, Routledge, London.

Giuliani, MV 1991, 'Towards an Analysis of Mental Representations of Attachment to the Home', *Journal of Architectural and Planning Research*, vol. 8, pp. 133-46.

Gleick, J 1999, *Faster: The Acceleration of Just About Everything*, Random House, USA.

Glendinning, S 1998, *On Being with Others: Heidegger - Derrida - Wittgenstein*, Routledge, London and New York.

Gonzalo, R & Habermann, KJ 2006, *Energy Efficient Architecture: Basics for Planning and Construction*, Birkhauser, Basel, Boston, Berlin.

Gooch, MJ 2003, 'Voices of the Volunteers: An Exploration of the Influences that Volunteer Experiences have on the Resilience and Sustainability of Catchment Groups in Coastal Queensland', Griffith University.

Green, M 2008, 'Zero-emissions living ready for take off', *The Age*, December 7, 2008.

Guba, EG 1990, 'The Alternative Paradigm Dialog', in EG Guba (ed.), *The Paradigm Dialog*, SAGE Publications, Newbury Park, London, New Delhi.

Gubrium, JF & Silverman, D (eds) 1989, *The Politics of Field Research: Sociology Beyond Enlightenment*, Sage, London.

Harries, K 1983, 'Thoughts on a Non-Arbitrary Architecture', in D Seamon (ed.), *Dwelling, Seeing and Designing: Toward a Phenomenological Ecology*, SUNY Press, Albany, New york.

Harvey, D 1989, *The Condition of Postmodernity*, Basil Blackwell, Oxford.

---- 1996, *Justice, Nature and the Geography of Difference*, Blackwell Publishers, Cambridge, MA.

Hasselgren, B & Beach, D 1997, 'Phenomenography — a "good-for-nothing brother" of phenomenology? Outline of an analysis', *Higher Education Research & Development*, vol. 16, no. 2, pp. 191 - 202.

Hayden, D 1984, 'Domesticating Urban Space', in S Wheeler & T Beatley (eds), *The Sustainable Urban Development Reader*, Routledge, London, pp. 150-6.

Head, L & Muir, P 2005, 'Living with trees – Perspectives from the suburbs', paper presented to Proceedings 6th National Conference of the Australian Forest History Society Inc, Rotterdam.

---- 2006, 'Edges of connection: reconceptualising the human role in urban geography', *Australian Geographer*, vol. 37, no. 1, pp. 87-101.

Head, L, Trigger, D & Mulcock, J 2005, 'Culture as concept and Influence in Environmental Research and Management', *Conservation and Society*, vol. 3, no. 2, pp. 251-64.

Heidegger, M 1951, 'Building Dwelling Thinking', in DF Krell (ed.), *Basic Writings*, Routledge, Oxon, pp. 343 - 64.

---- 1956, 'The Origin of the Work of Art', in DF Krell (ed.), *Basic Writings*, Routledge, Oxon, pp. 139-212.

---- 1958, 'An Ontological Consideration of Place', in *The Question of Being*, Twayne Publishers, New York.

---- 1962, *Being and Time*, 1st English edn, Blackwell Publishing, Oxford, UK.

---- 1969, *On Time and Being*, Harper and Row, New York.

---- 1971, *Poetry, Language, Thought*, Harper and Row, London.

---- 1977, *The Question Concerning Technology and Other Essays*, Harper and Row, London.

---- 1978, *Basic Writings*, Routledge, Oxon.

Hillman, J 1996, *The Soul's Code*, Random House Australia Pty Ltd, Milson's Point.

---- 2004, *Archetypal Psychology*, Spring Publications, Inc, Putnam, Connecticut.

Howard, E 1898, *Garden Cities of To-morrow*, Second edn, Faber and Faber, London.

Hudnut, J 1949, *Architecture and the Spirit of Man*, Harvard University Press, Cambridge.

Hughes, M 2007, *The Slow Guide*, Affirm Press, Mulgrave, Victoria.

Hume, D 1984 (reprint), *A Treatise of Human Nature*, Penguin Books, London.

Husserl, E 1931, *Ideas: General Introduction to Pure Phenomenology*, Library of Philosophy, George Allen & Unwin Ltd, London.

---- 1970, *The Crisis of European Sciences and Transcendental Phenomenology*, Northwestern University Press, Evanston.

Jenks, M, Burton, E & Williams, K (eds) 1996, *The Compact City: A Sustainable Urban Form?*, E & FN Spon, London.

---- (eds) 2000, *Achieving Sustainable Urban Form*, Spon Press, London.

Jung, C 1959, *The Archetypes and the Collective Unconscious*, Second edn, Routledge, London.

---- 1995, *Memories, Dreams, Reflections*, Fontana Library, London.

Katz, P 1994, *The New Urbanism: Towards and Architecture of Community*, Print Vision, Oregon.

Kinsella, WJ 2007, 'Heidegger and Being at the Hanford Reservation: Standing Reserve, Enframing, and Environmental Communication Theory', *Environmental Communication: A Journal of Nature and Culture*, vol. 1, no. 2, pp. 194 - 217.

Klein, S 2007, *The Secret Pulse of Time: Making Sense of Life's Scarcest Commodity*, Scribe, Melbourne.

Krebs, W (ed.) 1981, *Collins Australian Pocket Dictionary of the English Language*, Collins, Sydney, London, Glasgow.

---- (ed.) 2004, *Collins Australian Dictionary and Thesaurus: A Dictionary and Thesaurus to Speak Your Language*, 1st Australian edn, HarperCollins Publishers, NSW.

Krell, DF 1991, *Martin Heidegger*, 2nd edn, Routledge, London and New York.

---- 1993, 'General Introduction: The Question of Being', in DF Krell (ed.), *Basic Writings*, Routledge, Oxon, pp. 1 - 36.

Lamont, C 2008, 'Senate Confirms Need for Action on Affordability', *HIA Members News*, viewed December 12, 2008.

LeCompte, MD & Goetz, JP 1982, 'Problems of Reliability and Validity in Ethnographic Research', *Review of Educational Research*, vol. 52, pp. 31-60.

Lefebvre, H 1991, *The Production of Space*, Blackwell, Oxford.

Lewis, M 1999, *Suburban Backlash*, Bloomings Books, Melbourne.

Lincoln, YS & Guba, E 1985, *Naturalistic Enquiry*, Sage, Beverly Hills, California.

---- 2000, 'Paradigmatic Controversies, Contradictions and Emerging Confluences', in N Denzin & YS Lincoln (eds), *Handbook of Qualitative Research*, 2nd edn, Sage Publications, Thousand Oaks, California, pp. 163 - 88.

Lukerman, F 1964, 'Geography as a Formal Intellectual Discipline and the Way in Which It Contributes to Human Knoweldge', *Canadian Geographer*, vol. 8, no. 4, pp. 167-72.

Mallett, S 2004, 'Understanding Home: A Critical Review of the Literature', *The Sociological Review*, vol. Editorial Board, pp. 62-89.

Malpas, JE 1999, *Place and Experience: A Philosophical Topography*, Cambridge University Press, Cambridge.

Marc, O 1977, *Psychology of the House*, Thames and Hudson, London.

Marcus, CC 1995, *House as a Mirror of Self: Exploring the Deeper Meaning of Home*, Conari Press, Berkley.

Marton, F 1981, 'Phenomenography - Describing Conceptions of the World Around Us', *Instructional Science*, vol. 10, pp. 177-200.

---- 1986, 'Phenomenography: A Research Approach to Investigating Different Understandings of Reality', *Journal of Thought*, vol. 21, pp. 28-49.

---- 1994, *Phenomenography*, 2nd edn, Pergamon, London.

Marton, F & Booth, S 1997, *Learning and Awareness*, Lawrence Erlbaum Associates, Publishers, Mahwah, New Jersey.

Marton, F & Saljo, R 1984, 'Approaches to learning', in F Marton, D Hounsell & N Entwistle (eds), *The Experience of Learning*, Scottish Acadmic Press, Edinburgh, pp. 36-55.

Mascia, MB, Brosius, JP, Dobson, BC, Forbes, L, Horowitz, MA, McKean & Turner, NJ 2003, 'Conservation and the Social Sciences', *Conservation Biology*, vol. 17, no. 3, pp. 649-50.

Massey, D 1994, *Space, Place and Gender*, Polity Press, Cambridge.

McDowell, L 1999, *Gender, Identity and Place*, Polity Press, Cambridge.

McPhail, I 2008, *State of the Environment Victoria 2008*, Commissioner for Environmental Sustainability, Melbourne.

Miles, MB & Huberman, AM 1994, *Qualitative Data Analysis*, 2nd edn, SAGE Publications, Thousand Oaks, London, New Delhi.

Moncrief, M 2008, 'Brumby expands Melbourne's boundary as population explodes: Go-ahead for urban sprawl', *The Age*, December 3, 2008.

Moore, T 1992, *Care of the Soul*, HarperCollins Publishers Inc, New York.

Moustakas, C 1994, *Phenomenological Research Methods*, SAGE Publications Inc, Thousand Oaks.

Murcutt, G 1984, 'Foreward', in P Drew (ed.), *Leaves of iron: Glen Murcutt Pioneer of Australian Architectural Form*, The Law Book Company Limited, Melbourne.

Newman, P & Kenworthy, J 1999, 'Traffic Calming', in S Wheeler & T Beatley (eds), *The Sustainable Urban Development Reader*, Routledge, London, pp. 97-103.

---- 2000, 'Sustainable Urban Form: The Big Picture', in K Williams, E Burton & M Jenks (eds), *Achieving Sustainable Urban Form*, Spon Press, London, pp. 109-20.

Noble, G 2004, 'Accumulating Being', *International Journal of Cultural Studies*, vol. 7, no. 2, pp. 233 - 56.

Norberg-Schulz, C 1965, *Intentions in Architecture*, MIT Press, Cambridge, Massachusetts.

---- 1971, *Existence, Space and Architecture*, Studio Vista, London.

---- 1975, *Meaning in Western Architecture*.

---- 1980, *Genius Loci: Towards a Phenomenology of Architecture*, Rizzoli International Publications, Inc., New York.

---- 1985, *The Concept of Dwelling: On the Way to a Figurative Architecture*, Rizzoli New York, New York.

Oakes, T & Minca, C (eds) 2006, *Travels in Paradox: Remapping Tourism*, Rowman & Littlefield Publishers, Ic., Oxford.

Our Common Future, 1987, Oxford University Press, Oxford.

Payne, M, Bartlett, A, Colbeck, R, Fifield, M, Lundy, K & Moore, C 2008, *A Good House is Hard to Find: Housing Affordability in Australia*, Department of the Senate, Canberra.

Pratt, G 1999, 'Geographies of Identity and Difference: Marking Boundaries', in D Massey, J Allen & P Sarre (eds), *Human Geography Today*, Polity Press, Cambridge.

Pred, A 1984, 'Place as Historically Contingent Process: Structuration and the Time-Geography of Becoming Places', *Annals of the Association of American Geographers*, vol. 74, no. 2, pp. 279-97.

Rapley, T 2004, 'Interviews', in C Seale, G Gobo, JF Gubrium & D Silverman (eds), *Qualitative Research Practice*, SAGE Publications Ltd, London, pp. 15-33.

Ravetz, A 1995, *The Place of the Home: English Domestic Environments, 1914 - 2000*, Spon, London.

Read, P 2000, *Belonging: Australians, Place and Aboriginal Ownership*, Cambridge University Press, Cambridge.

Relph, E 1976, *Place and Placelessness*, Pion, London.

---- 1979, 'To See With the Soul of the Eye', *Landscape*, vol. 23, pp. 28-34.

---- 1985, 'Geographical experiences and being-in-the-world: The phenomenological origins of geography', in D Seamon & R Mugerauer (eds), *Dwelling, Place and Environment: Towards a Phenomenology of Person and World*, Martinus Nijhoff Publishers, Dordrecht.

Relph, E, Tuan, T-F & Buttimer, A 1977, 'Humaism, Phenomenology, and Geography', *Annals of the Association of American Geographers*, vol. 67, no. 1, pp. 177-83.

Richardson, JTE 1999, 'The Concepts and Methods of Phenomenographic Research', *Review of Educational Research*, vol. 69, no. 1, pp. 53-82.

Rigby, K 2003, 'Tuning in to Spirit of Place', in J Cameron (ed.), *Changing Places: Re-Imagining Australia*, Longueville Books, Double Bay, NSW.

---- 2004, 'Tuning in to Spirit of Place', in J Cameron (ed.), *Changing Places: Re-Imagining Australia*, Longueville Books, Double Bay, NSW.

Rose, G 1993, *Feminism and Geography: The Limits of Geographical Knowledge*, Polity, Cambridge.

Rybczynski, W 1987, *Home: A Short History of an Idea*, Viking Penguin Inc, New York.

Sack, R 1997, *Homo Geographicus*, Johns Hopkins University Press, Baltimore.

Sandbergh, J 1997, 'Are Phenomenographic Results Reliable?' *Higher Education Research and Development*, vol. 16, no. 2, pp. 203-12.

Seamon, D 1979, *A Geography of the Lifeworld: Movement, Rest, and Encounter*, St Martin's Press, New York.

---- (ed.) 1993, *Dwelling, Seeing, and Designing: Toward a Phenomenological Ecology*, SUNY Series in Environmental and Architectural Phenomenology, State University of New York Press, Albany.

Seamon, D & Mugerauer, R (eds) 1985, *Dwelling, Place and Environment: Towards a Phenomenology of Person and World*, Martinus Nijhoff Publishers, Dordrecht.

2008, *Housing Affodability in Australia*, Senate.

Sharr, A 2007, *Heidegger for Architects*, Thinkers for Architects, Routledge, London and New York.

Shellenberger, M & Nordhaus, T 2004, *The Death of Environmentalism: Global Warming Politics in a Post-Environmental World.* .

Shove, E 2003, *Comfort, Cleanliness and Convenience: The Social Organisation of Normality*, New Technologies/ New Cultures Series, Berg, Oxford.

Sibley, D 1995, *Geographies of Exclusion: Society and Difference in the West*, Routledge, London.

---- 1999, 'Creating Geographies of Difference', in D Massey, J Allen & P Sarre (eds), *Human Geography Today*, Polity Press, Cambridge

Stansfield-Smith, C 1994, 'The Built Technology of the Learning Environment', in J Steele & JG Hedberg (eds), *Learning Environment Technology: Selected papers from LETA 94, Adelaide 25-28 September*, AJET Publications, Canberra, pp. 326-9.

Stretton, H 1991, 'The Consolidation Problem', *Architecture Australia*, vol. 80, pp. 27-9.

Sullivan, LH 1896, 'The tall office building artistically considered', *Lippincott's Magazine*, March 1896.

Sutton, I 1999, *Western Architecture: A Survey From Ancient Greece to the Present* World of Art, Thames and Hudson, London.

Svensson, L 1997, 'Theoretical Foundations of Phenomenography', *Higher Education Research & Development*, vol. 16, no. 2, pp. 159-71.

Tacey, D 2003, 'Spirit Place', in J Cameron (ed.), *Changing Places: Re-Imagining Australia*, Longueville Books, Double Bay, NSW.

Till, K 1993, 'Neotraditional Towns and Urban Villages: The Cultural Production of a Geography of 'Otherness'', *Environment and Planning D: Society and Space*, vol. 11, no. 6, pp. 709-32.

Tolle, E 2005, *A New Earth*, Penguin Group, Australia.

Troy, P 1996, *The Perils of Urban Consolidation*, The Federation Press, Annadale, NSW.

---- 1997, 'Social Aspects of Urban Consolidation', *Historic Environment*, vol. XIII, no. 1, pp. 18-26.

Tuan, Y-F 1974a, 'Space and Place: Humanistic Perspective', *Progress in Human Geography*, vol. 6, pp. 211-52.

---- 1974b, *Topophilia: A Study of Environmental Peception, Attitudes, and Values*, Prentice-Hall, New Jersey.

---- 1975, 'Place: An Experiential Perspective', *Geographical Review*, vol. 65, no. 2, pp. 151-65.

---- 1977, *Space and Place: The Perspective of Experience*, University of Minnesota Press, Minneapolis.

---- 1991, 'A View of Geography', *Geographical Review*, vol. 81, no. 1, pp. 99-107.

Vitruvius, P 1999, *Ten Books on Architecture*, Cambridge University Press, Cambridge.

Webb, C 2008, 'Big house on the hill is a dream come true', *The Age*, viewed December 5, 2008.

Weil, S 1952, *The Need for Roots*, Routledge, London and New York.

Welch, B 2007, *Housing Sustainability for all Victorians*, Master Builders Association of Victoria, Melbourne.

Wheeler, S & Beatley, T (eds) 2004, *The Sustainable Urban Development Reader*, Routledge, London.

Williams, DE 2007, *Sustainable Design: Ecology, Architecture, and Planning*, John Wiley & Sons, Inc., Hoboken, NJ.

Zaborowski, H 2005, 'Towards a Phenomnology of Dwelling', *Communio*, vol. 32, pp. 492-516.

Scientific Publishing House

offers

free of charge publication

of current academic research papers, Bachelor´s Theses, Master's Theses, Dissertations or Scientific Monographs

If you have written a thesis which satisfies high content as well as formal demands, and you are interested in a remunerated publication of your work, please send an e-mail with some initial information about yourself and your work to *info@vdm-publishing-house.com*.

Our editorial office will get in touch with you shortly.

VDM Publishing House Ltd.
Meldrum Court 17.
Beau Bassin
Mauritius
www.vdm-publishing-house.com

Made in the USA
Lexington, KY
09 January 2012